CULTURE,
MULTICULTURE,
POSTCULTURE

CULTURE, MULTICULTURE, POSTCULTURE

Joel S. Kahn

SAGE Publications
London • Thousand Oaks • New Delhi

Extracts from *The Treasure of the Sierra Madre*, screenplay by
John Huston, edited with an introduction by James Nevemore.
© 1979 The University of Wisconsin Press

'I Got Plenty O' Nuttin' by G. Gershwin/I. Gershwin/
D. Heyward © 1935 Gershwin Publ. Corp, USA, Warner
Chappell Music Ltd, London W1Y 3FA. Reproduced by
permission of IMP Ltd.

First published 1995

SAGE Publications Ltd
6 Bonhill Street
London EC2A 4PU

SAGE Publications Inc
2455 Teller Road
Thousand Oaks, California 91320

SAGE Publications India Pvt Ltd
32, M-Block Market
Greater Kailash - I
New Delhi 110 048

British Library Cataloguing in Publication data

A catalogue record for this book is
available from the British Library

ISBN 0 8039 7564 3
ISBN 0 8039 7565 1 (pbk)

Library of Congress catalog card number 95-074609

Typeset by Photoprint, Torquay, Devon.
Printed in Great Britain by The Cromwell Press Ltd,
Broughton Gifford, Melksham, Wiltshire

For Sophie

Contents

Preface

Culture is a word on everybody's lips these days. Hardly a moment seems to pass when we do not hear on the radio or television, see in newspapers and magazines, or read in academic texts some account of the world of the cultural. Governments at all levels announce cultural policies and provide funding for cultural activities; intellectuals announce the need for cultural initiatives or bemoan the loss of traditional cultural values; famous cultural icons – musicians, artists, novelists – themselves culture makers, are increasingly sought out for their opinions on the state of the world; the new field of cultural studies takes the academy by storm. And small wonder – the image, the representation, things quintessentially cultural have, as cultural theorists like Jean Baudrillard and Frederic Jameson have argued, quite literally taken over our lives.

But if, as evidenced by the proliferation of simulacra, our lives have become fully culturalised, there is increasingly another way in which culture can be seen to have come to the fore. Here I refer to culture in its more anthropological sense, used to refer to the systems of signs, meanings and world views of *particular* groups of human beings. When we hear talk of cultural mosaics, diversity, difference; of the threats to indigenous ways of life; of subcultures and multiculturalism; of ethnicities, identities and nationalities – we have entered a different cultural domain. And just as cultural theorists from the early 1980s could speak of the culturalisation of everyday life as being a defining feature of a new, postmodern age, so now we can and should speak of an age characterised not just by the dominance of the sign, but of particular kinds of signs, those that serve to mark off groups and subgroups of humans one from another. And perhaps even more clearly than was the case in the early 1980s, this new wave of culturalisation – of the culturalisation of culture to play on the two meanings of the term – is self-evidently global, if by that we mean not necessarily a new world-wide reality, or even a new language shared by the whole of humanity, but a discourse that *purports* to treat the world as a single field.

It is now very difficult to travel very far in the world of the simulacrum without running into the signs of 'cultural difference' – where commodities such as restaurant meals or items of clothing draw our attention to their supposedly 'ethnic' origins; photography, painting, novels, films, and dance tell stories of cultural identity or multiculturalism; where an increasingly popular 'world music' infuses western popular music with

African, Asian or Latin American influences; where western architects seek to build on what they take to be non-western understandings of domestic or urban space; or travel brochures and tourist destinations for the discerning 'cultural tourist' promise glimpses of indigenous life styles in remote parts of the world; where cosmetics companies promote themselves and their products by associating them with attempts to rescue threatened indigenous peoples; to say nothing of books, films and television programmes by 'serious' ethnographers which provide us with 'authentic' glimpses of the lives of exotic others.

Nor is everything so cosy. The news reports of a world in crisis to which we have grown so accustomed confirm that we live in a world of difference by reading major global conflicts – in Eastern Europe, Asia, Africa, the Middle East and Brooklyn – through the grid of culture conflict. Far from signalling the end of history, the collapse of communism has, we are told, allowed cultural/civilisational conflict to become the defining feature of the new world (dis)order.

As a reluctant anthropologist with a particular interest in the history of anthropology, I have found this evidence of a sensitivity to culture and difference interesting; as an ethnographer who has carried out research in Southeast Asia I have been struck by both parallels and differences between the fetishisation of culture there and in the West; as an American who has lived outside the United States for more than twenty years I have found the developing obsession there with culture and difference both intriguing and, at times, alarming; as a resident of Australia I have watched multiculturalism turned into an often anodyne national ideology. Why has there been this turn to culture, in both senses of that term? And what should we make of the current obsession with cultural diversity?

In an attempt to come to grips with questions such as these I have been led beyond the restrictive boundaries of my own discipline, and of at least that variant of area studies that I have most frequently encountered, for neither has seemed capable of treating concepts of culture and difference as both problematic and worthy objects of study in their own right. For example, anthropology seems in general to have reacted to what looked like being a healthy engagement with such issues in the mid-1980s by re-dedicating itself to the traditional project of interpreting cultural otherness. The assumption appears to be that the textual qualities of cultural otherness, the significant role played by anthropologists in constructing these other cultures, can be overcome by once again purging the discipline of ethnocentric assumptions. Perhaps this has been encouraged by the time-worn anthropological appeal to 'fieldwork' as the source and guarantee of its truth claims. The opportunity provided by the call for greater reflection on the role played by anthropological knowledge in the world it sought to represent, to implicate anthropology and anthropologists more directly in the situations within which it was embedded – not just in the momentary fieldwork encounter, but in the national contexts within which that fieldwork took place – appears to have been lost. Once again we have the rather unedifying sight of the ethnography, today especially the theoretically highly-sophisticated ethnographic text, being torn from its context, and evaluated, debated and emulated far from the site of its production.

As a consequence I have been led to the relatively new fields of cultural studies, globalisation theory and, especially, postcolonial theory. Here I found a greater willingness to deal with these issues, and in particular, to borrow a term favoured by Roland Robertson, explicitly to *thematise* the discourse of culture and difference. People like Robertson himself or Appadurai, for example, have shown how notions such as 'nation', 'ethnic group', 'indigenous culture' are as much contemporary as they are reflections of a pre-existing global cultural mosaic. They are as a consequence shaped by the imperatives of a global system of states and, in Appadurai's terms, the emergence of 'postnational social formations' (Robertson, 1992; Appadurai, 1993). And critics such as Talal Asad, Edward Said and subsequently a new generation of postcolonial theorists have traced the links between discourses of difference and power, specifically those systems of power deemed imperial. All this serves to render the project of interpreting cultural difference highly problematic, and does not suggest that escaping into the world of the other is something that can be accomplished, before and after a relatively brief stay 'in the field', merely by thinking oneself out of the economic, political and social contexts within which such knowledge is produced.

However, while these approaches do help us to thematise culture by allowing us to focus on its discursive characteristics in ways that traditional disciplines do not, they are not without fault. There is one problem in particular that has provided me with my starting point, a problem that might be stated in three only apparently different ways. On the one hand we might ask how it is that if the discourse of cultural difference is so closely implicated in the project of European empire, and if empire is so all-pervasive a feature of the modern condition, what is it that permits the postcolonial theorist to step outside the relationships of empire? For even to identify a discourse, much less to criticise it, one presumably first needs to be able to escape its clutches even if momentarily to see that it is discourse.

On the other hand we could ask whether, granted that 'cultural difference' is always discursively constructed, all such discourse is therefore identical. The more one reads the postcolonial deconstructions of *certain* texts (those by Jane Austen and Joseph Conrad seem to come in for an inordinate amount of attention), the more one wonders why these texts and not others have been singled out for attention.

Finally, perhaps in particular given the important role played by the theories of either Gramsci or Foucault, we might ask whether it is not too crude to categorise all discursive phenomena as *either* dominating/ hegemonic *or* resistant/counterhegemonic. Such a formulation, by associating cultural expression with the 'interests' of either a dominant or a subordinate/subaltern class appears in particular to completely miss the specific sociological positions occupied by those who are the main producers and consumers of these images of culture and difference, namely the modern intelligentsia. Neither, as their radical critics would have it, the chief architects of global capitalism or western empires; nor, as they and perhaps some of their conservative critics would have us believe, the direct spokespersons or voices of the (voiceless) subaltern classes they seek to represent, intellectuals (or the holders of 'cultural capital', according to a characterisation currently in vogue) generally occupy a social position somewhere 'in between' the two. Surely an analysis of the discursive formations of the intelligentsia requires greater attention to their somewhat ambiguous sociological positions within the social constellation of twentieth century modernity that is provided in much of the current discussion of the topic.

In what follows, therefore, I have attempted to take some of the insights provided by contemporary cultural theory into notions of 'culture' and 'difference' somewhat further by examining a number of textual accounts of 'other cultures' that appeared in the early decades of the twentieth century. The initial choice of texts – a film about Bali made with the expert advice of the German artist and musician Walter Spies; a novel about Mexico by B. Traven, the pen-name of a man presumed to have been the Austrian anarchist Ret Marut; and a novella about southern African Americans by the Charleston-born writer DuBose Heyward – might at first appear somewhat random. However, the reasons for this initial selection, and for the subsequent discussion of a mixed group of cultural intermediaries like Béla Bartók, A.V. Chayanov, Zora Neale Hurston, Julius Herman Boeke, George Gershwin, Diego Rivera, Wifredo Lam, and Carl Van Vechten, should become clearer as the reader progresses through a discussion of the different concepts used to construct cultural difference as well as the different contexts within which such constructions have taken place. I have, for example, focused largely on a particular period in the history of modernism, namely the years between the two World Wars, a period which I shall suggest was formative of much of contemporary debate about culture and difference. I have chosen largely not to focus on anthropologists, although some are discussed, and I suggest that the emergence of modern anthropology was intimately bound up with this broader intellectual development. Instead I have focused on figures whose involvement in the situations they sought to describe was longer lasting, and often more influential than that of the anthropological fieldworker.

Finally, apart from trying to achieve a relatively broad geographical sweep, using examples from Europe, Asia, Latin America and North America, I have also tried to achieve a relatively broad coverage of the areas where notions of cultural otherness have come to play significant roles – in literature, music, architecture and the arts; in the fields of peasant studies, economics, the social sciences, urban studies and jurisprudence; in urban and rural, first world and third world contexts. But in no way have I achieved anything like a 'global' approach. Failing that, I have instead anchored the discussion by means of the three texts with which I began. The result is not, and is not intended to be, a neat general 'theory' of how and why it is that the discourse of cultural difference has achieved the degree of dominance that it has, nor a definitive, once and for all answer to the question of whether this is a good or a bad thing. Instead I hope to have taken some of the existing debates a little further, and to raise questions which, however awkward, need to be considered more carefully than they currently are. And, it has to be admitted, in taking time out from an anthropological career devoted to the writing of 'ethnography', I have also had a lot of fun. If nothing else, I hope this sense comes through here, although I fear that I have been insufficiently successful in escaping the constraints of much social scientific discourse to fully convey here the enjoyment this project gave me.

Obviously I am indebted to a large number of people and organisations who helped, wittingly or unwittingly, with the writing of the book. The material on Malaysia and Indonesia discussed here was collected in the course of other research projects, and I have acknowledged the support given for these projects elsewhere. The writing was made possible by the generosity of La Trobe University and the Australian Research Council which provided relief from the rewarding, but very time consuming tasks associated with undergraduate teaching, without which I would never have found the time. The Ashworth Centre for Social Theory at the University of Melbourne provided me with space during my study leave. Thanks are due especially to the acting director, Dr John Rundell, for organising that. Two people at different times, Gillian Robinson and Francesco Formosa, provided me with research assistance – preparing bibliographies, summarising texts, chasing down references – that helped me tremendously with the preparation of the manuscript. Francesco Formosa, moreover, was more than a research assistant. He also gave me advice, encouragement, feedback and ideas. His engagement with and enthusiasm for the project was absolutely invaluable, and I want to express my gratitude here. It is probably poor reward, but I can only list some of the large number of other people who offered useful advice, references, comments, or who provided other kinds of assistance equally important: Maila Stivens, Jonathan Friedman, Johann Arnason, John Rundell, Joanne Finkelstein, Alberto Gomes, Martha Macintyre, Jeremy Beckett, Suvendi Perera, Win Stivens, Sanjay Seth, Beryl Langer, Peter Beilharz, Clive Kessler, Yoshio Sugimoto, Jessica Kahn, Stephen Mennell, Richard Fardon, Beth Robertson, Manolete Mora and Adrian McNeil. I have also greatly appreciated the professionalism of Rosemary Campbell and Robert Rojek of Sage who helped turn the manuscript into a book.

Finally, I want to take this opportunity to express my thanks and gratitude to Chris Rojek. From the time we first met to discuss the project, and through subsequent meetings and correspondence Chris has been consistently enthusiastic. He expressed confidence in the book even when it was a poorly-formed initial idea, his comments and encouragement sustained me throughout the writing, and his advice on the manuscript has been extremely helpful. It is difficult to express how important his support has been to me – there is no question that without it the book would not have been written.

1

Culture, Hegemony, Representation: A Postcolonial Empire?

I want no gold and I want no silver. I have enough to eat and I have a good and beautiful wife and a son whom I love and who is strong and well formed. What is gold to me? The earth brings a blessing; the fruits of it and my herds of cattle bring blessings. Gold brings no blessing and silver brings no blessing. Does it bring the blessing to you white Spaniards? You murder each other for gold. You hate each other for gold. You spoil the beauty of your lives for gold. We have never made gold our master, we were never its slaves. We said: Gold is beautiful. And so we made rings of it and other adornments, and we adorned ourselves and our wives and our gods with it, because it has beauty. But we did not make it into money. We could look at it and rejoice in it, but we could not eat it. Our people and also the peoples of the valleys have never fought or made wars for gold. But we have fought much for land and fields and rivers and lakes and towns and salt and herds. But for gold? Or silver? They are only good to look at. I can't put them into my belly when I am hungry, and so they have no value. They are only beautiful like a flower that blooms or a bird that sings. But if you put the flower in your belly, it is no longer beautiful, and if you cook the bird it sings no longer. (Traven, 1980: 115f.)

'De buckra sho gots nigger figgered out tuh a cent!' said Peter philosophically, and even with a note of admiration in his voice. ''Dem knows how much money wagon make in er week; an' de horse man, de furniture man, an' de lan'lo'd mek dey 'rangement accordin'. But I done lib long 'nough now tuh beat 'em all, 'cause money ain't no use tuh a man attuh he done pass he prime, nohow.' (Heyward 1953 [1925]: 55)

The film *Island of Demons* was made in 1931 by two Germans, Victor Baron von Plessen and Dr Dahlseim, but relied heavily on the expertise and advice of the German painter and musician Walter Spies. The film is

a love story about two peasants whose harmonious village life was destroyed by a *Rangda*-like witch, who created an epidemic which devastated the happy village community. Only exorcistic rituals could stop her, and return the village to its normal state . . . [The film contains] beautifully filmed scenes of rice-terraces reflecting the sky, and of hard-working and happy peasants in the fields. Then [comes] the ideal community, disrupted by a bitter woman whose shifty looks [betray] her evil nature, who [is] eventually revealed in the form of *Rangda*. Throughout the scenes of witchcraft and exorcism [are woven] documentation of Balinese dances and rituals. This documentation [guarantees] the authenticity of the scenes, showing that they [are] giving insight into the 'real' Bali behind the superficial tourist images. (Vickers, 1989: 107)

What do these passages have in common? As it turns out a great deal. But we might start this examination of difference and modernity by exploring what is commonly described as their textuality. In the language of cultural theory, the 'Mexican Indians' of B. Traven's novel, *The Treasure of the Sierra Madre*; the 'Negroes' who populate DuBose Heyward's *Porgy*; and the 'Balinese' in the German film *Island of Demons* are all *representations*. They are, moreover, representations of a particular kind: *of* what at least now we have come to call other cultures, *by* representatives of what we have come to see as a 'dominant', 'hegemonic', 'western' culture. Walter Spies, the man most responsible for the images of Bali that circulate in *Island of Demons* was a German painter and musician; the mysterious B. Traven was in all likelihood an Austrian anarchist, Ret Marut; and DuBose Heyward was a white poet and novelist who lived most of his life in Charleston, South Carolina.

In other words *Treasure*, *Porgy* and *Island of Demons* are all 'anthropological texts' in the broad sense of that term. While neither Traven, Heyward nor Spies was a professional anthropologist, they all nonetheless were performing the intellectual function which their contemporaries – like Bronislaw Malinowski, Franz Boas, Margaret Mead and Marcel Mauss – were claiming for themselves, namely the textual representation by and for westerners of non-western 'cultures'. And, it must be said, as such they all enjoyed a good deal of success and influence, either at the time, or subsequently. Traven's *Treasure* sold a large number of copies when it originally appeared in German in 1926. It was subsequently translated into English in 1935 and, together with his later novels of Mexico, has enjoyed a steadily growing popularity since that time. It became, moreover, the basis for a film by John Huston starring the director's father, Walter, and Humphrey Bogart which has come to occupy the status of a cult classic, at least among members of my own generation.

Porgy, too enjoyed a good deal of initial success. And while Huston's version of the Traven novel significantly altered Traven's own representations of Mexican Indians, Heyward's dignified images of southern African Americans were only slightly modified in the Broadway play by Heyward and his wife Dorothy, and then, most successfully, in the 'folk opera' *Porgy and Bess* with music by George Gershwin.[1] Heyward himself is credited as the librettist and he collaborated with Ira Gershwin in the writing of the lyrics. Since 1935 when *Porgy and Bess* was first performed in Boston, and on Broadway, Gershwin's opera has been revived numerous times, notably in a number of successful performances after Gershwin's untimely death, then for the 1959 Hollywood film version starring Sydney Poitier and Sammy Davis Junior, and subsequently in productions by the Houston Grand Opera, New York's Metropolitan Opera, and in Trevor Nunn acclaimed Glyndebourne production. And this is to say nothing of the commercial success of some of the 'songs' extracted and separately recorded. Most popular among these have undoubtedly been 'Summertime', and the irreverent 'It Ain't Necessarily So', but perhaps closest in spirit at least to the above passage from the novel is a song that was written according to Gershwin only for a bit of light relief,

> Oh, I got plenty o' nut-tin'
> An' nut-tin's plenty fo' me.
> I got no car, got no mule,
> I got no misery.
> De folks wid plen-ty o' plen-ty
> got a lock on dey door,
> 'Fraid some-bod-y's a-goin' to rob 'em
> while dey's out a-mak-in' more.
> What for?
> I got no lock on de door,
> (dat's no way to be).
> Dey kin steal de rug from de floor,
> Dat's o-keh wid me,
> 'Cause de things dat I prize,
> Like de stars in de skies,
> all are free. —
> Oh, I got plen-ty o' nuttin',
> An' nut-tin's plen-ty fo' me.
> I got my gal, got my song,
> got Heb-ben de whole day long.
> No use com-plain-in'!
> Got my gal, —
> got my Lawd, —
> got my song. —

(from *Porgy and Bess*. Music by George Gershwin. Libretto by DuBose Heyward. Lyrics by DuBose Heyward and Ira Gershwin. Gershwin Publishing Corporation/Chappell and Co: New York.)

Walter Spies might at first sight appear to be different, his paintings of Java and Bali being largely unknown in Europe, at least until 1980 when Amsterdam's Royal Tropical Museum mounted the first systematic exhibition of his work in the West. However from behind the scenes, as it were, Spies has done probably more than anyone else to shape the western image of Bali, not just as tropical paradise, but as a land of mystery, spirituality, sexual tolerance, art and culture. This is because in the late 1920s and 1930s from his base in Ubud in Bali Spies acted as the key cultural broker for other westerners visiting Bali – people like Noel Coward and Charlie Chaplin; but also the anthropologists Margaret Mead and her husband Gregory Bateson; the Mexican caricaturist and travel writer Miguel Covarrubias and his American photographer wife Rosa Rolanda; the popular novelist Vicki Baum – all of whom contributed to a European and American Balinese imaginary that is in substantial ways still with us today.[2]

These texts are 'anthropological' in another sense as well – all bear the stamp of 'authenticity' established by the experience of their authors as close observers of, if not participants in, the cultures being represented. The dust jacket on Heyward's novel establishes him as uniquely qualified to interpret the culture of southern African Americans. He was descended, we are informed, from a signer of the Declaration of Independence, and was born, reared and spent a large part of his life around Charleston, South Carolina. He was, we are told, categorised as 'folks' which allowed him freedom to be at once white and coloured.

> He understood the language of Porgy in the wide sense of the word, spoke it in the narrow, an impossibility to anyone outside the low country. Gullah, the language they speak, is a dialect peculiar to Negroes who live along the Carolina Coast low country. More than any other it retains trace, words and intonation, of Africa. . . .

Beneath this, we are further informed also were the 'gesture', the laughter, the 'turn of an eye' which Heyward learned in his childhood from servants, playmates and neighbours. This intense interaction was possible, we are told, because there was no Negro ghetto in Charleston at that time. George Gershwin, it is said, was equally immersed in African American culture, especially its musical culture – although his musical influences would largely have stemmed from his experience of the New York music scene during his Tin Pan Alley days, and, with many other New Yorkers, as a frequent visitor to the nightclubs of Harlem in the 1920s. But in preparing for the composition of *Porgy and Bess* Gershwin also felt it necessary to spend time on South Carolina's Folly Island, experiencing first hand the music of the 'Gullah Negroes' and becoming, so the story goes, more adept at the 'shouting' that was such a feature of this 'folk' tradition than many of these American 'peasants' were themselves.[3]

The case of Traven is somewhat different, largely because so little is known about his life in Mexico. Indeed this sense of mystery, that Traven himself did so much to preserve, is clearly an important part of his appeal. But for whatever reason this, by our best account (see Wyatt, 1980), German-born anarchist, forced to flee Austria and then Europe, and who arrived in Mexico in the summer of 1924 and then may (or may not) have changed his name, first to B. Traven and then to Hal Croves, is assumed to have 'gone native' for much of the time, spending a good deal of time in Chiapas, a place that since that time has been assumed to be a privileged site of Mexican indigenous (Mayan) culture.

Walter Spies, Russian-born, but of German nationality, was interned by the Russians in the Urals during the First World War. He studied and practised painting and music in Russia, Germany and then the Netherlands from which, having discovered the 'lure of the East' within the walls of Amsterdam's Tropical Museum, he boarded a ship bound for Java. Appalled by what he saw as the ugliness of the colonial rulers and the beauty of the Indonesians,[4] he visited and then became chief musician at the court of the Sultan of Yogyakarta, and then moved to Bali. There he painted, taught painting to young Balinese and associated with Balinese and Europeans with an interest in art and culture until his arrest for homosexuality, in 1938, by a Dutch regime in the throes of a puritan revival. Released, he was then interned by the Dutch during the Second World War as an alien national and was killed by Japanese bombs while being transported by ship to another prison in Indonesia.

To qualify as genuine anthropological monographs of the period, our texts would obviously have had to carry with them the kinds of justificatory social-scientific language with which many modern ethnographies are replete. But fortunately Traven, Heyward and Spies spare us that. While contemporary ethnographies were mouthing platitudes about ethnocentrism, objective reporting, controlled comparison and the like, Traven, Heyward and Spies were doing what they all aspired to do – producing sensitive 'portraits' or representations of other cultures for avid consumers 'back home'. As exemplary 'texts', the works of Traven, Heyward/ Gershwin and Spies therefore allow us to begin a journey into the realm of 'anthropological' representation, a realm that has increasingly come under the critical gaze, not just of cultural theorists, but of artists, politicians, theologians and intellectuals in both East and West in recent years. The critique takes the form of a challenge, mounted by, but more often in the name of, the Balinese, the indigenous American, the African American – the subjects it is said not so much of western or European economic exploitation, but more of a 'cultural hegemony' by which these non-western or non-European peoples have had their cultures denigrated, their voices silenced, while they have been appropriated to and by the goals of empire. These are important objections to the anthropological project of a DuBose Heyward, a B. Traven, a Walter Spies. How valid are they?

Postcolonial Empires?

Edward Said's *Orientalism* (1978) is correctly seen as a watershed in the recent thinking about cultural difference, and specifically as a foundational text for the development of what has since come to be called postcolonial thought. The book has stood as a challenge to the way the West has heretofore conceptualised its relationship to the non-West, demonstrating the extent to which existing discourses of otherness, even those that saw themselves as emancipatory, were embedded, indeed implicated, in the imperial processes by which for more than a century the West has treated the globe and its peoples as both plaything and object to be exploited, ruled and studied – it all amounts to the same thing. Combining powerfully with insights from poststructuralism, postmodernism and cultural studies – especially as read in the United States and its cultural colonies like Australia – the result was a radical perspectivism focused on the culture/ power nexus and its relation to the production of knowledge of cultural otherness.

Some fifteen years on, however, a number of writers with sympathy with the original Saidian project (to say nothing, of course, of the representatives of a traditionalist backlash, particularly in the United States) have begun to remark on the problems in the project that has formed under the banner of postcolonialism, suggesting that far from producing the opening/ rapprochement with the other that was urged in Said's first major work on the theme, postcolonial assumptions are now themselves implicated in a renewed project of empire.

A number of observers, for example, have noted the way in which some of the key premises of postcolonialism have been appropriated by the American Right, which has now apparently accepted the postcolonial argument that what were previously assumed to be universal values were, in fact, western ones. But having accepted the contingency of the old universalisms, the Right now maintains that 'western values' must be quarantined against those whose cultures are at odds with them – accepting, in other words, certain key diagnoses of postcolonial analysis, namely that 'western' society stands or falls on the hegemony of a particular 'culture' (the white, Anglo-Saxon culture of its elites) (Giroux, 1993; Rieff, 1993).

An example of this kind of thinking is found in traditionalist responses to the immigration flows that followed the lifting of the so-called 'White Australia' policy by which migrants were chosen on racial grounds. In typical vein a letter to the editor of the national newspaper wrote:

> The question, however, concerns not immigrants' race but their culture. In the course of our immigration debate it is vital for us to recognise that some cultures offer ideas, values and beliefs which are appropriate in Australian society, while the ideas prevalent in certain other cultures are inappropriate.
> We are talking about cultures some of which hold drastically different beliefs about moral codes, systems of justice, clerical influence in politics and the law, and women's rights, as compared with the views of most Australians. . . .

In Europe, too, there is a growing feeling that a postcolonial language of culture and difference has been re-appropriated by the Right in a renewed racism, as is pointed out by Silverman when he writes that

> [t]he colonial logic of universalism and assimilation has given way to the postcolonial logic of pluralism and difference.
> In this pluralist context, 'culture' has become the major site of struggle for new racist and anti-racist formations. It can be mobilized both to reinforce and to challenge exclusion and racism. This has clearly been a problem for anti-racism, whose language of 'difference' has been appropriated by the new racism and turned back on the anti-racist movement itself. Anti-racism has therefore been faced with the problem of how to challenge the essentialist concept of difference used by the New Right without reinforcing an essentialism of its own or slipping back into a universalism which it was at pains to challenge in the first place. (Silverman, 1991: 2)

Guillaumin, another commentator of the European scene, also suggests this by explaining that

> [t]he cultural Right (now known as the 'Nouvelle Droite') which has made use of a Gramscian approach to culture, has occupied a rather special position in intellectual and political life during the last twenty years . . . the 'cultural' Right is making a marked attempt to distance itself from the established conception of 'racism', claiming left-wing theoretical roots (for example Gramsci) and emphasizing the cultural over the parliamentary or extra-parliamentary struggle. It claims to work on an intellectual rather than classically political or directly

interventionist level. It energetically denies accusations of racism and claims to reject notions of a fixed hierarchy of human groups. It is the self-proclaimed advocate of the right of 'difference', of culture and roots. A fascinating semantic cluster . . .

The right to be different is also inherited from left-wing discourse. In fact, the 'droit à la difference' was a priority during the 1970s for the anti-racist movements and, subsequently, international organizations. This new approach was extremely fortuitous for the Right which promptly appropriated the crucial term 'difference'. The New Right then used the idea of difference as the backbone for a so-called 'cultural' rather than racial argument. It cultivates revulsion at the use of the term 'race', replacing it with 'culture'. (Guillaumin, 1991: 9)

The extent to which propositions first advanced in the postcolonial critique of the West have now entered the general language at least of cultural debate leads one to suspect that at least certain parts of the postcolonial critique of empire have become re-embedded in an imperial project. To quote Anthony King, a sympathetic participant in the debates:

We might begin by recognizing what a very colonial, or neocolonial, term 'postcolonial' actually is, not least when used to describe 'all the culture affected by the imperial process from the moment of colonization to the present day . . . Conceived in the first instance either by liberals in the European or American academy or by post-colonial intellectuals now resident in academic institutions of 'the West', the discourse on colonialism has itself become a form of academic colonialism, expanding outwards to fill the academic journals, publishers' catalogues, and the presses of a global publishing industry. I am suggesting that this discourse on colonialism may be seen as colonial because, like much of 'scientific knowledge' itself, it stems predominantly from the colonializing or post-imperial countries themselves. (King, 1992: 340f.)

What are the claims of postcolonial theory, and why should they have given rise to problems such as these? Said's original formulation, that is that towards the end of the eighteenth century European (mainly French and British) intellectuals invented new ways of conceiving of the Orient (the Arab world) which, while partly indebted to earlier European ideas about Islam, now constructed a much more passive Orient, the essence of which was seen to lie in its ancient past (the present is a crude degener-ation), is now well known. A central insight of Said's analysis is into the ways orientalist discourse, by constructing a passive and backward or even decadent orient, generated what he calls a will to govern over it, justified as a 'civilising' project by which the Orient can be brought into the modern world. Said's central proposition – that Europe's Orient is best understood not as a reflection in thought of a real Orient out there in the world, but, following Foucault, as a discourse, that is as a set of propositions/ significations/representations that derive their truth value not from corre-spondence to reality but from the power relations they imply and are implicated in – is now common currency, having been elaborated by Said and others in different disciplines and for other national and historical contexts. And clearly postcolonialism as critique has a number of appeal-ing features, capturing as it does in a particularly acute way a series of significant problems in existing knowledge complexes – especially the obvious failings of realist and objectivist epistemologies of cultural representation and the now, thanks in part to Said, equally obvious relations between knowledge and power.

But postcolonialism has become more than a critique of existing (western) knowledge. Instead it sees itself increasingly as a counter (post) colonial discourse, that is able to destabilise existing systems of signification of otherness seen as falsely universalist and hence imperial and replace them with new ones that are pluralist. And here postcolonial theory gives rise to a number of conundrums with which it has yet to deal in any satisfactory way.

These problems are manifest in the fact that despite (or perhaps even because of) taking on board the postcolonial critique, we cannot seem to escape the representation of cultural difference in realist and/or essentialist modes. Could it not be that the project of representing 'cultures' in the way Said suggests is as saturated with power as were earlier representational practices, even though we now choose to represent cultures as historically constituted rather than ontologically given? Who is to say that there could not be a postcolonial empire?

That in spite of the insights of postcolonial theory we seem wedded to the kinds of realist representations of cultural differentiation that we have already noted in the works of Traven, Heyward and Spies, is evident in the thoughts of even the most sophisticated of new theorists. An illuminating example is provided by Jean-François Lyotard who, in an article first published in 1985 entitled 'Histoire Universelle et Différences Culturelles', repeats his by now familiar denunciation of the grand narratives of traditional philosophy and social theory, arguing now that they do a kind of violence to non-western cultures. All such modern emancipatory narratives are for Lyotard distasteful precisely because they speak of/are implicated in the process whereby 'other cultures' are dominated and then destroyed by the advance of the West. In particular they do so by means of their 'cosmopolitan' nature, by which all particularity is dissolved into universalism. Lyotard secures this postcolonial conclusion by means of the example of 'savagery' provided by the Cashinahua of South America,[5] whose narratives, unlike those of the imperial West, are characterised by the meticulous naming of places, heroes, destinations and narrators. Lyotard concludes this brief ethnographic detour by maintaining that:

> This kind of organisation is completely opposed to the grand narratives of legitimation that characterise western modernity. These latter are cosmopolitan in Kant's terms. They are concerned precisely with the overstepping/surpassing of particular cultural identity towards a universal civic identity. (1985: 566)

But who are the Cashinahua? Are they really another culture located outside modernity? Or is this a case of a clearly postcolonial argument relying on the rhetorical form of the sorts of anthropological texts with which we have been dealing, with their essentialised and realist representation of a cultural otherness as if the representations were mere reflections of an already existing cultural mosaic out there in the world?[6]

One might well ask, of course, whether if those other cultures are indeed so persistently alien, how we could know them even well enough to assert their alterity. Modern anthropology has its own conceit, asserting an intuitive understanding through 'participant observation', and securing this authenticity in text by the rhetoric of 'I was there'. Much the same sort of aura around the works of Heyward, Traven and Spies contributes, as we have seen, to their 'authenticity'. Postcolonial theorists are rightly sceptical of such claims. And yet it is interesting that in spite of all their appeal to the discursive dimensions of knowledge of cultural otherness, ideas of intuitive understanding acquired through the shedding of 'ethnocentric' presuppositions are still brought into play. While admitting that it is difficult, JanMohammed has suggested that: 'Genuine and thorough comprehension of Otherness is possible only if the self can somehow negate or at least severely bracket the values, assumptions, and ideology of his culture' (JanMohammed, 1985: 65). But of course because 'this [would entail] in practice the virtually impossible task of negating one's very being precisely because one's culture is what formed that being' (ibid.), by implication the authority of the postcolonial interpreter is more often established by his/her cultural identity. Contrary to the view that postcolonialism is a genuinely pluralistic, that is non-power laden discourse, power is here once again reintroduced into postcolonial discourse: first, by establishing specific criteria – the ability to 'bracket' one's own cultural values and/or the possession of a particular cultural identity – as prerequisites for the creators of interpretation, hence empowering some and not others as capable of authenticity; and, second, by introducing culture, as Said has reminded us a concept inevitably saturated with power, once again into the equation (this time the cultural identity of the author).

Foucault has maintained that all power implies resistance, that therefore particular languages of power imply particular languages of resistance to that power, an insight on which Said has drawn in a recent contribution to the debate (Said, 1993). While it seems ultimately far too simplistic to consider all discourse on cultural difference as *either* hegemonising *or* resistant, as Said has done here, it might nonetheless be fruitful to speak of colonialism and postcolonialism as standing in just such a relationship of interiority one to another, that is as partaking of a single discursive field that is constructed by a single language of culture, identity and power, rather than to assume that postcolonialism is a discourse which marks a radical break with existing languages of empire/counter-empire. To do so might make it easier to understand the continuities in the modern imperial/counter-imperial project. How otherwise can we account for the fact that postcolonial theorists themselves presume the persistence of imperial thinking into the postcolonial age?[7] And if there were no such continuities in colonial/anti- colonial thought, how is it that postcolonial theory, in spite of its purported rejection of European or western notions of cultural otherness, at the same time brings western theory in by the back door in its reliance on particular variants of contemporary European theory – notably poststructuralism, deconstructionism and the like? If there were no continuity with 'western' discourses of empire/counter-empire, how otherwise could we explain the obvious links between contemporary postcolonial writing, and that long-standing expressivist challenge to techno-rationalist modernism that we examine later on?

There is a particular reason why the question of whether or not postcolonialism participates in a longer-standing language of culture, difference and identity cannot be asked and that is that these links are typically obliterated in much postcolonial writing by means of an equation of 'western' thought with techno-rationalism, and particularly with its nineteenth century form, commonly called 'social Darwinism'.[8] JanMohammed for example describes as colonial literature that which articulates the 'manichean opposition between the putative superiority of the European and the supposed inferiority of the native . . .' (1985: 63). But it is not just the inferiority, but the 'perfectibility' of the savage that, more than anything else, characterises this discourse, the overt aim of which 'is to "civilize" the savage, to introduce him to all the benefits of western cultures' (ibid.: 62). It has been argued similarly that European social theory in the nineteenth century invariably interpreted otherness as anteriority (McGrane, 1989), hence justifying the civilising claims of colonialism.

Quite clearly then it is the utilitarian evolutionism of a Spencer, rather than nineteenth century social theory in general, with which we are dealing here. In other words, for many postcolonial theorists 'imperial ideology' refers to the idea that all peoples are capable of achieving the liberal ideal of emancipation, and that they are in fact destined to do so. The links between this particular nineteenth century vision and the imperial project, particularly as it was conceived by Britain and France in the specific conditions of 'free trade imperialism' obtaining prior to the 1870s, has been well established (see for example Asad, 1973).

But as an overall characterisation of all modern discourse on the other, 'social Darwinism' is, as we shall see, problematic for a number of reasons, not least of which is the fact that 'anthropologists' like Heyward, Traven and Spies, to say nothing of 'real anthropologists' like Boas, Malinowski et al., saw their own rhetoric as distinctly anti-utilitarian and/or anti-civilizational.[9] The above quotes from *Treasure of the Sierra Madre* and *Porgy* articulate an anti-instrumentalism of which a postcolonialist might be proud. Nor is there any doubt that all three writers were variously critical of colonialism/imperialism, precisely for the way in which it forced a utilitarian instrumentalism onto cultures that, unlike our own, had a proper appreciation of the place of material goals. Porgy's refrain, 'I've got plenty o' nut-tin' ', echoing Peter's altogether healthy valuation of money and material goods echo the words of Traven's Indian chief who, unlike the Spaniards, knew the true rather than fetishised value of gold.

Moreover, all three writers bemoaned the processes by which their 'other cultures' would be debased by the spread, through western domination and civilising missions, of 'western', that is instrumental, values. We have already had occasion to refer to Spies's aesthetic denunciation of colonialism. Heyward too, in similarly paternalistic vein echoes these sentiments when he observes:

> But one thing is certain: the reformer will have them in the fullness of time. They will surely be cleaned, married, conventionalized. They will be taken to the fields, and given to machines, their instinctive feeling for the way that leads to happiness, saved as it is from selfishness by humour and genuine kindness of heart, will be supplanted by a stifling strait-jacket. They will languish, but they will submit, because they will be trained into a habit of thought that makes blind submission a virtue.
>
> And my stevedore, there out of the window I look at him again. I cannot see him as a joke. Most certainly I cannot contrive him into a menace. I can only be profoundly sorry for him, for he sits in the sunshine, unconscious, awaiting his supreme tragedy. He is about to be saved. (From an 1923 essay 'And Once Again – the Negro', cited in Slavick, 1981: 30)

Traven, as befits his European anarchist background, was far more radical in his denunciation of American, indeed all western, cultural imperialism in Mexico, describing the American 'faked civilization' that infiltrates Mexican ceremony as the 'vomit of our culture',[10] and Christianity as a systematically perverse influence in the lives of all Mexicans.

There are a number of reasons why the use of the label 'social Darwinism' and the conflation of it and 'western' thought is misleading. First, the term social Darwinism is itself rather misleading. To the extent that the term refers particularly to the social evolutionism of Herbert Spencer, in fact many of the key notions pre-date Darwin's own work. While we might not choose to go so far as to label Darwinian biology 'biological Spencerism', it might not be less adequate than attaching the label social Darwinist to Spencer. Perhaps more significantly, Spencerian evolutionism probably owes a good deal more to pre-Darwinian, particularly Lamarckian biology than it does to the Darwinian version.

Second, even setting aside what may appear to some mere semantic quibbles, the use of the term even to refer to all nineteenth century theories of social evolution is misleading. For example there are significant differences, especially vis-à-vis the treatment of racial differences between a Lewis Henry Morgan who tended to see a strong link between the social and the biological stages of human evolution at one extreme, and an E.B. Tylor at the other, who always emphasised a disjuncture, arguing for stages of social or cultural evolution at the same time as he spoke of the 'psychic unity of mankind'. Spencer's own theory may be said to lie somewhere in between (see for example Stocking, 1982). Morgan's theory would as a consequence have made a poor foundation for a civilising colonial mission in so far as it would have denied the possibility of perfectibility at least in the short run.

Third, there is the presumption in much postcolonial theory that some form of social Darwinism emerges as an ideal 'justification' of colonial rule. But to maintain the justificatory function of imperial ideology is inevitably to assume that it needed justifying at the time. Justification implies credible resistance, and a discursive arena of justification and resistance which may not have always existed, or may have taken divergent forms in imperial situations. A neat illustration of this point is provided by Stephen Jay Gould who shows how defenders of slavery in the southern states of the United States in fact saw little need for the justifications of slavery being provided to them by the scientific racism of biologists like Louis Agassiz and Samuel George Morton. On the contrary, wrote a South Carolina parson in the 1850s:

> In intellectual power the African is an inferior variety of our species. His whole history affords evidence that he is incapable of self-government. Our child that we lead by the hand, and who looks to us for protection and support is still of our blood notwithstanding his weakness and ignorance. (cited in Gould, 1981: 70)[11]

But fourth, perhaps the main difficulty with the use of the blanket label 'social Darwinism' to characterise modern thought is that it fails to capture other, often overtly anti-utilitarian and counter-Enlightenment trends in modern thought. In particular, it fails to address an equally significant expressivist heritage in 'western' discourse, a heritage which has been mobilised in different places and different times in critiques of techno-instrumental modernism. One such instance was during the interwar years when proponents and critics of European empire alike attacked the 'social Darwinist' foundations of earlier advocates, and critics, of empire. Thus the equation between 'social Darwinism' and 'western' thought fails to recognise the continuities in modern imperial/counter-imperial discourse, continuities that are concealed in much writing characterising itself as 'post colonial'. Viewed this way, so called postcolonialism might be seen as the contemporary manifestation of the expressivist critique of western civilisation that is also articulated in earlier 'anthropological' representations of cultural difference such as those of Spies, Heyward and Traven.

Fifth, recognising these continuities also helps us deal with the key question of how it is that postcolonial theorists are able to achieve the vantage point, apparently *outside* existing thought, from which to criticise existing knowledge as imperial. Again this is a particular problem for a theory which is so 'perspectival', in other words within which vantage point plays such a key role in the determination of knowledge.

This difficulty in Lyotard's perspectivism has been exposed in the following terms:

> What is interesting . . . is that despite Lyotard's argument that we are all subjects of language, positioned in and by a communication system which precedes and shapes us, and that our life and freedom come in knowing how to play and disorient the game, Lyotard nevertheless ultimately appeals to 'justice'

and defends 'values' which are here identified with otherness and irreducible heterogeneity. Yet he gives no explanation of *why* or *how* a player would make that very first act of 'renunciation of terror', or subdue that desire to overpower the game and obliterate the opposition. Nor does he explain what conditions would allow the agonistic players to first even *agree* to the contract that sets up the rules. If language is agon, conflict, and war game, how could any player ever step 'outside' it to appeal to justice, or to agree to a set of constraining rules? At bottom, this model ultimately continues to pit one form of aggression against another, one violence against the next. Is the game ultimately judge of the game, to paraphrase Hegel? (Handelmann, 1991: 195)

The problem of vantage point is particularly evident when we consider the explanation offered by postcolonial theorists for the emergence of a (their) postcolonial sensibility in the first place. Rightly criticising Lyotard for having no explanation for the rise of his own 'incredulity towards metanarratives', and dismissing Rorty's intercultural dialogues for their sociological naivety, or naivety about the power relations involved in contemporary 'cross cultural' dialogue, Said explains the new sensitivity as an imperative caused by the emergence of an identity politics among those previously denied a voice by orientalism. He argues that there is, therefore, an intimate connection between an emerging postmodern sense of identity, one that sees identity as contingent and subject to playful subversion and the rise of a postcolonial sensibility among the colonised. The former, in Said's view, represents an attempt on the part of the former colonisers to recapture the high ground, and, in so doing, once again acts to denigrate the voices of the colonised (Said, 1989). Said's comments bring to mind the project of those other main contributors to postcolonial theory, namely the Indian subalternists. Here we must assume that subalternism is itself developed by the pressures being exerted on hegemonic/colonial discourses on the part of subalterns themselves. But since postcolonial theorists are not themselves subalterns,[12] but part of a growing 'non-western' intelligentsia, a postcolonial analysis strikes one as incomplete at best. Particularly within a perspectival theory such as postcolonialism, we need to demand an explanation which takes account of the 'speakers of subalternism' themselves before we could say we had an adequate account of the emergence of their own position. Once again, the vantage point from which postcolonial theorists claim to speak becomes a problem precisely because they posit such a radical break with earlier imperial/counter-imperial discourses.

The same problem arises when we begin to examine perspective sociologically, as it were. To see Heyward, Spies and Traven as apologists for, or spokespersons of, empire is odd given their own social location. Certainly they were not 'natives', and thus it is not surprising that, in spite of claims to the contrary, their texts do not represent that 'native point of view' which anthropology has always claimed to represent. But neither were any of them in any sense imperial power holders. At best their social positions might be described as 'middle class', even impoverished middle class. And far from associating directly with the cultural project of empire, their cultural positions were at best marginal. Traven was, as we have seen, a political radical fleeing imprisonment first on the continent and then in England. Walter Spies ran into difficulties in Europe and later in Indonesia because his nationality was always marginal – no German nationalist, he was nonetheless imprisoned by the Russians in the First World War and the Dutch in the Second World War. His well-publicised homosexuality, moreover, more often than not made him *persona non grata* to the colonial authorities in the Netherlands East Indies. And if DuBose Heyward was merely an 'impoverished southern gentleman', George Gershwin grew up in prewar New York, when, largely as a consequence of a prolonged period of 'Americanisation', Jews were as likely to, indeed most often did, see themselves as part of an embattled group of minorities, immigrant and American-born, than as part of a dominant American culture with its roots in the pioneers' days. This surely explains why people like Gershwin, Traven and Spies were all critical of the civilisational implications of the techno-instrumental modernism of the 'social Darwinists'.

Contrary then to the spirit of much postcolonial rhetoric, I want here to suggest that what we have come to call postcolonialism is in fact part of an earlier expressivist discourse on culture and difference mobilised within a more general critique of techno-rationalist, bureaucratic and evolutionary modernism. This is a language of culture, alterity and identity that, I would argue, is shared by advocates of colonialism and anticolonialism in the twentieth century.

But to the extent that postcolonial discourse shares in this language of culture, identity and alterity, it also tends to draw a firm boundary between 'indigenous' and 'western' cultural representations. An important characteristic of the orientalist project according to Said and others is, as we have noted, the way it authorises certain people and not others to speak authentic oriental culture, as it were. It does this by maintaining that the essence of the Orient lies not in its present, but in its past.[13] Therefore knowledge of the 'true' Orient can only be gleaned through study of the classical texts, and, not surprisingly, only European scholars were thought to have the proper linguistic and archival resources to examine these texts. By authorising European scholars in this way, orientalism denies the other even the possibility of knowledge of his or her own culture, hence denying him/her a voice even in the construction of knowledge about him- or herself.

While this seems to be an accurate characterisation of much nineteenth century 'imperial' ideology, the question is does the position change in the twentieth? Are the representations of people like Heyward, Traven and Spies orientalist in this sense of the term? This is an issue to which we shall return. Suffice it to point out here that 'westerners' by the 1920s certainly had no monopoly on the representation of cultural otherness, either at home or abroad. For every Traven there is a Diego Rivera, for every DuBose Heyward or Carl Van Vechten there is a W.E.B. Du Bois, for every Walter Spies there is a Sukarno. And what should we make of Béla

Bartók, the evolution of whose musical style owed so much to his ethnological studies of the folk musics of his native Hungary, but also Slovenia, Algeria and Turkey? Is he indigene or imperialist? And what of Miguel Covarrubias, a Mexican by birth who in words and drawings produced influential representations of New York's Harlem and Bali, as well as of Mexico's indigenous peoples? Or, in the more mundane field of agricultural economics, what do we make of someone like A.V. Chayanov, the Russian 'neo-populist' who argued for the integrity of his country's own 'indigenous' (peasant) economic system in the face of Stalinist collectivisation. Is Chayanov's an 'indigenous voice' in Russia? But then what do we make of the fact that his work was seized upon by a whole generation of Dutch colonial advisers seeking ways of 'preserving' at least elements of Indonesia's 'native' agrarian systems? Who is the colonial, who is post-colonial?

In the light of these difficulties with the postcolonial project, it is interesting to note that elsewhere Said has himself anticipated a broader one. On precisely the issue of culture and difference – and particularly of the flaws of essentialism – he has suggested:

> If we no longer think of the relationship between cultures as perfectly contiguous, totally synchronous, wholly correspondent, and if we think of cultures as permeable and, on the whole, defensive boundaries between polities, a more promising situation appears. Thus to see others not as ontologically given but as historically constituted would be to erode the exclusivist biases we so often ascribe to cultures, our own not least. Cultures may then be represented as zones of control or abandonment, of recollection and of forgetting, of force or dependence, of exclusiveness or of sharing, all taking place in the global history that is our element. (1989: 225)

Said's recognition of the contingency of culture and difference seems to me to open the way to a more nuanced consideration of the context of discourses of cultural pluralism than is permitted in much of what passes for postcolonial critique (including it must be said some of Said's own), as well as opening up the possibility of a greater degree of reflexivity, so that one does not simply absolve oneself of any involvement in the phenomenon under scrutiny. What follows is just such an attempt to assess the project of cultural representation. And contrary to the claims of much recent cultural theory, in what follows I shall suggest that these discourses of cultural alterity, multiculturalism and the like came largely to replace the nineteenth century language of civilisation, the temporal anteriority of the other, and the emancipation of human beings as autonomous subjects already by the early twentieth century.

Nor even then did the language of culture and multiculture simply appear from nowhere. Instead it was already implied in a post-Enlightenment, but still mainly European, expressivist critique of utilitarianism and social Darwinism, leading one to suspect that against the claims of both its conservative defenders and its multicultural critics, 'western' modernism has been 'multicultural' from its very inception. This allows us to see more clearly than do many contemporary cultural commentators that the discursive shift within twentieth century modernism was not in any unambiguous sense a good or a bad thing, for certainly in this century culturalism and multiculturalism have been implicated in both imperial *and* counter-imperial projects, have been embedded in totalitarian as well as emancipatory movements.

It may now be time to recognise the interiority of the relationship between modernism and multiculturalism, and hence to abandon the vain search for a means of time or space travel to facilitate our escape from the shackles of modernity, instead once again dedicating ourselves to the rather different project of attempting to transcend it.

Notes

1 It is not certain that this would have been the case if Jerome Kern and Al Jolson had managed to produce their own musical version of *Porgy*. Fear that they would turn it into just another 'blackface' musical made the Heywards reluctant to sell the rights, but their financial circumstances made it necessary.

2 For an English-language account of Spies's paintings, see Rhodius and Darling (1980). For an excellent account of the developing European image of Bali as island paradise, and of the significant role played by Spies in this development, see Vickers (1989).

3 For an example of this treatment of Gershwin's musical 'fieldwork' see Alpert (1990: 88ff).

4 He wrote to a friend : 'The people . . . are so incredibly beautiful, so delicately built, brown and aristocratic, that all who do not resemble them should hang their heads in shame' (cited in Rhodius and Darling, 1980: 19).

5 Lyotard's account of the Cashinahua is based on an ethnography by André-Marcel D'Ans entitled *Le Dit des Vrais Hommes*.

6 It is instructive to note in this regard B. Traven's remarks on the 'particularism' of Mexican Indian thinking, as opposed to the abstract universalism of westerners. On memory and the importance of the naming of particular places (destroyed by colonialism) see the passage in *Treasure* (1980: 115); for the importance of concrete as opposed to abstract thinking, consider the passage in which the Indians tell Curtin that they don't know what 'figures', i.e. abstract numbers, are, one says: ' "You can't say ten. You must always say ten what. Ten trees, or ten men, or ten birds. If you say ten or five or three without saying what you mean, there's a hole and it's empty" '(1980: 130).

7 Spivak, for example, in her 'Three Women's Texts and a Critique of Imperialism' (1987), like Said, tackles the traces of empire in the English literary canon, and then goes on to argue that contemporary defence of that canon amounts to a refusal to come to terms with its imperial context, and hence a reinstatement of empire in the contemporary world. But this assumption about the persistence of empire is not unproblematic, since if orientalism is a specific knowledge effect of a particular *imperial* relationship of culture and power, then it would follow that the end of the empire will lead to other forms of knowledge. If imperial discourse is still with us, then surely so must also the economic/political dimensions of empire. The problem is that in most postcolonial theory these latter are envisaged almost entirely in terms of the political economy of nineteenth century English and French colonies. If such forms of colonial institution are gone, then how can imperial discourse persist into the late twentieth century? Perhaps the problem lies in a sociologically highly naive understanding of empire.

8 Nicholas Thomas has, in a somewhat different way, also attempted a critique of the tendency of at least some postcolonial theorists to treat ' "colonialism" as a unitary totality,

and to related totalities such as "colonial discourse", the "Other", "Orientalism and imperialism" ' (see Thomas, 1994: ix). Similarly, Thomas suggests that the existing critique of colonialism 'must deal with a wider range of events and representations, including some in which the critics themselves are implicated' (ibid: 2). It will be argued below that this implication is almost a necessity, that no critic is immune from it.

9 It was absolutely standard practice in introductory courses in Social Anthropology in Britain, at least in the 1970s when I did my training, to start off with a smug denunciation of 'social evolutionism' and those who practised it, the so-called 'armchair anthropologists'.

10 These terms are used to describe the influence of American popular music in Mexican funerals in *The Bridge in the Jungle*, first published in 1929 (Traven, 1980: 590). The polemical attacks on Christianity are scattered throughout the Mexican novels. See, for example, the discussion in *Treasure* in which banditry and barbarism in Mexico are explained as arising out of the introduction of Christianity (Traven, 1980: 91ff.). See also Cynthia Steele, 'The Primitivist as Anarchist' in Schuerer and Jenkins (1987).

11 Abdul JanMohammed argues, somewhat more carefully than most, that 'justification' cannot be used as a blanket explanation in this way. In fact, he writes, in the nineteenth century there was little felt need to justify imperial ideology to the conquered, only to members of the colonising society at home (1985).

12 See Spivak (1988).

13 This 'degenerationist' vision of the non-West is not strictly speaking 'social Darwinist' at all, since most Victorian social evolutionists accepted Spencer's assumption that all societies moved inexorably from simple to complex, undifferentiated to differentiated. But it was nonetheless an important strand in nineteenth century evolutionary thinking, having (like the Spencerian variant) come into it from Christian debates about monogenesis and polygenesis, degeneration and progressivism, etc. (see for example Burrow, 1966).

2
Culture, Difference and the Expressivist Critique of Modernism

When reports began to appear in the English-language media of the confrontation between government troops and armed insurgents in the southern Mexican state of Chiapas on New Year's Day of 1994, the general impression created was one of both surprise and mystery. The report by the Latin American correspondent for *The Times*[1] captured the mood perfectly when he wrote of these 'surprise attacks' which caught residents and tourists in the small town of San Cristobal de las Casas completely 'unaware as they celebrated New Year's Day'. The rebels, he wrote, arrived from nowhere, 'moving under cover of darkness'. They disappeared just as silently 'to the remote hillsides' from which they had so mysteriously emerged just twenty-four hours earlier.

Who exactly was involved in the EZLN? What could they possibly want? Did the attacks speak to a general unrest in Mexico, or were they mounted by those old bugbears, outside agitators? Could there possibly any longer be people who still believed that globalisation, development and – yes now that we had reached the 'end of history' – liberal economic and political values would not lead to a better world for all? Was not the very day of the attack the proclaimed beginning of a new age of equality and cooperation between North and South, at least in the continent of North America? Had we not been told, even by people on the left, that the idea of the Third World was now outmoded (Harris, 1986)?

Some commentators were of course not so mystified; they had seen it all before. The staff writer for *The Christian Science Monitor*[2] knew that we were witness yet again to the effects of an alien ideology implanted in the minds of ignorant rural people by a clandestine band of subversives.

Not all reporters saw the actions of the EZLN as those of subversives. But many nonetheless read the events in Chiapas on New Year's Day 1994 through similar pre-established universal categories. Those more sympathetic to the socialist aspirations of the EZLN drew our attention to the poverty and landlessness prevailing in Chiapas, the huge gap between rich and poor, the land alienation and degradation by logging companies, and the deleterious effects of an economy oriented towards the export of oil and hydro-power. While during the Mexican Revolution land had been distributed to poor peasants elsewhere through the *ejido* system, these promises remained unfulfilled in Chiapas. The socialist character of the movement did not seem out of harmony with the universalistic aspirations of an emerging rural proletariat in Chiapas.

Others, less socialistically inclined, saw the EZLN as the vehicle for a general movement for basic human rights, and particularly for basic political rights in a country long subjected to one-party rule and political corruption. Urban sympathisers in Mexico City included members of opposition parties calling for political liberalisation and democracy.

But these attempts to subsume the Chiapas affair to universalistic emancipatory languages seem flawed. Such discourses are the bread and butter of our own political debates; they are part of our world. But to read the reports of the events in Chiapas is to read not just of our world, but of a culturally alien one. This sense of a mysterious world and of the uniqueness of its inhabitants is found in almost all the reports that appeared in the immediate aftermath of 1 January 1994. The rebels, we were told, were more than simply normal citizens demanding their rights, farmers demanding land to farm – they were 'peasants' or, more often, indigenous peoples, a unique and alien form of humankind who slip in and out of their very particular worlds, often unnoticed, but occasionally violently and for reasons which we can never truly understand. The inhabitants of this alien world are steeped in a traditional culture that is radically different from our own, an 'indigenous' culture inimical to modernity. The peasants of Chiapas have been exploited and made landless by 'development', but the need for land is more than the need to have access to means of subsistence. As the *Guardian* correspondent put it, a plot of land (*milpa*) in Chiapas is more than a guarantee of economic subsistence. It is also a 'symbol of the right to live. For many Ch'ol, Tzeltal and Tzotzil indians in Chiapas, land ownership is a condition of 'indian-ness'. Those without usually leave their villages, severing ancestral ties, religious customs and languages to begin the process of *mestizaje* – westernization.[3]

The peasants of Chiapas, this article went on to explain, are culturally, socially and politically part of Guatemala, and they 'follow the same customs in the same isolated villages as their ancestors who built the Mayan pyramids in Guatemala and Mexico' (ibid.). Indeed members of the EZLN played their parts well, donning balaclava masks and furthering the sense of mystery. These masks, we were told later, sold like hotcakes in Mexico City, snapped up by those who saw the leaders of the movement as liberators from the corrupt and undemocratic government of the PRI.

Most reports by outside observers, accordingly, did not stress the universalistically emancipatory nature of the revolt so much as they continually drew our attention to the fact that the participants were not mere modern citizens. Chiapas has a large 'native Indian population of Mayan descent'.[4] The indigeneity of the people of the region was continuously stressed in accounts of the affair. The apparent survival of age-old cultures in the rural lacunae of the modern world makes terms like 'peasant', 'tradition', 'alien', 'indigenous' – in short, terms that convey radical cultural alterity, seem peculiarly apt here. Such terms frame the alien world of Chiapas by drawing a boundary between our own and alien worlds – crossed here one way by rebels and the other by reporters (or the 'experts' on Mayan culture to which our reporters refer). But, the reports imply, the crossing of the border will not substantially affect life on either side. The world of Chiapas remains clouded in mystery. It may perhaps continue to be the home of cultural otherness. Or it may be destroyed either suddenly or gradually by the encounter. If the latter happens then of course Chiapas will no longer be an alien world, and the reporter interested in cultural alterity will have to seek fresh fields for study. The crucial assumption then is of the radical cultural alterity of places like Chiapas.

The current preoccupation with, even consuming passion for, culture and difference in the 'West', to which reporting on the Chiapas affair speaks so eloquently, is characterised by the curious presupposition that cultural difference lies somehow outside modernity. In spite of the fact that modern society has been, from its very inception, both discursively and sociologically 'multicultural', despite the fact in other words that what we have in the late twentieth century come to call multiculturalism could be said to have been constitutive of both modernism and modernisation, we continue to think of 'other cultures' as though they somehow constituted a mode of existence outside ourselves.

Lest this be misunderstood, let me be clear on what I mean by this statement. In positing an interior relationship between difference and modernity, I have no intention of denying the existence of what might be called a radical cultural alterity, that is a difference that genuinely lies outside or beyond our economic, political and/or discursive reach.[5] On the contrary, I presume such alterity from the start. But the fact is that once we even seek to name that alterity, we thereby begin to integrate it to the self by bringing it back within modernity's reach. And at a very general level it is this process of naming difference, of thereby constructing alterity within modernity, that I see as constitutive of the modern world view. Why otherwise would the Chiapas of the European and North American news media be so mysterious? Is it really because we do not know what goes on over there? Is Chiapas really such unknown territory? Surely if previous reporters had brought back authentic knowledge of this alien culture, it would not be so alien to us.

Curiouser and Curiouser

In fact a cursory examination of the history of such encounters reveals that, contrary to the impression given by the media, January 1st was *not* the first time that the border between Chiapas and the modern world had been crossed by modern travellers seeking to provide us with knowledge of their cultural otherness. Chiapas is far from being unknown territory. On the contrary it has been one of the most reported-upon parts of the entire globe.

Even if we restrict ourselves to the last few decades we find that the industrialised world has been bombarded with information about the indigenous peoples of Chiapas. To quote one authority writing over ten years ago:

> Perhaps more than any other social group in recent memory, native people in highland Chiapas have been subjected to prolonged and continuous anthropological scrutiny, an unrelenting examination of the most intimate details of daily life. The outpouring of scholarly literature on such topics has been correspondingly prodigious: during the past quarter century, no less than 30 books and monographs on Indian communities in the area have been published; perhaps 20 of these have appeared in the last dozen years alone. (Wasserstrom, 1983: 1)

But then perhaps Chiapas remains alien territory because nobody reads anthropological monographs any more. The days are long past when books by the likes of Margaret Mead or Ruth Benedict were on the bookshelves of a large proportion of the educated middle classes. While we may have intimate knowledge of Chiapas, maybe it is stored away in obscure libraries, knowledge being limited to a small number of us.

Yet lack of familiarity with the anthropological literature on Chiapas is on its own an inadequate explanation for the sense of mystery the place seems to generate. For here is a case, rather typical in fact, where the anthropological literature itself seems to generate a sense of profound otherness in Chiapas. To the American anthropologist Sol Tax, the doyen of the anthropology of Mesoamerica, and his followers, Chiapas:

> appeared to offer an almost unique opportunity to test anthropological tools and concepts, to observe Indian society in a virtually uncontaminated setting, to develop paradigms for application and extension to other regions and problems. [The indigenous communities of Chiapas] permitted ethnographers to imagine how indigenous life might have been organized and conducted before the intrusions of Europeans. To this end, Tax and his followers soon devised a unique style of anthropological writing that (in keeping with professional standards of the day) placed heavy emphasis upon the ways in which local beliefs and practices reinforced communal solidarity'. (Wasserstrom, 1983: 3)

Far from dispelling the mystery of Chiapas, anthropologists have only contributed to it. But professional anthropology's contribution to the exoticisation of places like Chiapas must not be overestimated, or at least it must be seen in the context of a more general tendency to produce and consume cultural alterity in the West. Exoticised or othering knowledge of the indigenous culture of Chiapas, for example, is not restricted to the small public for anthropological monographs. Without wishing to suggest that the North American public is fully conversant with the details of indigenous lifeways in Chiapas, we can nonetheless point to other ways in which they have at least encountered 'traditional Mayan culture' in this part of Mexico, either directly as tourists, or indirectly as consumers of media imagery. We have already had occasion to mention John Huston's *The Treasure of the Sierra Madre*, which presents us with images of peasant life in Mexico[6] some time after the Mexican revolution.

But the Huston film shows something else at work. While particularly in the scene towards the end of the film where we encounter Howard – the old prospector played by Walter Huston – living an idyllic life among Mexican peasants, Huston's *Treasure* provides us with images of the otherness of Mexico's indigenous inhabitants, its main function is to transfer that alterity back home, to the San Joaquim valley where Curtin hopes to retire:

[What are you going to do with your share of the fortune?]

Curtin: I figure on buying some land and growing fruit – peaches maybe.

Howard: How'd you happen to settle on peaches?

Curtin: One summer when I was a kid I worked as a picker in a peach harvest in the San Joaquim Valley. It sure was something. Hundreds of people – old and young – whole families working together. After the day's work we used to build big bonfires and sit around 'em and sing to guitar music, till morning sometimes. You'd go to sleep, wake up and sing, and go to sleep again. Everybody had a wonderful time . . .

. . .

[and what about you Dobbsie?]

Dobbs: First off I'm going to the Turkish bath and sweat and soak til I get all the grime out of my pores. Then I'm going to a barber shop and after I've had my hair cut and 've been shaved and so on, I'm going to have 'em douse every bottle on the shelf. Then I'm going to a haberdasher's and buy brand new duds . . . a dozen of everything. And then I'm going to a swell cafe – and if everything ain't just right, and maybe if it is, I'm going to raise hell, bawl the waiter out, and have him take it back . . . (He smiles, thoroughly enjoying this imaginary scene at the table.)

Curtin: What's next on the programme.

Dobbs: What would be . . . a dame!

Curtin: Only one?

Dobbs: That'll depend on how good she is. Maybe one – maybe half a dozen.

Curtin: Dark or light?

Dobbs (the liberal):   I don't care what her nationality is just so long as she's kind of small and plump . . . you know . . . (his hands describe an hourglass) . . . with plenty of wiggle in 'er.

From John Huston's screenplay *The Treasure of the Sierra Madre*, Scene 47 (in J. Nevemore, 1979)

Typical of discourses of otherness in the modern age, 'cultural difference' seems to be only loosely attached to geographical locale. It manifests an uncanny ability to be relocated wherever its author, or reader, wishes to find it.

Huston's film was, as we have seen, 'based upon' another text, the novel of the same name written by one B. Traven and published first in German in 1927. In Traven's work, cultural alterity is located firmly in Chiapas.

A vehement critic of North American imperialism in Mexico, Traven would have been extremely reluctant to accept that an earthly paradise could have existed in the imperial heartland. Huston, equally critical of the 'bolshevism' of people like Traven, was just as determined that it could, although he could justifiably have argued that Traven's book did provide examples of camaraderie among his gringo 'workers'.

Less 'authentic' but equally influential as far as western school children from the 1920s onward are concerned were the various versions of the Zorro story, beginning with the first book by Johnston McCulley in 1919 which generated images of life in Spanish America.[7]

Yet hard as it may be to believe, there are doubtless members of the intelligentsia who read neither adventure stories nor anthropological monographs. But then they may have acquired some familiarity with the 'ancient' Mayan peasant culture of Mexico through the paintings of Diego Rivera who, disillusioned with the current high modernist style of European painting of the time (Abstract and Synthetic Cubism), returned to his native Mexico in the 1920s and rediscovered both figuration and indigenous Mayan motifs, producing along with several other Mexican painters a series of murals that at least for a time became the height of artistic fashion among progressive North American aesthetes.

The point of all this should now be evident. Chiapas is not an alien world at least to the intelligentsias of the North. Almost certainly 'we' know more about Chiapas than we do about the more 'mundane' regions of Mexico, and perhaps than we do of most parts of the cities in which we live. Indeed Chiapas seems to be one of those places, Bali being another, that becomes more mysterious the more information we have about it. Awe, wonder, mystery, alienness – these are not characteristics of a radical alterity at all, they appear to stem from the very appropriation of that alterity to modernity.

But it should not after all surprise us in this age of postmodern ethnography and postcolonial critique to find evidence of slippage between representations of cultural otherness and the real world. Chiapas by the 1920s, indeed from the sixteenth century, was after all very much part of the world that surrounds it – the object of Spanish conquest, revolutions and North American economic exploitation. Looked at from this perspective it might appear more curious that Chiapas should still be considered somehow *pre*-modern or at least *non*-modern.

But, of course, the naming of alterity has been a more or less universal dimension of human existence. It is the naming of cultural difference, and its reincorporation within the modern sensibility in general, and the modern subjectivity, in particular, that is a constitutive element of the modern condition. And it is precisely with this element of the modern condition with which we shall be concerned here.

A clue as to the role played by Chiapas in the modern imagination is provided in the contrast between the attitudes of Curtin and those of Dobbs. Dobbs is here taken to be the archetypal modern man, whose main concerns in life appear to be purely the satisfaction of personal desire. He wants nothing more than clothes, food, drink and sex, as much as he can get. His calculus is a purely instrumental one. Curtin, on the other hand, wants more out of life than the pure egoistic pursuit of pleasure. He wants, instead, the meaning expressed in family, community and nature. This implied critique of the modernism of a Dobbs, and subsequent modern attempts to come to grips with otherness take shape in what we might call the first central critique of modern culture. But while this critique appears in the period of the formation of a modernist sensibility, it has up to now remained unresolved, or better, following Charles Taylor, its effects have been contained in 'modern Western civilization'. It is this which accounts in part for the fact that this particular critique continues to resonate among modernism's discontents. I have here in mind of course what is often called romanticism, although it is debatable whether the term is precise enough to have any particular meaning. Moreover the use of the term is likely to be misleading since it is commonly employed as a term of abuse, to refer to a discourse as 'merely romantic' is to attempt to rob it of its critical cutting edge. More particularly therefore I have in mind what Taylor calls the 'expressivist' conception of human life that develops as a reaction and hence alternative to the Enlightenment vision of man based upon an 'associationist psychology, utilitarian ethics, atomistic politics of social engineering, and ultimately a mechanistic science of man' (Taylor, 1975: 539). But the critique cannot itself be called anything but modern since when consistently developed it does not merely advocate a return to a pre-modern age.

The instrumental mode of evaluation, inherited from the Enlightenment, and against which expressivism develops, has, argues Taylor, become endemic to modern society. In it

> [t]he major common institutions reflect . . . the Enlightenment conception in their defining ideas. This is obviously true of the economic institutions. But it is as true of the growing, rationalized bureaucracies, and it is not much less so of the political structures, which are organized largely to produce collective decision out of the concatenation of individual decisions (through voting) and/or negotiation between groups. (1975: 541)

At the same time the Enlightenment vision has also informed 'many . . . conceptions of society which have been invoked to mitigate the harsher consequences of the capitalist economy . . . [such as] notions of equality, of redistribution among individuals, of humanitarian defence of the weak' (ibid).

Taylor wants to argue that as a consequence 'expressivism' has been more or less banned from public life, and confined to the sphere of the private where 'Romantic views of private life and fulfilment' proliferate. I, on the other hand, am particularly interested in those periods when the expressivist critique of instrumentalism resonates more strongly beyond the discourse of personal fulfilment, that is those periods when tropes such as 'cultural difference' are marshalled against the very structures of the modern state and modern economy. For we are going through just such a period now, and this explains the seductiveness of invitations to 'listen to the voices' of the cultural other.

The expressivism that B. Traven speaks through his Mexican peasants, and John Huston through the fruit pickers of California, therefore appears first to have been clearly and publicly articulated by those unhappy either with what they took to be the Enlightenment attitudes towards man, or to the perceived threat of the emancipatory rhetoric of the French Revolution particularly in its Jacobin phase. This ground has been covered so many times in recent attempts to specify the nature of modernity in general, and of modern conceptions of the self, that it is not necessary to retrace the various strands of the argument here. Suffice it to say that what we, with Taylor, are calling expressivism developed against the perception that an increasingly larger number of humans in the grip of modern ideologies (philosophical or, more important for the masses, theological) were beginning to think of themselves as self-defining rather being defined from a cosmic order outside themselves. If, however, human subjectivity comes to be seen as self-definition, the relationship between humans and the world is radically transformed. Rather than humanity and nature together representing a deeper meaning whose source is the same, individuals are now seen as autonomous subjects who stand apart from the natural (and social) world which now becomes so many facts which can be known only by the sensations we have of it as autonomous subjects. This view of the world of nature Taylor characterises as 'objectified', by which he means a vision of nature as lacking in any inherent meaning and purpose, as characterised merely by contingent relations or patterns that we can uncover through the processes of observation. With Newton man now gives up the search for final causes in nature, and looks instead merely for efficient causes among separately observable 'facts'.

But in this view humans do not merely stand outside nature, for since the observable world is now totally naturalised, then man must also be part of nature, and therefore understandable in the same way that we understand the movements of the planets. Discovering the nature of humans was conceived by Enlightenment scholars to be a process like all other forms of scientific inquiry, since it was assumed that humans were part of that rational and understandable natural order which it was the task of philosophers to study.

There were, argues Weyant (1973), three kinds of approach to the investigation of human nature during the eighteenth century, which he terms 'biological', 'psychological' and 'anthropological'. The first was concerned with the properties which set the human creature apart from other creatures. Inheritors of the Christian category of Man as a separate creation of God, these scientists were, not surprisingly, concerned with biology, not theology.

Second, there were attempts to analyse human nature into a small number of basic abilities, processes or faculties which combined in lawful ways to produce the complex observable phenomenon of human behaviour. These Weyant describes as psychological theories.

Finally there were those who focused on the question of what Man would be, or had been, in a state of nature, without the complications of social contracts or customs. These anthropological (in the philosophical sense) studies aimed at the determination of Man's original nature, as a prelude to criticising social institutions which did not enhance or further that nature.

What were the results of these studies? First, although largely unified in their approaches to the study of human nature, it cannot be said that Enlightenment philosophers came to any very sophisticated, or even agreed upon, understanding of the 'nature of human nature'. Second, it is clearly possible with the benefit of hindsight to see that this is quite clearly a consequence of the naive way in which they set about studying it. What is perhaps more important to a characterisation of the age is that there were widely shared views, namely that:

1   There *is* a fundamental human nature.
2   That it is shared by *all of humanity*.
3   That it is the proper task of science to investigate it just like any other aspect of the natural world.

To this it is important to add two more points of summary. First, and somewhat paradoxically, it can be argued that Enlightenment philosophers believed that 'it is the nature of Man to have no nature'. While not strictly speaking accurate (cf. Weyant, 1973) this belief does follow on logically from an extreme version of Lockian sensationalism, a view that Man has no innate ideas. This view holds, in other words, that everything about humans derives from their sensed experience, hence human character, social behaviour, and so on are totally *environmentally* determined. Such a view is, for example, implied by the remark of Helvetius who wrote: 'Born without ideas, without vice, and without virtue, everything in man, even his humanity, is an acquisition' (quoted in Weyant, 1973: 32).

But, second, if Lockian sensationalism tended to lead Enlightenment philosophers to the notion of 'natureless humans', most of them also did share a minimalist view of humans, like Huston's Dobbs, as seekers of pleasure and avoiders of pain. Even Locke and Helvetius, with their minimalist notions of human nature, accepted the universality of pleasure/ pain in human nature. Beyond this minimum there were two main tendencies in Enlightenment anthropology, described by Weyant as *egocentric* and *sociocentric*. According to the first of these, human behaviour stems entirely from personal needs and desires; for the latter, while some human behaviour stems from personal needs and desires, there is also a natural affection for others, a 'social love'. An example here is the Earl of Shaftesbury's distinction between the mutual affections which lead to the good of the public, and the self affections which lead to the good of the private. This view of an innate human morality, what Weyant calls a view of human nature as essentially *sociocentric*, is also found in the writers of the Scottish Enlightenment, including Adam Smith in his *Theory of Moral Sentiments* (a view which he changed later in his better-known work on human economic egoism) and in the thought of Thomas Jefferson.

It is important to see the connection between this Enlightenment anthropology and the new understanding of human freedom that arose in the period. Freedom now becomes the freedom of the individual subject to express his/her human nature most fully, that is, for the minimalist to be free to maximise pleasure and minimise pain. This means that all social, political and religious institutions need to be judged according to whether they do or do not hinder the autonomy of the individual subject. It does not, of course, follow that all such institutions must be destroyed. Instead they must be evaluated according to the principles of reason as to their effects on human individuality. Naturally those who see human nature as largely egocentric, such as Jeremy Bentham, will find the need for political institutions, even highly repressive ones, in order to maximise the sum total of human happiness rather than the happiness of particular individuals which may lead to a decrease in the happiness of the whole.

Indeed this combination of naturalism and atomism brings a new way of making moral judgements based now not on religion but on scientific reason itself.

Now, rather than simply rejecting this Enlightenment formulation of modern subjectivity, and advocating a return to the vision of human subjectivity as a mere expression of a cosmic order that is also expressed in nature and in human social arrangements, expressivists in general retained, even if unconsciously, the vision of a self-defining subjectivity. What they appeared to object to most was instead the separation between subjectivity and the world, between meaning and being, hence between mind and body posited by Enlightenment anthropology. This is, of course, most radically posited by Kant in his argument that there can be no internal connection between the thing in itself and the knowledge we have of it. But it is generally present in most eighteenth century philosophy which, as we have seen, abandons final for efficient cause and hence sees meaning as a property not of the world itself but only of our propositions about it.

What Taylor calls expressivism takes a view of human life quite different from that implied by Enlightenment anthropology. Rather than seeing human life and activity as essentially without any meaning, expressivism sees them as 'expressions', as realisations of a purpose or an idea. This notion was unlike pre-modern notions of expression, in two main ways. First, for the pre-moderns the meaning or purpose of human life is pre-given, that is it is already established outside human subjectivity, while for modern expressivism the meaning unfolds within human subjectivity – hence the notion of the self-defining subject is retained. Second, that meaning is not necessarily known in advance, that is humans may grasp it or recognise it as their own only once it has been realised. It could not have been known in advance. To quote Taylor:

> the notion of human life as expression sees this not only as the realization of purposes but also as the clarification of these purposes. It is not only the fulfilment of life but also the clarification of meaning. In the course of living adequately I not only fulfil my humanity but clarify what my humanity is about. As such a clarification of my life-form is not just the fulfilment of purpose but the embodiment of meaning, the expression of an idea. The expression theory breaks with the Enlightenment dichotomy between meaning and being, *at least as far as human life is concerned.* Human life is both fact and meaningful expression; and its being expression does not reside in a subjective relation of reference to something else, it expresses the idea which it realizes. (1975: 17; emphasis added)

This expressivist critique of Enlightenment anthropology can and has led to a number of somewhat diverse projects: an intuitionist critique of reason, an extreme romantic individualism, a particular romantic aesthetics (perhaps the central project of Romanticism), a pantheistic nature worship, and so on with which we shall not be concerned here (this explains my emphasis on the above quote from Taylor). Instead, to bring this back to the particular critique of instrumental reason with which we are concerned here, it is important to see how expressivism lay at the foundation of two ideas – first, what we might call the meaning of human cultural life and, second, the diversity of human groups – which in turn provide the basis for the kind of anthropological (now using the term in our twentieth century sense) critique of the commodity with which we began.

As Taylor demonstrates, these ideas are first clearly articulated by Herder, and it is therefore worth looking briefly at his discussion of them.[8] In Enlightenment philosophy language is seen simply as a set of arbitrary signifiers whose meaning is those objects and ideas to which it refers. The idea that language could itself have a meaning or purpose would have been nonsensical within this view. It is this instrumental understanding of language as 'referential sign', as a mere tool-kit with which Herder took issue. For him language is not just a way of operating in an objectified world, it is itself an expression of human capacity or potential, more than that it is its embodiment. Language does not merely represent thought, in some sense it actually is human thought. As part of the world, it is outside us, but it is also our expression, and as such a system of human expression that cannot be reduced to its instrumental function. It has purpose in the pre-modern sense, but that purpose is not divinely pre-given but created by human subjectivity.

It is significant that Herder used language as his main example of human expression for a number of reasons. First, language is of course intrinsically social and hence, more clearly than would have been the case for art, it can be seen to be not just the expression of a highly individualised romantic subjectivity, for it is of necessity created by humans in social groups. Second, the recognition of the interior relationship between language and human thought leads one to reach conclusions about other spheres of shared meaning similar to those reached about language – in other words recognition of the non-instrumental, expressive dimensions of language leads almost inexorably to a view of human culture as a whole as expression in the romantic sense (a conclusion drawn by successive generations of linguists and anthropologists). Third, there are of course many languages in the world which leads the expressivist, unlike the instrumentalist, to the view that humanity or better modes of thought/ systems of meaning can be differentiated. Combined with our first point this leads less to a private or highly individualised expressionism but a public one, a division of the public into different linguistic and, hence, cultural groups. This in turn marks the beginning of a second, if related, critique of Enlightenment anthropology, that is of its universalistic pre-suppositions. That the English, French and Germans have different languages is no longer just an accident, an arbitrary or contingent point of difference among them. It is a fundamental difference since in Herder's system linguistic differences speak of differences in the modes of thought, or *Volksgeist* of different peoples.

As we have suggested, expressivism represents a critique of an Enlightenment anthropology in which the world is objectified and subjected to human reasoning and manipulation. But it is more than epistemological critique – expressivism is also a heartfelt despair at the world view propounded by eighteenth century philosophy. To quote Taylor once again:

> The Enlightenment developed a conception of nature, including human nature, as a set of objectified facts with which the subject had to deal in acquiring knowledge and acting. [It created a] rift . . . between nature, whether as plan or instrument, and the will which acted on this plan.
>   It was this rift which the originators of expressivist theory . . . could not tolerate. They experienced this vision of things as a tearing apart of the unity of life in which nature should be at once the inspiration and motive force of thought and will. It was not enough that nature provide the blueprint for the will, the voice of nature must speak through the will. (1975: 22f.)

But this rift between humans and nature was not the only rift decried by expressivism. As the discussion of Herder shows expressivism also decried the rift among humans themselves created by the Enlightenment vision of human nature. As Taylor points out:

> what has been said of communion with nature applies with the same force to communion with other men. Here too, the expressivist view responds with dismay and horror to the Enlightenment vision of society made up of atomistic, morally self-sufficient subjects who enter into external relations with each other, seeking either advantage or the defence of individual rights. They seek for a deeper bond of felt unity which will unite sympathy between men with their highest self-feeling, in which men's highest concerns are shared and woven into community life rather than remaining the preserve of individuals. (1975: 27f.)

The very notion of freedom espoused by the Enlightenment and the French revolutionaries was, according to expressivism, only negative, and hence meaningless. For the former freedom meant only that unshackling of the individual free to pursue his/her own private ends. But where did these ends come from if not from the communities/languages in which they were embedded? And if so then unshackling all human bonds in the name of freedom is to create a new kind of slavery in which humans are now left only with their natural desires and inclinations, pursuing these goals and these goals alone in purely instrumental fashion. This is what is left by Enlightenment reason and the emancipation promised by the French Revolution.

It can now, I think, be seen fairly clearly that the trope of cultural difference represents a direct development out of the expressivist critique of the instrumental rationalism of the eighteenth century. Dobbs's pursuit of base self-interest embodies all that the expressivists were reacting against – a crude materialism, a desire to satisfy the baser wants against the higher potential of human subjectivity, competitive/atomistic individualism, conflict and competition, and so on. It should come as no surprise that more radical expressivism should find inspiration in Marx, and not so much the Marx of *Capital*, but the Marx of the 1844 manuscripts who had come into direct contact with expressivism. Although decidedly not part of the movement for a Romanticist and highly individualised aesthetics,[9] Marx was through Hegel very much in touch with the expressivist critique of Enlightenment instrumentalism. This stance in Marx is most clearly expressed in his earlier work in which alienation is the key theme.

The notion of alienation represented Marx's own ambivalence towards the freedom and emancipation promised by the French Revolution and articulated by the philosophers of the French Enlightenment. Like many German intellectuals of the early nineteenth century Marx embraced the ideal of human emancipation, but also wondered whether the French 'freedom of the individual' was really any kind of freedom at all. For to maintain that freedom of the individual was equivalent to human emancipation was to assume that 'the individual' as known to Enlightenment philosophy was really the autonomous, pre-social being posited by French and British philosophical constructions of humans in a state of nature. Or rather was this autonomous self itself something artificial, that is a socially constructed being whose character derived from the society and culture from which he or she (but mostly he) emanated? In fact, argued Marx very early on, freeing the individual is not to give free expression to basic human needs at all, but merely to give full flight to an individual *alienated* from his or her true 'species being' or nature, free to compete, to do down his neighbour. Human 'species being', for Marx, was not therefore defined by a Hobbesian or Smithian state of nature. On the contrary what such philosophers took for humans in a state of nature was really humans in a social state – alienated from each other by the imperative to compete with each other. That social arena Marx, following Hegel, termed modern civil society (the label capitalism was to come later). And reading through the early manuscripts one is constantly struck by the extent to which for Marx, as for Hegel, civil society is defined as the sphere of economic exchange.

Hegel, as we know, therefore saw the path to emancipation through an institution that stood outside civil society, for only in this way could the selfishness imposed on man by the norms of civil society be curbed and true reason (as opposed to understanding) find its fullest expression. That institution for Hegel was of course the State. Marx and his fellow left Hegelians, having observed the development of the Prussian state,[10] rejected this solution, arguing that the State, far from being altruistic and standing outside civil society, in fact had its own particular agendas and in any case was the captive of powerful forces emanating from civil society.

We know how later on Marx was to discover an alternative vehicle of emancipation in the class of proletarians, that one group within civil society for whom the universal interests of human emancipation corresponded with self-interest. However this mode of characterising civil society – as class society – appeared somewhat later on in Marx's career. His earlier critique of modern notions of freedom rested instead almost entirely on the notion that money, markets, exchange, commodities and, hence, individualism as competition for individual advantage represent the main alienating forces in modern society. 'Practical need or egoism' he wrote 'is the principle of civil society and appears as such in all its purity as soon as civil society has completely given birth to the political state. The god of practical need and selfishness is money' (Marx, 1971: 112). And this influence is corrosive and corrupting of all forms of human social arrangement. Referring to religion, for example, Marx writes that:

> Man emancipates himself politically from religion by banishing it from the field of public law and making it a private right. Religion is no longer the spirit of the state where man behaves, as a species-being in community with other men albeit in a limited manner and in a particular form and a particular sphere: religion has become the spirit of civil society, the sphere of egoism, the *bellum omnium contra omnes* ['the war of everyone against everyone']. Its essence is no longer in community but in difference. It has become the expression of separation of man from his common essence, from himself and from other men, as it was originally. (1971: 95)

That in some of his earliest writings Marx subscribed wholeheartedly to the narrative of demon commodity, a narrative which derives in part from his own attachment to a version of expressivism is here clear. And in this, it must be added, Marx did not depart very far from either his teacher, Hegel, or from his contemporaries, the so-called Young Hegelians.

Hegel himself was less critical of civil society than was Marx, for true to his dialectical understanding of history he saw individualisation and freedom as necessary to the emergence of a synthetic *Sittlichkeit* that would surpass that of the Greek polis that he admired so much. But precisely because civil society is driven by selfish calculation:

> it also leads to the intensification of the division of labour, the increasing subdivision of jobs, and the growth of a proletariat. . . . This proletariat is both materially impoverished, and spiritually as well by the narrowness and monotony of its work. But once men are reduced in this way materially and spiritually they

lose their sense of self-respect and their identification with the whole community, they cease to be integrated into and they become a 'rabble'. (Taylor, 1975: 436)

As a result for Hegel, as for Marx, it is less a question of turning back than of transcendence, and for Hegel civil society will 'be kept in balance by being incorporated in a deeper community. It cannot govern itself. Its members need allegiance to a higher community to turn them away from infinite self-enrichment as a goal and hence the self-destruction of civil society' (ibid.: 438).

Further Adventures of a Trope

If the expressivist critique of modernity that arose first in late eighteenth century romanticism has been more or less contained by the increasing dominance of techno-rationalism in the public sphere on the one hand and the pre-eminence of the Enlightenment project of emancipation in the aims of the most significant opposition movements, including Marxism, on the other, it must not be assumed that it has disappeared. On the contrary it is my contention that expressivism remains a constitutive element in the formation of a modern (and postmodern?) culture, not confined solely to private life as Taylor suggests. Instead expressivism, particularly in the form of the critique of commodification and instrumental reason, has been a more or less constant presence in the history of modern culture, never resolved, taking different forms and being articulated by radically different political forces, but always an undercurrent that resonates particularly in times of perceived crises of modernity. That expressivism continues to resonate in modern culture (at least among intellectuals) is evident as I have suggested in the reception accorded the works of 'anthropologists' like B. Traven, Walter Spies and DuBose Heyward, and, more recently, the writings of postcolonial and multicultural theorists. Marx's account of the alienating qualities of modern civil society was not the end but only the beginning of this expressivist current in modern thought.

While the Hegelian version of expressivism may not have survived the disasters of 1848, the negative vision of commodification and instrumental reason did not disappear even, or especially in nineteenth century Germany. And of course the expressivist critique of the commodity has re-emerged in this century in different forms and in different places. This is not the place for further detailed exposition, but the following are deserving of mention:

1 Combining the concerns of the Young Hegelians and of Weber characteristic of all Frankfurt School exponents, Adorno's critique of mass culture and Habermas's critique of instrumental rationality. For Adorno protection against infection by instrumental reason is to be found in high art, for Habermas in the sphere of communicative action.
2 More direct heirs of the German economists include: the Russian 'neo-populist' A.V. Chayanov arguing for the unique features of the

peasantry which cannot be subsumed to general economic theory that presupposes a universal homo œconomicus (either liberal *or* Marx); Karl Polanyi who brought many of the ideas of Historical Economics into American anthropology, instigating the so-called substantivist critique of 'formalism' (once again a critique of instrumental rationality, and especially of attributing it to non-western peoples), leading in turn to Marshall Sahlins's critique of 'practical reason' and Clifford Geertz's attack on economism.

3   Critiques of the 'consumerism' of western, particularly American, society, from Thorstein Veblen to the so-called 'institutionalists' and also to the *Monthly Review* economists, particularly Paul Baran and Paul Sweezy.

4   The anthropological heirs of Durkheim in France, especially Marcel Mauss whose analysis of the gift was formulated in direct opposition to the instrumental mode of commodity exchange

5   Finally, the more recent globalisation of the critique of 'western' individualism. Of particular interest here are the ways this critique has become embedded in an Asian critique of western modernity. In Malaysia, for example, we see it both in the notion of a particularly Malaysian, or Asian, path to modernity which avoids the materialism and instrumentalism of the West, and in the discourse of an Islamic economics where greed is replaced by moral relations within the Islamic *ummat*.

Community as Human Expression

Among B. Traven's 'Mexican Indians', DuBose Heyward's 'Negroes', Walter Spies's 'Balinese' we see the significance of the concept of community to the early twentieth century discourse on difference – communities are seen as social matrices that serve at least to contain and at most negate human egoism. Not surprisingly twentieth century ideas of *other communities* are as much influenced by western notions of community as they are informed by the facts of non-western community life, although they acquire a certain specificity in so far as they have been projected upon the non-West.

As we have already suggested early modern expressivist discourses on human subjectivity imply from the outset notions of human communities conceived in opposition to those agglomerations of self-interested individuals that were so central to Enlightenment philosophy. But while for twentieth century writers community is, more often than not, a property of the social life of the other, for early modern expressivism communities characterise – or must come to characterise – the social life of modernity itself. Yes, community life is endangered by the spread of instrumental rationality. But it can nonetheless be preserved against the corrosive effects of commodity circulation, or new forms of community can and must be established to avoid the *bellum omnium contra omnes* that is promised by the rise of modern civil society.

It is once again in Hegel that we find the parameters laid down for a concern with the communal that was to arise, if in different forms, time and time again throughout the nineteenth century – a concern that perhaps finds its most influential spokesman in Ferdinand Tönnies. But while, perhaps influenced by the rapid pace of late nineteenth century industrialisation and urbanisation, Tönnies and many others like him yearned for a lost community, the Hegelians, along with other early nineteenth century thinkers were considerably less nostalgic and considerably more optimistic that new forms of community could be created either as uniquely modern human expressions or, as in Hegel's case, expressions of a human-like transcendental subject – the absolute spirit of history.

If Hegel was uninterested in a return to the ancient community, and while his notion of the modern political community (qua state) was more accommodationist in relation to the rise of capitalism and instrumental rationality, Marx, as many have remarked (see Berman, 1983), was somewhat more ambivalent. There is, on the one hand, the almost celebratory modernism of *The Communist Manifesto*, and, on the other, the nostalgia of, for example, the 1844 manuscripts. But equally clearly, community is an absolutely necessary part of Marx's critique of civil society. In fact, the extent to which he shared such notions with the whole range of his fellow German philosophers cannot be stressed too much. A case in point is his one-time ally Moses Hess whose notions of community clearly informed his later Zionist writings. Of all the German philosophers in the years before 1848 it is perhaps only Max Stirner who rejected any form of communitarianism in his relentless attack on all appeals – whether traditional or modern – to loyalties beyond the ego, although even in the case of Stirner it can be argued that there is a notion of the communal in his recognition of the extra-individual determinants of subjectivity itself. This in any case was the view at least of some who, like Landauer, chose to resurrect Stirner's 'anarchism' in the critique of orthodox social democracy at the turn of this century. And it is through Landauer's anarchism that the Young Hegelian concern found its way into the contrasting image of community among Mexican peasants, for Ret Marut/B. Traven was a disciple (see Essback, 1987).

So central was the notion of community to nineteenth century expressivism, and so important was expressivism to the formation of classic modern social theory that we can with Robertson speak of *Gemeinschaft* as *the* central problematic of classical sociology (Robertson, 1992).

Culture, Difference and Expressivism

The language of empire and counter-empire is, by definition, a language of culture and alterity. Note how Edward Said's very definition of empire, as something over and above profit, is couched instead in terms of profound cultural difference:

> There was a commitment to them [empires] over and above profit, a commitment in constant circulation and recirculation, which, on the one hand, allowed decent men and women to accept the notion that **distant territories** and their **native peoples** *should* be subjugated, and, on the other, replenished metropolitan energies so that these decent people could think of the *imperium* as a protracted, almost metaphysical obligation to rule subordinate, inferior, or less advanced **peoples** (1993: 10; bold emphasis added)

Even the most passionate of contemporary critics of empires is forced to use their language – a language of immense distances, cultural as well as physical, that separate rulers from 'natives' – in order to define them. Without these terms there is only 'normal' state power over its citizens. Why is or was the French republic not an empire? Surely it has not been democracy that differentiates modern states from empires. No, it is the profound difference between ruler and ruled – a difference that is and has to be acknowledged by imperialist and counter-imperialist alike.

And while there is no doubt, as a whole host of postcolonial theorists have hastened to point out, that the discourse of racial hierarchies, of superior and inferior peoples, of the civilising mission of the West, has been handed down to us by nineteenth century apologists for colonialism, we also have the nineteenth century to thank for the very language by which we continue to define, and to criticise empire, that is the language of that profound cultural alterity without which empires could not even be seen to have existed. While it may have been 'social Darwinism' that gave us the modern language of dominance and subordination, it was quite clearly a form of expressivism that defined for the imperialist who was to dominate and who to be subordinate. And it was that same language in which the challenge to 'alien' rule and domination has since then had to be phrased. In this the discourses of empire/counter-empire in the nineteenth century spoke the same language of culture, difference and destiny, just as they have in the twentieth.

At least with the benefit of hindsight, it may not be altogether surprising to find that, just as Victorian Britain gave us that supreme cultural justification for imperial rule now known as social Darwinism, so it was most clearly in Germany in the first part of the nineteenth century that our modern language of culture and difference was first articulated. Germany was, after all, the world's first modern colony, 'emancipated' by Napoleon, and exploited by the world's foremost economic power, Great Britain, in the name of free trade. Subsequently Germany both threw off French political domination to become the modern world's first 'new nation state', and overcame British economic hegemony to become the world's first 'newly industrialised country' – all this ultimately to compete with these metropoles as a fully-fledged imperial power itself.

This is not the place for an exhaustive cataloguing of nineteenth century treatments of human difference in general, or the cultural differentiation of humanity that is a feature of so much nineteenth century social theory in particular. Instead, in examining a number of examples, I want to demonstrate a number of things: that simplistic formulae such as those brought to bear by McGrane, Said and others are bound to be inadequate; that while the vision of a multicultural globe that developed in the interwar years is in many ways unique, it was built up from elements that were given to it by nineteenth century discourses on human difference; and that it was particularly from what I have, with Taylor, been calling expressivist currents in European thought that the modern (and to an extent also postmodern) discourses of cultural difference have been fed. For these reasons, and also because developments within Anglo-Saxon positivism have already been so thoroughly documented (see for example Burrow, 1966; Hawthorn, 1976; McGrane, 1989), that I shall restrict myself here to the role played by notions of cultural difference in the expressivist currents in European, especially German, thought particularly in the period before the disasters of 1848.

If culture is understood as a complex of meanings that is unique to a particular group of human beings, then there is little doubt that this mode of conceiving of humanity as a fragmented rather than universal category has its origins in the late eighteenth century critique of Enlightenment instrumentalism. We have already had occasion to remark on the way Herder's theory of language led to the notion of human systems of symbolic communication as *expressions*, hence as possessing a meaning in their own terms (rather than finding meaning only in that which they stand for or signify). And while the expressions that interested some romantics were art, or even nature itself, an equally important expressivist tendency was concerned with what we might term the symbolic expressions of humans in social groups, what Herder called *Volksgeist*.

Now it has to be said that it was less the symbolic codes of other human groups, and more the symbolic expressions of their own groups that interested most turn-of-the-nineteenth century Europeans. Specifically of course this is the time when one kind of cultural expression, that is the nation, was drawing the most attention. In this Herder was in no way untypical of his time or place, an intellectual living in a region that was perceived to be on the fringes of the emerging modern world, the economic and political centre of which was located in Britain and France respectively. It has been argued convincingly by Peter Murphy that the Romantic nationalist project is the first and perhaps the most radical of modern attempts to conceptualise human alterity (see Murphy, 1993). To this one might add, contra Murphy, that the ways in which modern Europeans came to conceive of nations has been perhaps the dominant influence on the way they came to conceive of a single world made up of a diversity or mosaic of cultures. For the claims to nationhood, while often advanced in opposition to the supposed shortcomings of eighteenth century universalism, nonetheless employed universalist language, arguing for the rights of *all* peoples to their own unique national traditions:

In [Herder's] eyes, nations and their traditions were living wholes existing in organic cohesion and yet, simultaneously, individuals whose uniqueness should be recognized. He saw history as the natural history of 'living human force', as a process in which *one* mankind presented itself in multiple forms and expressions while, at the same time, the very idea of humanity acted as a regulatory force. 'Because *one* form of humanity and *one* region of the earth were unable to contain it, it spread out in a thousand forms, it journeyed – an eternal Proteus – through all of the areas of the earth and down through all the centuries. (Halbfass, 1988: 69)

Herder and the other early imaginers of German nationhood formulated their views, significantly, before Germany was itself a nation state, but a 'loosely organized confederation of some 250 sovereign territories' the most prominent of which were the eight electoral states, including Austria, Bavaria, Prussia, and Saxony, the remainder belonging 'to twenty-seven spiritual members of the College of Princes, thirty-seven lay princes, ninety-five imperial counts, forty-two imperial founders, and fifty free or imperial towns' (Linke, 1990: 121). Nor was Germany at this time in any sense an economic unit, each local fiefdom and principality jealously protecting itself against external competition by a complex web of protective measures. It is not surprising, then, that Germany, and by extension all the other 'forms and expressions' of humanity should have been conceived first not as a political or economic but as a linguistic/cultural unit, the original 'imagined community' (cf. Anderson, 1983).

The Road to India

But the idea of German nationhood led to notions of culture and alterity in another way as well – for in their critique of the rise of (French and British) instrumentalism, many German intellectuals found a somewhat unlikely counterweight in an India that:

became the focal point of an enthusiastic interest, occasionally bordering on fanaticism, within the German romantic movement. Here, the motif of origins and unspoiled pristineness shared by the Enlightenment became effective in a different, more exalted way. The very idea of India assumed mythical proportions; the turn towards India became the quest for the true depths of our own being, a search for the original, infant state of the human race, for the lost paradise of all religions and philosophies. 'The "eternal Orient" was waiting to be rediscovered within ourselves; India was the "cradle of humanity" and our eternal home'; it was the 'home and youth of the soul'. It represented the 'spirit of infancy', which Schelling evoked in his early programmatic work *Über Mythen, historische Sagen und Philosopheme der ältesten Welt* ('On Myths, Historical Legends and Philosophemes of the Most Ancient World', 1793). For something was missing from the European present – the sense of unity and wholeness – and this was mourned as the affliction of the time. There was hope that a return to the Indian sources would bring about a change for the better. (Halbfass, 1988: 72–3).

In the romance of the Orient that is as much a feature of the history of European thought as is its demonisation, India and China have for some considerable time played contrasting roles. Typical of the China worship is the eighteenth century, particularly French, admiration of all things Chinese – from Voltaire to the physiocrats to the consumption of Chinese design in the movement known as *chinoiserie*. Here China played the role of earthly, rational and enlightened civilisation, precisely the kind of civilisation to which the *philosophes* themselves aspired. When India's turn came, it once again played the role of mystic and organic foil to Europe's supremely cold, rationalistic and instrumental civilisation [11]

Among the authors who contributed to the development of the (German) 'Romantic understanding of India' were Schelling, Novalis, Görres, Creuzer, Goethe, M. Claudius and, 'more than any of the others, the Schlegel brothers' (Halbfass, 1988: 73).

Stressing India's infancy and antiquity, J. Görres wrote:

> And do you know the land where infant mankind lived its happy childhood years, where stood the pillars of fire in which the gods descended to their darlings and mingled in their spirited play? . . . Towards the Orient, to the banks of the Ganges and the Indus, it is there that our hearts feel being drawn by some hidden urge, – it is here that all the dark presentiments point which lie in the depths of our hearts, and it is there that we go when we follow the silent river which flows through time in legends and sacred songs to its source. In the Orient, the heavens poured forth into the Earth. In the primitive cultures of this earth, the original force must still appear undivided; in them everything must be contained in the same homogeneity which would later become separated into the various camps. (Görres cited in Halbfass, 1988: 73–4).

In *Die Christenheit oder Europe* ('Christendom or Europe', 1799), Novalis, the greatest of the early Romantics, wrote of an idealised medieval world, of a time in which God, man, and the world were united in harmony and mankind was filled with a 'childlike trust'. This was the standard against which he measured his criticism of the present. Because of Herder's influence, however, the Orient and especially an idealised India also became associated with the idea of an original state of harmony and a childlike, unbroken wholeness:

> Poesy-garbed India, where the people were still 'dozing' and dreaming, appeared to be the antithesis of the cold, prosaic Europe of the Age of Enlightenment. The poesy sought in India was at once religion. 'Religion is the great Orient in us, which is seldom obscured'. Still, for Novalis [like a number of other Romantics] India never attained the central importance that would have led him to strive after a more detailed knowledge. (Halbfass, 1988: 74)

For Friederich Schlegel the critique of Europe through the lens of an Indic imaginary was even sharper. European Man, he wrote 'cannot sink any deeper; it is impossible. Man has indeed come very far in the art of arbitrary division or, what amounts to the same thing, in mechanism, and thus man himself has almost become a machine' (ibid.: 74). India ' "from where every religion and mythology up till now has come", where the "possibility of enthusiasm" could never be completely obliterated' provided a way out (ibid.: 74f.). Summarising the role played by India in Romantic thought, and particularly that of the Schlegels, Halbfass writes:

> [T]he Romantic interest in India was inseparable from a radical critique of the European present. The preoccupation with the merely useful, the calculable, rational, precisely determinable, the loss of faith, enthusiasm, and the sense of unity and wholeness, were seen as symptomatic deficiencies of this present. As a remedy for such spiritual impoverishment, Friedrich Schlegel proposed a return to the sources of Indian wisdom. Yet in order to bring about such a return, he felt that linguistic studies alone would not suffice; they had to be supplemented by 'research', by the historical and philological methods of his time. The types and methods of Indological research which Friedrich and August Wilhelm Schlegel eventually applied proved to be aspects and symptoms of precisely that present, which the *yearning* for India had initially sought to overcome [in other words, the sort of Indological interest and research as advocated and pursued by such Romantic figures as the Schlegel brothers not only allowed rational thinking back in, but also allowed it to acquire even more sophisticated and developed forms]. There is no way which leads out of the present: what had appeared as a promise of retreat and return, as a possible escape from the present, itself became the object and goal of a program of historical and critical research that was committed to the spirit of that present and oriented around classical philology and the ideal of 'objectivity'. Instead of the desired ascent from the cold and prosaic world of 'numbers and figures' (Novalis) to the world of 'fairy tales and poems', a process of 'objective' research, of scientific and very prosaic exploration of such 'fairy tales and poems' was inaugurated. (Halbfass, 1988: 83).[12]

India continued to play the role of critical foil in the thought of subsequent generations of German philosophers. For Hegel, of course, there was no question of a return to India. True to his philosophy of history earlier/different cultural and intellectual traditions are viewed not merely as sources of interesting, even if fallacious, thinking, but as evolutionary stages and dialectically inflected components in the development of western philosophy, of an increasingly complex and encompassing 'thought process' and 'system'. In Hegel's system the greater complexity of European/western philosophy represents the latest (even if not the last and definitive) *synthesis* of the dialectical resolution of historical-philosophical contradictions. Furthermore, the greater complexity of western philosophy (or of whatever system that precedes any other along the developmental axis) is capable of containing, subsuming, translating, comprehending and interpreting all earlier, incomplete, simpler, lower-level forms of thinking, but the opposite is not possible. Hegel's philosophy is thus stacked against the 'Orient', so to speak, since Hegel externalizes Indian thought vis-à-vis western history-philosophy by imputing to Indian thought the following characteristics: that it is static, irrational and primordial; that it lacks the full separation between philosophy and religion; that it denies reason its rightful developmental and liberating role; that it obstructs the emergence of individuality and personal freedom; that it perforce corresponds to backward social-political 'realities'; that it is literally *pre-historical* (before philosophy/rational history); that it cannot possibly provide any serious solution or alternative from the perspective and position of what Hegel considered to be the latest and most complex and comprehensive 'thought process' to date, the western philosophy of his time (especially his own philosophical theories). This is perhaps a pure form of Said's 'Orientalism'. Indeed, while Germany had at the time no imperial ambitions in the subcontinent, Hegel even expressed the opinion that European colonialism was historically necessary and justifiable if one wanted to spread the rationality and superior rewards of western modernity (and its philosophical system/foundations) to the rest of the world. This distinguishes Hegel from most so-called Romantic thinkers.

On the other hand, precisely because Hegel treats Indian thought as an anterior, simpler, incomplete, stage in the historical development of western philosophy, Indian thought becomes, in a sense, internalised by western history-philosophy. It acquires a necessary genetic, developmental, dialectical linkage to western philosophy – Hegel even stresses how Indian thought has melted or fused into western philosophy; how the process of development that has led to western philosophy has absorbed and metabolized Indian thought, physiologically 'cancelling' its original (or earlier) contents and characteristics, and kneading it anew into a more evolved and complex system (see Halbfass, 1988: 96). This internal connection with India is something Hegel shared with the Romantics.

Hegel's 'evolutionism' could be, and was certainly challenged, not just by Romantics before him, but by subsequent writers. The argument that contra Hegel the West does *not* subsume the non-West historically represents a challenge to the justificatory function of the Hegelian schema. But, significantly, this counter-imperial message is still delivered in a language of radical Indian alterity.

A case in point is the philosopher Schopenhauer who

> rejected the Hegelian integration of the system and history of philosophy, and saw no scheme of reflection according to which a succession of cultural traditions and philosophical theories could be constructed and following which Indian and European thought could legitimately be coordinated with or subordinated to one another. His approach to Indian philosophy was, so to speak, that of a 'recognitive historiography of philosophy' ('wiedererkennende Philosophiegeschichte') which remained open to the possibility of finding the same insights in the most diverse historical contexts. Schopenhauer felt that the basic ideas of philosophy, and an apparent projection into spatiotemporal multiplicity, could be found among the Indians, and not just in the form of historical antecedents, but in a sense of truth which knows no historical and geographical restrictions. (Halbfass, 1988: 110)

Schopenhauer's

> critique of European tradition shows us the other side of the nineteenth century . . . he showed an unprecedented readiness to integrate Indian ideas into his own European thinking and to utilize them for his articulation of the doctrine of the 'will' and its 'negation' which implies a critique of the European confidence in representational and rational thinking, in calculation and planning, science and technology. (Halbfass, 1988: 436)

While Schopenhauer's schema challenged the necessity of a western supersession of the East, hence radically undermining its function as imperial ideology while still speaking a language of a radical Indian alterity, India played a different role in Nietzsche's thought.

> In a somewhat simplifying fashion, we may say that there are basically two perspectives in which Indian thought and culture became significant for Nietzsche. On the one hand, it provides him with examples of a superior 'yea-saying', a degree of commitment to, and acceptance of this world which is higher than what is found in the Christian tradition; on the other hand, it provides him with expressions of a more advanced and refined denial of the world, a more mature pessimism and nihilism. (Halbfass, 1988: 125–6)

Unlike earlier Romantic and Hegelian philosophy, Nietzsche's did not find in India an inherent justification for Germanness – either because India acted as stand-in for the critique of instrumental reason, or because of the interiority of German and Indian civilisational history. Instead, in a project that anticipates that of much twentieth century anthropology, India functioned as a terrain from which Nietzsche could launch his critique of Germany itself: 'Although Nietzsche usually ranks the foreign higher, his concern lies for the most part with his "own" *as criticized from the perspective of the foreign*. We hardly ever come across observations of a foreign culture in Nietzsche without being related back in this way' (Scheiffele, 1991: 42: emphasis added). As a consequence : 'Nietzsche speaks of his "trans-European eye" which enables him to see that "Indian philosophy is the only major parallel to our European philosophy" ' (Sprung, 1991: 76).

For his own reasons, therefore, Nietzsche provided a critique of Eurocentrism and European pretensions to imperial superiority, striking 'a blow against occidental arrogance when he emphasizes that there have been "more thoughtful times, and times more distracted by analytic thinking than ours" . . . (Scheiffele, 1991: 40–1).

Marx would at first sight appear to have been much more straightfor-wardly orientalist, both because, under the sway of Hegel, he characterised India as a stagnant, *pre*-capitalist oriental backwater, and because he defended British colonial rule as the only means of bringing India into the modern age. This certainly is the central thrust of his best-known writings on India published in an early series of articles written for *The New York Daily Tribune*. But elsewhere even Marx is a less unambiguous apologist for empire. Of the image of India contained in his 'mature' works, *Capital* and *Theories of Surplus Value*, for example, it has been observed that:

> Marx moves back and forth from a more originary view of the Asiatic mode, focusing on the self-sufficient communities and then on the relationship among these communities and between them and the state, between the state and manufacturers' external trade. In this way the Asiatic mode is conceived of as having an *historical dimension*, with a specific dynamic. The AMP is *not considered stagnant* . . . it is pictured as an historically differentiated whole which never spontaneously evolved into capitalism. (Bailey and Llobera 1981: 33–4; emphasis added)

And still later, in his ethnological researches and the correspondence on the Russian commune there is evidence that Marx was beginning to consider **non**-capitalist social and economic formations in a more positive light, seeing the Russian *mir* and the Indian village, because of their 'ethnocentricity' (by which he meant their concentration on human needs rather than production for profit) and inherent democracy now at least as possible alternative routes to socialism.[13]

Two further cases of nineteenth century 'postcolonialism' are provided by the German poets Gustav Kleist and Henrich Heine. According to a recent commentator, Kleist's novella *Die Verlobung in St. Domingo*, an account of the Haitian revolution (1791–1803) represents

> a critique of [contemporary European thought, particularly Enlightenment philosophy, and] . . . the contemporary political relationship of Napoleonic France to Prussia (a kind of master–slave relationship) . . . [and] also a larger cultural critique in which the perspectives of the white characters are ultimately revealed as no longer *the normative*, or authoritative, mode of reading this *Novelle*. (Fleming, 1992: 306)

Kleist's highly sympathetic reading of the revolution represents a reaction to

> eighteenth century philosophical assumptions that excluded the culturally Other as fully human for [the novella's black characters Babekan, Congo Hoango, Toni and so on] . . . are not the benighted black subhumans of Kant and Hume any more than they are like the romanticized Native American noble savages of Chateaubriand or James Fenimore Cooper'. (Fleming, 1992: 307)

But there is something else in Kleist's account that deserves mention. While as we have suggested German thought in the nineteenth century may, by calling into question the superiority of European culture and, hence, the necessity of European empire, have been counter-imperial, it, like a good deal of what is in this century called postcolonial theory, nonetheless retained orientalism's language of the radical cultural alterity of places like India. Poets such as Kleist, Heine and Wieland, certainly challenged the presumption that these other cultures needed western domination to bring them up to civilised standards. One is reminded of Heine's realisation in his poem 'Das Sklavenschiff' of 'European responsibility for the evils of slavery, colonialism, and exploitation of indigenous peoples' (Holub, 1992: 335).

But more than this they further undermined the very language of alterity. As Fleming observes, in *Die Verlobung* Kleist depicts the

> perspectives of the white world as represented by the narrator and by [the character of the white plantation owner, Gustav, to be inadequate [in] com[ing] to terms with the experience and values of the people of color whom they encounter [and hence] . . . seems to be revealing . . . how experience solely or largely within the confines of one's racial culture and values places one at a disadvantage in dealing with and understanding the experience, values and perspectives of others who do not belong to that same race and culture – a notion that would seem a truism now, though the racial attitudes of such figures as

Hume, Kant, Burke, and Napoleon show us that Kleist's open-mindedness did not characterize his age. (Fleming, 1992: 308)

As the story unfolds, we therefore learn that 'love, infatuation, or passion can triumph over racial or cultural solidarity [and difference]' (Fleming, 1992: 310), that, in other words, difference is itself experiential or contingent, not an absolute given of human existence. One is reminded here of Edward Said's own project by which he seeks to 'to see others not as ontologically given but as historically constituted [which] would be to erode the exclusivist biases we so often ascribe to cultures, our own not least' (1989: 225). For without such a caveat the language of culture, difference and alterity spawned by expressivism contains its own dangers. While, as postcolonial theorists point out, 'social Darwinism' provides a justification for a particular kind of empire within which the stated aim is the project of 'civilising' the natives. But the civilising project is not all there is to empire. There is instead a side to modern imperialism that is, if possible, far darker than this. I refer, of course, to genocide. While ethnocide may be implied by civilising ideologies, it is important to note that a radical culturalism may be implicated in genocide. If the other is seen as unredeemably other, then empire becomes a project of eliminating the other.

Without wishing to suggest that the seeds of the Holocaust can necessarily be found in all nineteenth century German thought – an argument that would itself amount to an extreme form of cultural or racial essentialism – it must nonetheless be pointed out that it was in the country that produced perhaps the first and most sophisticated understanding of cultural difference that six million of its own citizens were killed on account of their radical alterity. No account of the German contribution to the culture of modernism can be complete without a consideration of the roots of German anti-Semitism.

Back to the 'Jewish Question'

What Karl Marx and his fellow Young Hegelians were wont to call the 'Jewish Question', and what a more recent commentator has suggested is more properly called the German Question, namely 'how far could – and should – Jews become assimilated in (or, in the words of some of the participants in the controversy, amalgamated with) German society?' (in Pulzer, 1992: 2). The question was first posed within the theological debates associated with the so-called Jewish Enlightenment or the *Halakah* during the eighteenth century. Of particular significance was an essay written by Moses Mendelssohn – 'Über die Frage: was heisst Aufklären' – which appeared just a few months before Kant's 'Was ist Aufklären?' (1784).

It is generally maintained that Mendelssohn's enthusiastic endorsement of the Enlightenment was generally shared by most German Jews who can thus be thought of as highly assimilated to or by European culture. In this sense, Karl Marx was by no means untypical of German Jews, or should we say was no more than an extreme proponent of the ideas expressed from Moses Mendelssohn onwards, that Jews, while they should hang on to their religion in the private sphere, should otherwise adapt to the universal principles of the French Revolution in the public sphere. Marx's father, again not untypically, went one step further and was baptised a Christian (though, as in other cases, it is not clear the extent to which this was instrumental, considering that as a public servant he could not hold office as a Jew).

The support given by German Jews to nineteenth century German liberalism, and to national liberation (in a unified Germany to override local political loyalties) is fully in keeping with this image of a cosmopolitan, universalist and emancipated community. As a result nineteenth century German Jews are considered archetypes of the 'West European type' Jewish communities described by Ezra Mendelssohn as having:

> a high degree of acculturation and aspirations to assimilation, a general tendency to abandon both Yiddish and Orthodoxy. . . . Such Jewish communities tended to be middle class [and] highly urbanized, though they rarely constituted a remarkably high proportion within the general urban population. The typical western European Jewry possessed a low birth-rate and high rate of inter-marriage; its sense of Jewish identification was usually religious, not national secular. (quoted in Pulzer, 1992: 2)

And, one must add, Judaism itself changed under such circumstances. It was not just relegated to the sphere of the private, but there were also doctrinal and ritual adaptations to 'modernism' Enlightenment-style – hence the growth of what has come to be called Reform Judaism.

As a result, the debate particularly among Jewish thinkers and writers after the Holocaust has tended to proceed from the assumption that assimilationism was itself part of the problem, that Jews should have held on to their culture, religion and nationhood, since German anti-Semites made no allowance for, indeed were positively scornful of, their assimilationist aspirations.[14]

But there are a number of problems with this debate. Most positions are informed by a notion of otherness as *pre*-modern – hence Jewishness to the extent that it existed in nineteenth century Germany is taken to be a 'survival', a result of 'incomplete assimilation' and the accompanying belief that anti-Semitism was itself the result of an incomplete modernisation of German Christians.

1   Not all nineteenth century German Jews were advocates of Enlightenment, liberalism and religious reform. Take the voting percentages in 1848 estimated in Mosse et al. (1981): 30–25 per cent conservative; 25–30 per cent loyalist; 30–35 per cent moderately liberal; 14 per cent Radical-Democratic, and 1 per cent Socialist.[15] Consider for example also the large and important groups of 'eastern' Jews – migrants from Poland and Russia who remained orthodox, brought Hassidism, and

who, as aliens would not be included in the above figures (see for example Wertheimer, 1987).

2 The concept of a 'western Jewry' must not be taken at face value. It was instead not so much a direct reflection of reality, but an aspect of the self-identity of German Jews, from Mendelssohn through to liberal Jews in the early twentieth century, and can be said to have been part of a discourse also about the loss of identity.

3 As an important study by Sorkin (1987) shows, even 'assimilated Jews' in fact formed a distinctive 'subculture' in nineteenth century Germany, defined in part culturally/religiously and also significantly in patterns of social life and interaction. In other words the 'western Jews' were still others in German society, no matter how much they themselves, their Jewish critics or non-Jewish Germans tried to portray them otherwise.

This otherness has been largely misrecognised, at least up until Sorkin's important study, by those subscribing to the narrative of the necessary alterity of cultural difference within modernity. Put another way, the post-Holocaust critique of Jewish 'assimilationism' presumes that there *were* essential differences between Jewish and German culture, that, in other words, Germanness really was what nineteenth century German Romantics claimed it to be. It was not just Heine, Kleist and others who questioned the absoluteness of cultural distinctions. Even earlier, the poet and dramatist Friedrich von Schiller 'questioned the romantic assertion that such oral traditions expressed collective or national German sentiments', as did others like August Wilhelm Schlegel and Johann Heinrich Voss (see Linke, 1990: 121). The problem, in other words, lay perhaps not in 'assimilation' to an Enlightenment ideal so much as in the counter-Enlightenment discourse of culture and difference that seems to have been accepted by most Germans, Jews and Christians alike.

From its inception, then, modernism has been characterised by an internal debate over the nature and future of the human subject. Should humanity aspire to the universal emancipation of autonomous subjectivities, free as much as possible to pursue their own internally-generated goals? Or is this very notion of personhood, embedded in utilitarianism and, subsequently, social Darwinism, both false and, to the extent that it informs modern consciousness, profoundly alienating? Concepts of the cultural dimensions of human existence, of course, shape both sides of the debate. Culture, for what we might call instrumental modernism, is the tool-kit – understood both literally and metaphorically – with which nature provides us to facilitate our pursuit of individual pleasures and avoidance of pain. But for its expressivist critics culture is something far more – on the one hand, it is that which shapes human subjectivity and defines its goals, and, on the other, it constitutes humanity's highest form of expression.

Not surprisingly it is in this latter form that culture came to shape the emerging discourses of human difference, themselves intimately linked with the various projects for national political and economic self-determination that emerged in the aftermath of the French Revolution and the rise of British economic supremacy. However, as Taylor has reminded us, this expressivist critique never looked like displacing instrumental modernism which came increasingly to take on the role of a 'defining idea' in the realm of economic life, in the growing bureaucracies, and in the more influential political movements whether of the right or the left. Moreover, as Said and others have so clearly demonstrated, 'social Darwinism', an example of an instrumentalist discourse *par excellence*, was also globalised in the second half of the nineteenth century, when it became the central plank of the ideology of European empire as well.

Expressivism, and with it the language of culture and cultural difference increasingly took a back seat. However, it was never completely relegated to the private sphere. As we shall see, it instead re-emerged in the early decades of the twentieth century, so that during the interwar years this other side of modernism once again became a significant element in a continuing debate over instrumentalism and techno-rationalism, in general, and social Darwinism, in particular. In the following three chapters we shall look at three arenas where expressivist notions of culture and difference played especially significant roles in twentieth century thought: in debates over the 'peasantry', in accounts of cultural otherness outside the West, and in images of 'multicultural' cities in the new heartland of modernism, the United States

Notes

1 'Mexico sends in tanks to crush peasant rebellion' by David Adam, *The Times* (London), 3 January 1994.

2 In a front page article entitled 'Mexican Rebels Reject Talks, Vow to fight to Death for Socialism', *The Christian Science Monitor*, 7–13 January 1994.

3 From a background article explaining the roots of the unrest in Chiapas that appeared in *The Guardian Weekly*, 6/1/1994 entitled 'Land that time forgot'.

4 This phrase comes from *The Times* article quoted above.

5 There has been too easy a slippage between anthropology's 'other' and the other of contemporary French philosophy, between, in other words what we call cultural difference and *différance*. I will, following Levinas and others, defend here the notion that our attempts at knowledge should rightly always be oriented towards a radical alterity, at the same time arguing that anthropological notions of 'other cultures' are in no way capable of playing that role in contemporary thought.

6 As we shall see shortly, while the Huston film is based on a novel that locates the action in Chiapas, the film itself was shot elsewhere in Mexico. An interesting characteristic of the film is the way it continually elides the link between culture and place.

7 The character of Zorro first appeared in Johnston McCulley's novel, *The Curse of Capistrano* (1919).

8 Others have seen in Herder an antecedent of contemporary notions of cultural and linguistic relativism. Darcy, for example notes the similarities between Boasian notions of culture and Herder's ideas about *Volksgeist* (1987), while Whitton (1988) has seen Herder's early work on language as anticipating in significant ways the ideas of Lyotard (and, one might add, the earlier ideas of Wittgenstein, Sapir and Whorf).

9 Marx saw such romantics as enemies from very early on in his university career (see McLellan, 1974).

10 Taylor gives the lie to the simplistic assumption that Hegel's philosophy represented merely a defence of the Prussian state (Taylor, 1975: Ch. 16).

11 See for example Mackerras (1989) for an account of European images of China, and particularly the admiration for things Chinese in the eighteenth century – a trend which seems to be re-emerging in different circumstances today, after a prolonged period of Indic romance in postcolonial and cultural studies.

12 See also Wilson (1964).

13 For this re-evaluation of Marx in the light of his ideas on the Russian *mir*, see Shanin (1983).

14 For some of the main debates, see for example Stein and Loewe (1978) and Jospe (1981); and for accounts of relationship between German liberal thought and Judaism see Bach (1984), Bronsen (1979), Tal (1975) and Reinharz and Schatzberg (1984).

15 For another discussion of variation in Germany see Cahnman (1987: Ch. 1) and also for individual accounts of memoirs see Richarz (1991).

3

Peasants, Difference and the Commodity's Malcontents

In a speech he gave in 1928 the Hungarian composer Béla Bartók told his audience:

> Some twenty-five years ago a few quite young musicians . . . began to turn their attention to the Hungarian peasant classes. An urge toward the unknown, a dim incline that true folk-music was only to be found in the peasant class, induced them to make their first superficial tests. These first essays yielded rich and hitherto entirely unknown material. . . . Those days which I spent in the villages among the peasants were the happiest days of my life. (quoted in Króo, 1974: 77f.)

Bartók was of course only one of a number of composers who in the early decades of this century turned to popular or folk musics for inspiration, a group that included Ravel, Manuel de Falla, Szymanowski, Janáček, and Bartók's good friend Kodály in Europe, Aaron Copeland in the United States and Carlos Chavez in Mexico. Moreover European music had just emerged from an earlier romantic period in which composers sought to articulate unique national musics in more universalistic musical languages. What makes the case of Bartók and his contemporaries so different?

To answer this question it is useful to look more closely into Bartók's own career and the reception accorded his music both in his native Hungary and elsewhere. Born in 1881, Béla Bartók,[1] like other aspiring European musicians of the period, received his early musical training in the then dominant German musical tradition. His early training and knowledge was 'deeply rooted in the German tradition', he is said to have had a distinctly Brahmsian style and on top of that Wagner's 'chromatic scores' (Antokoletz, 1988: xviii).

There followed, however, a burst of cultural nationalism in the period leading up to the First World War during which time continental composers began to react against the ultra chromaticism of Wagner and Strauss, turning against German musical hegemony. Bartók too became disillusioned with the Germanic tradition, his disillusion only temporarily resolved by his discovery of the music of Richard Strauss – which brought harmonic and tonal influences into his music.

During the 1903 resurgence of the Hungarian patriotic movement, Bartók expressed his sympathies by wearing national dress, and speaking

Hungarian rather than German. At this time he wrote the distinctly Lisztian patriotic symphonic poem, *Kossuth*.

In 1904 Bartók, somewhat accidentally, came into contact with Hungarian peasant music when he heard a young peasant woman singing. He was particularly struck by the fact that her rendition of a popular Hungarian folk song differed significantly from standard 'gipsy-style café' versions, which both Brahms and then Liszt had represented as the authentic folk music of Hungary. The discovery of this other folk style led Bartók to investigate the musical traditions of the Transylvanian villages from which the folk singer came, research which he carried out with his friend Kodály. The first results of these researches were the *Eight Hungarian Folk Songs* for voice and piano (1907–17) among the first Bartók prepared for concert performance (the first five were collected in 1907, the rest between 1916 and 1917).

Developing a research methodology as he went along, Bartók extended his ethnomusicological research – first among Slovaks and Romanians in Hungary and in neighbouring countries, then in 1913 in Algeria, and finally in Turkey. Apart from recordings and notations, from this research he also wrote *Four Slovakian Songs* for voice and piano (three in 1907, the fourth in 1916); the fifth piece of the *Fourteen Bagatelles* (1908) based on a Slovakian folk song; the *Sketches* of 1908–10 which were based on Romanian folk songs; the third movement of the *Piano Suite*, Op. 14 (1916) which was influenced by North African folk music; and the *Second String Quartet* (1915–17).

In this period he also wrote an opera, *Bluebeard's Castle* (1911), hoping to bring 'authentic' Hungarian peasant music to the Hungarian public. But the opera was not performed, partly because those who had heard it, used to the Germanised/gipsy version of Hungarian music, did not recognise any 'Hungarianness' in Bartók's juxtapositions of Germanic and peasant musics (see Antokoletz, 1988: xxiv). Discouraged, Bartók withdrew from public performance. Cut off from his ethnomusicological research by the First World War he spent his time transcribing and composing which led to a significant change in the nature of Bartók's compositional creativity.

In his earlier compositions Bartók generally combined peasant and German musical traditions largely by means of juxtaposition. From around 1912, however, he began to produce syntheses or fusions of 'European' (that is German) and folk musics. Early examples of this new style are the 1916 ballet *The Wooden Prince*; the *Piano Suite* of 1915–17 and the *Second String Quartet*. In *Eight Improvisations on Hungarian Peasant Songs* (1920) elements of the underlying folk tunes are systematically developed and modified, transformed into the highly abstract pitch sets and interactions for which Bartók is probably best known. The *Fourth Quartet* (1928) manifests a move towards ever greater abstraction and synthesis of divergent art- and folk-music sources.

In the 1930s Bartók continued his folklore research, withdrawing once again from performing his works in Budapest because of the increasingly repressive political atmosphere. Finally conditions became so bad that he left Hungary for the United States where he lived until his death in 1941. While he had numerous admirers and a string of successful performances during his lifetime, it is typically only since his death that he has come to be recognised in three somewhat different ways: first, as the founder of a modern and distinctively Hungarian musical tradition in his country of origin; second, as a pioneer of modern ethnomusicology; and third, as one of the leading modern (western) composers of the twentieth century.

I want to use the example of Béla Bartók's 'discovery' of, first, the Hungarian peasant, and subsequently the peasantry more generally as a route into the modern constitution of the peasantry as, paradoxically, both a unique and a generalised/globalised form of human existence in the early decades of this century. In so doing I will begin the project of seeing cultural otherness in the twentieth century, in the words of Edward Said, 'not as ontologically given but as historically constituted'. For, as will become evident, there have been specific times and particular places when different groups – western and non-western intellectuals, colonial officials, nationalist and/or populist leaders, Marxist activists, novelists, painters, musicians and, indeed peasants themselves – conceived of a peasant mode of existence as a peculiarly alien one in the modern world.

In this context, the example of the musical peasantism of Béla Bartók provides an interesting starting point, not because it is necessarily typical, but because it serves to raise the issues in an interesting way.

First, Bartók viewed peasant music as radically different from the 'modern' or 'western' musical tradition. 'The study of [Hungarian] peasant music was', he said, 'of decisive importance for the reason that it revealed the possibility of a total emancipation from the major-minor system'.[2] 'Peasantry' describes an existence of radical cultural alterity – in Bartók's case a musical alterity – outside the dominant/hegemonic culture. For Bartók and many of his contemporaries that dominant culture – both musically and otherwise – was German, part and parcel of the rule of Hungary by a Germanised Habsburg elite. The German tradition had even managed to corner the market on Hungarianness itself through the appropriation of 'gipsy' themes by the German, Brahms, and the Germanised Hungarian Franz Liszt.

Second, and following on from this, Bartók brought to the task of studying peasant music a seriousness of purpose absent in the use of folk themes in nineteenth century romantic music. Describing his method of study, Bartók maintained that it was useless to attempt to study peasant musical traditions unless one immersed oneself in peasant life and culture. Such music, he wrote, needs to be:

> studied in the country as part of a life shared by peasants. It is not enough to study it as it is stored up in museums. . . . It must be pervaded by the very atmosphere of peasant culture. Peasant motifs (or imitations of such motifs) will only lend our music new ornaments; nothing more.[3]

The search here is for an authentic encounter with a radically different peasant music – as it is embedded within peasant life and culture. Until one is immersed in the totality of peasant life one is at best lifting motifs, and at worst mere imitations of motifs. Peasant music, like peasant culture in general, does not allow for any superficial understanding. Precisely because it is so alien to those immersed in hegemonic traditions it requires the kinds of empathic immersion in peasant culture also advocated by contemporary anthropology, as we have had occasion to note. Significantly it is precisely out of this empathic encounter with the peasant other that one recovers the 'essential' Hungarian music. Only dilettantes, it is implied, could think that tacking a few gipsy motifs onto what is otherwise merely German romantic music would result in a genuine Hungarian national music. This tremendous emphasis on first-hand experience was directly implicated in the development of the idea of the professional cultural interpreter or translator who situated him/herself as a serious student of cultural otherness against 'amateurs' who, in Bartók's words, copied or imitated mere motifs, or learned his or her trade in dusty and lifeless museums. The parallels with professional anthropologists particularly in Britain railing against 'armchair anthropology' are striking.

Third, Bartók, having carried out his studies of Hungarian peasant music, then went on to make studies of the regional folklores and musics of Romania, Slovakia, Algeria, Bulgaria, Yugoslavia, the Ukraine and Turkey – hence gradually expanding the notion of peasant music beyond a simple concern with a nativistic revival of his own cultural roots (a significant aspect of nineteenth century peasantism as part of nationalist discourses). In this, Bartók broke with his friend Kodály, and indeed from nineteenth century European approaches to peasant culture in general. While Kodály, an anti-German Hungarian nationalist, was interested only in the music of the Hungarian peasantry, Bartók, the humanitarian anti-fascist, was concerned with peasants in general.[4]

Fourth, Bartók in the first instance as we have seen produced 'compositions', or elements within compositions, that were more or less direct transcriptions of the peasant songs he had studied. But from the later 1920s he went on to write new compositions 'in the style' of such folk songs, as well as music in which there is some kind of fusion or synthesis of different musical traditions. While clearly up until late in his life, as a research fellow at New York's Columbia University, Bartók continued to see himself as an ethnomusicologist, faithfully representing pre-existing peasant musical traditions in Europe and North Africa, the compositional works for which he is now most admired do not pretend to speak the authentic voice of the heretofore silenced Hungarian peasant. Far from being *representations*, Bartók's mature compositions are quite self-consciously *constructions*. The language of fusion and synthesis is extremely important here. A piece like the *Eight Improvisations on Hungarian Peasant Songs* does not pretend to represent within it a musical mosaic. Instead it is, borrowing George Gerswhin's description of his music for the folk opera *Porgy and Bess*, 'all of a piece'. It is important to note the ways in which this dimension of Bartók's representational practice parallels in significant ways the radically modernist claims of a hermeneutics of cultural interpretation, particularly the assertion that all cultural interpretation is new knowledge rather than a mere appropriation in thought of an already existing cultural otherness already out there in the world.

There has, not surprisingly perhaps, been a good deal of debate over the role played by Bartók's musical peasantism in his own original compositions. Adorno, for example, attacked Bartók, among others, for engaging in the 'reactionary' practice of folklorism, a practice that according to Adorno was implicated in the rise of fascism in eastern and central Europe. Such a claim would have appalled Bartók, a committed humanist and antifascist. It seems that here Adorno misrepresented Bartók, largely missing the significance both of the more generalised (rather than purely nationalist) dimensions of Bartók's peasantism and of the degree to which his mature music spoke a language of fusion and synthesis, rather than one of peasant authenticity and essentialised cultural purity.[5]

Fifth, it is I think very significant that the 1928 speech in which Bartók described the joys of living in peasant villages was not delivered in Hungary to an audience eager to stoke up its nationalist fires, but in fact on a tour of the United States. What this reminds us is that there were at least two if not more distinct audiences for Bartók's music. In Hungary there were of course nationalists seeking to reaffirm their own cultural roots – by listening to 'authentic' Hungarian peasant music as opposed to German or Germanised Hungarian music – although as we have seen these audiences did not immediately recognise, even in Bartók's more or less faithful versions of peasant songs any Hungarianness, used as they were to the idea that Hungarian music equalled gipsy tunes. But later on, especially after the Second World War, Bartók was elevated to the status of national hero, as founder of a modern *Hungarian* musical tradition.

Elsewhere, in the United States, Britain and France, there were what modernism insists on seeing as audiences with 'universal' tastes and standards, in this case eager to consume 'peasants' as exotic beings wherever they come from, or to listen to the results of the fusion of 'peasant' and 'universal' musical languages. Anthropology, broadly understood as a set of discourses of cultural otherness, had in this period come of age, reaching broad sections of the educated middle classes at least in the West – people who consumed the texts with very little concern for the role played by such images in the places they purported to be about, but a great deal of concern for the way they articulated their own tastes and feelings.

If Bartók was attacked by Adorno for a 'reactionary' turn away from modernism to folkloric sources, then he was lauded by his countryman Lukács for precisely the opposite. In an article published in 1971 in the *New Hungarian Quarterly*, Lukács praised Bartók for his (musical) critiques of capitalist alienation. How can this be? How can a journey outside modernity lead to its critique? What are the contours of this particular discourse of alterity, of the alienness of peasant worlds, that begins to emerge in the interwar years and what can its relation to modernism be?

The discourse of peasantism

If an alien peasant world is part of a modern imaginary, then the concepts with which many have sought to characterise its inhabitants are as well. One of a number of important concepts in the media reporting of the Chiapas affair for example (see pp. 18–20), the notion of 'peasantry', for some time now a word which has been used to convey the alterity of small-scale cultivators both at home and abroad, was frequently drawn upon. Yet, contrary to the impression of radical alterity generated by the media reports, the word itself of course is European. It has its roots in the Latin *pageisis* from *pagus* which meant a canton or district. 'Peasant' came into English from the French *paysan*, from the word *pays* or country. But as Raymond Williams (1976) points out, current European usage has been more profoundly shaped by the French Revolution and its aftermath. Accordingly in nineteenth century Europe peasants came to acquire a more positive evaluation, particularly in the emancipatory discourses of European nationalism that arose after the Revolution. It is it seems within these emancipatory nationalisms that the peasantry came to be seen as expressing the limitations of the existing universalistic discourses of freedom inherited from the Enlightenment and the French Revolution. For many nineteenth century European nationalists peasant life expressed that higher set of values, most frequently the values associated with the unique cultural heritage of the emerging nation, that would be lost in the pursuit of a cosmopolitan emancipation Enlightenment-style. In this sense nineteenth century peasantism was part of that expressivist critique of techno-instrumental modernism discussed in the previous chapter.

In the debates in Germany towards the end of the last century about the social and cultural consequences of industrialisation, for example, German critics of industrialism defended the so-called *Agrarstaat*, and saw in measures to promote the German peasantry a means of inoculating Germany against the dangers of untrammelled emancipation, and the evils of Manchester-style industrialism. Max Sering, for example, argued: 'We designate the people of the land as the source of eternal renewal of the physical strength of all classes. The fountain of youth of our national strength would be spent with the destruction of the peasantry' (cited in Barkin, 1970: 16).

The following definition by the economist Conrad shows clearly how this particular critique of modernity was in this way embedded in a conservative vision of German national development:

A peasant is the owner of a farm which is big enough to feed and employ the owner and his family. The peasantry is one of the most robust sectors of the

[German] population. Peasants have a special feeling of attachment to the soil; they are, in general, a conservative, anti-revolutionary political force; they have an advantage in times of economic crisis of being able to retreat from market relations, by increasing naturalised production. (Conrad, 1891)

The articulation of a similar notion of peasantry, this time within a language of emancipation is evident in the discourse of Russian populism. This time peasants were seen not as a bulwark against modernisation so much as the anticipation of a future socialist society that would provide a means of transcending the alienating practices of capitalism. Chernyshevskii, for example, if not a populist theorist then, with Herzen, one of its important ancestors, attempted a synthesis of French philosophy with 'some elements of historicism and Hegelian dialectics', considering himself a disciple of Feuerbach (Walicki, 1969: 14). As Walicki points out Chernyshevskii was on the one hand an ardent westerniser, a firm believer in progress and an advocate of the Europeanisation of Russia. On the other hand he defended the peasant commune against liberals who saw it as a major obstacle to Russian progress. He therefore argued for the protection of the Russian peasantry against the sufferings generated by development English-style. The classical populists Lavrov and Mikhailovski both questioned the optimistic belief in progress held by Russian adherents of the Enlightenment, at the same time rejecting the unilineal evolutionism of nineteenth century positivism. For liberal evolutionists like Spencer had, as we have seen, taken over more or less whole hog earlier utilitarian notions of freedom, differing only in that they postponed the day of the new age to the endpoint of the full development of the division of labour and the accompanying total differentiation of society.

Populism's admiration for the peasantry stems almost directly from a critical engagement with this nineteenth century version of Enlightenment liberalism. Populists like Mikhailovski saw Spencer's evolutionary process as regressive rather than progressive since it would result in precisely that alienating freedom of which the Young Hegelians were so critical. The very fact that peasants stood outside the capitalist market and the division of labour made peasant life a worthy foundation for a new and genuinely emancipated society. The populist image of the peasantry is summarised by Walicki in the following terms:

> the Russian peasant lives a life which is poor but full; being economically self-sufficient he is, therefore, an independent, 'all round', and 'total' man. He satisfies all his needs by his own work. . . . The peasant community is egalitarian, homogeneous, but its members have differentiated many-sided individualities. The lack or weak development of complex cooperation enables them to preserve their independence and simple cooperation unites them in mutual sympathy and understanding. This moral unity underlines the common ownership of land and the self-government of the Russian 'mir'. (1969: 53)

But in these late nineteenth century European usages the particular ambiguity which is manifest in contemporary usages of the term does not appear so clearly. I refer to that apparent contradiction between, on the one hand, the argument that the economic, social and cultural conditions of particular groups of peasants are unique and mysterious (that is untranslatable by the languages of modernism) and, on the other, the description or characterisation of those conditions by means of a term that can and has been used to describe unique or particular conditions in other places and at other times.

Neither the German advocates of an *Agrarstaat* nor Russian populists were especially concerned with the peasantry as a general category. Both at least purported to be talking about particular peasantries, Russian or German, and would not have been especially concerned about peasantries elsewhere.

It was not until the twentieth century that the critique of techno-instrumental modernism, together with an emphasis on cultural particularism, would be systematically combined with attempts to construct peasants as a general type of human existence, hence bringing about the ambiguities I have associated above with current uses of the term. This tension is evident in more recent attempts to define the peasantry in ways that are not evident in earlier writings. Retaining many of the characteristics attributed to peasantries by nineteenth century expressivism, for example, the anthropologist Robert Redfield wanted to argue that:

> Peasants are a *type* or *class* loosely defined. Their agriculture is a livelihood and a way of life, not a business for profit. . . . A peasant is a man who is in effective control of a piece of land to which he has long been attached by ties of tradition and sentiment. (1956: 25–9)

And more recently in introducing a book which made a significant impact in the field of peasant studies James Scott wrote:

> The basic idea upon which my argument rests is both simple and, I believe, powerful. It arises from the central economic dilemma of most peasant households. Living close to the subsistence margin and subject to the vagaries of weather and the claims of outsiders, the peasant household has little scope for the profit maximization calculus of neoclassical economics. . . . If treating the peasant as a would-be Schumpeterian entrepreneur misses his key existential dilemma, so do the normal power-maximizing assumptions fail to do justice to his political behavior. (1976: 4f.)

It is clear that, at least in *The Moral Economy of the Peasant* from which this quote comes, Scott envisaged that this thesis would be pertinent to a broad historical and temporal range of peasant societies.

Michael Taussig, in an influential study of South American peasants, makes the contrast between 'traditional' peasant culture and capitalist ideology even more explicit by arguing that:

> In two widely separated areas of rural South America, as peasant cultivators become landless wage laborers, they invoke the devil as part of the process of maintaining or increasing production. However, as peasants working their own land according to their own customs they do not do this. It is only when they are proletarianized that the devil assumes such importance, no matter how poor or needy these peasants may be and no matter how desirous they are of increasing

production. Whereas the imagery of God or the fertility spirits of nature dominates the ethos of labor in the peasant mode of production, the devil and evil flavor the metaphysics of the capitalist mode of production in these two regions. (1980: 13)

Moreover, what makes the demonised response particularly apt for Taussig is the fact that it appears better than ours to recognise the artificiality, and even moral bankruptcy of a world structured by exchange value. We in the industrialised West, according to Taussig (following Marx), apprehend a world in which distinctive objects and particular human beings are evaluated not for the practical uses to which we may put them or the individual ways in which we may relate to them, but also for a value which differs only quantitatively from the value of quite different objects and human beings. All particularity is reduced to mere quantitative difference. Moreover we take this world of exchange value to be in some sense natural instead of for what it 'really' is – that is an artificial way of arranging our social lives based on the dominance of the commodity form, that is the object or the labour power produced specifically to exchange for money. In this sense the critique of the commodity form parallels Bartók's critique of the major-minor system. Both critiques trace a path from a supposedly universal language to the peasantry and back again – discovering in that journey that what appeared first to be universal was, in fact, particular. In this way the peasantry becomes, like Nietzsche's foreign terrain, a place from which we can focus a critical gaze back upon ourselves.

Because we have learned to take our own discourses as natural we fail to see, in ways so clearly seen by South American peasants, that such are distinctly unnatural – more than this, alienating and demonic. Thus for example while some might suggest that the exotic devil-beliefs and rituals of South American peasants are 'a response to anxiety and thwarted desire' or that they are 'part of an egalitarian social ethic that delegitimizes those persons who gain more money and success than the rest of the social group', Taussig prefers to see them 'in their own right with all their vividness and detail', as 'poetic cadences that guide the innermost course of the world' (Taussig, 1980: 15, 17).

Here again the notion of a peasantry is almost inevitably bound up with notions of cultural and historical uniqueness. The reason Taussig chooses to call South American villagers peasants is precisely that they are in some sense culturally alien – part of another world, a world outside modernity where culture rather than money, profit and/or the individual pursuit of utility governs everyday life; where community guards against the alienating, one-off social encounters of modern society.

Yet to call South American villagers peasants is also to subsume them to a general category of human existence. There have been peasants in other places and at other times, in Germany, Central Europe and Russia, Japan, Southeast Asia, and even the southern United States. Moreover how can it be that having travelled so far to find a traditional peasantry in the lacunae of modern South America that they are found to be speaking the voice of classical European social theory, particularly that of the Young Hegelians in general and the Young Marx in particular for whom 'alienation' was what came of the promise of Enlightenment emancipation? Just as, according to Lukács (another heir of the Young Hegelian tradition), Bartók's journey outside modernity into the alien world of European and North African peasants allows Bartók to speak (their) critique of capitalist alienation, so Taussig has discovered the voice of the young Karl Marx in the hinterlands of South American capitalism.

While in important ways Bartók's musical peasantism serves to illustrate this new attitude, there are others who, like Taussig, come closer to Lukács' image of peasantist critics of the capitalist commodity form. One such was an eastern European contemporary of Bartók's who set out to generate a generalised understanding of the peasant condition, this time from the much more mundane perspective of economics.

A.V. Chayanov (Tschajanov) was a Russian agricultural economist whose theories of peasant economy made a significant impact in development studies when a translation of two of his essays – 'Peasant Farm Organization' and 'On the Theory of Non-Capitalist Economic Systems' – first appeared in English in 1966 (Chayanov, 1966). However Chayanov first formulated his theory of the distinctiveness of 'peasant economy' in a series of articles written in the 1920s, including an essay that appeared first in German in 1924 (Chayanov [Tschajanov], 1924).

Chayanov's arguments for the distinctiveness of peasant economy were based on the assertion that it differs from capitalist economy because categories of economic calculation normal in the latter are absent in the former. Specifically the absence of wages and profits means that peasant income takes the form of a 'labour product' or labour income which is indivisible. The result is that the organisation of the constituent units of peasant economy – the so-called 'family labour farms' – is determined by the interaction not of monetised costs of production and prices, but of the degree of labour effort on the one hand, and the consumption needs of the family on the other. As is well known, the specific variable which Chayanov introduced was the consumer/worker ratio, variations in which are seen to determine variation in the labour product/income.

This feature of the peasant economy is advanced as a general characteristic of 'natural economy'. But as Littlejohn (1977), among others, points out, Chayanov is best known for the contention that this basic proposition also holds for an economy dominated by family labour farms which is at the same time characterised by markets, exchange and commodity circulation. Peasant otherness, for Chayanov, thus exists both *within* and outside the modern exchange economy at the same time. In other words Russia from the 1880s to the 1920s, in which Chayanov was obviously most concerned, is amenable to, indeed is particularly suitable for analysis in terms of a general theory of peasant economy. From the basic model Chayanov derived theories of capital formation, rent, and the relationship between price and output fluctuations which he maintained were pertinent to a peasant economy and which ran counter to the wisdom of a marginalist economics which, Chayanov maintained, was appropriate only in a thoroughly capitalist economy.

While as some critics have pointed out Chayanov's theories depended on conditions such as partible inheritance and communal repartition of land that were in fact unique to the Russian countryside, it is quite clear that Chayanov saw his version of a uniquely peasant mode of (economic) existence as of far-reaching validity, and it is this extension of his findings beyond the historically unique situation obtaining in pre-Revolutionary Russia for which Chayanov has been most frequently criticised. We shall not enter into this somewhat technical debate here. Instead we need to note how once again a notion of peasantry emerges in the 1920s that first arises out of a nineteenth century particularist critique of commodification and modernity[6] But from this particularistic tradition Chayanov developed a notion of difference and otherness that at the same time was generalised – to peasants not just in Russia at the turn of the century, but peasants everywhere and at all times.

We do not of course need to place the peasantist critique of the commodity in the mouths of Russian or South American peasants, or even in the mouths of peasants at all. Some, like Marx, discovered the demonic qualities of the commodity without finding it necessary to leave home. John Huston relocates Traven's communally-organised Chiapas peasantry to the United States, thereby providing a domestic platform from which to launch an attack on the materialist calculus of modern men like Dobbs. And while 'I've got plenty o' nuttin' ' may have been added to the original *Porgy* as a light diversion in an otherwise serious story, it is by no means out of keeping with the tone of Heyward's novel, for the general contours of such a critique are sketched out by Heyward this time on the imaginary terrain of 'Catfish Row'.

While Peter's refrain quoted above represents the clearest articulation of the view that money, or better a particularly calculating attitude towards money and the good life, are mutually incompatible, much the same conclusion is suggested by the demeanour of the two 'bad guys', Crown and Sportin' Life – Crown, who kills Robbins during the dramatic opening when the latter has swept his crap winnings into his pocket before Crown can see the lie of the dice, and Sportin' Life, with his evil (if also laughable) New York ways, which includes inordinate pride in his (loud but presumably expensive by the standards of Catfish Row) clothing, and his constant search for clients to whom he can sell drugs.

Like other critics of the commodity form, Heyward is anxious to demonstrate that there are other less destructive ways by which goods and services might be distributed. That alternatives exist within Catfish Row is evident in the saucer burial. Here the money to bury Robbins is collected from the members of the community as a whole, and when it is still not enough, the black undertaker nonetheless agrees out of that same community spirit to perform the burial.

Similarly, many contemporary cultural critics employ the trope of demon commodity to great effect in their critique of consumer society and its corrosive effects on genuine cultural alterity. Susan Hegeman, for example, has produced a highly negative reading of an exhibition mounted in the 1970s by the Smithsonian entitled 'A Nation of Nations' which attempted to portray American cultural history, including or especially its 'multi-ethnic' characters by means of an exhibition of objects, as museums are wont to do. The problem with the exhibition, argues Hegeman was that the use of material objects such as 'folk artefacts' to represent cultural pluralism is bound to portray only a weak conception of ethnicity, a vision of a melting pot or cultural mosaic in which the 'strong ethnicity' (the racism and cultural resistance) that really characterises America's present and past is suppressed from view. The reason why a museum exhibit has this ideological effect lies in the very arrangements of objects which constitute the core of such exhibitions, since Hegeman, following Baudrillard, tells us

> Objects evoke other objects – and create a desire for more objects. This process does not change significantly whether the context is Baudrillard's French drugstore, an American shopping mall, or an exhibit (on that other 'Mall') at the Smithsonian. . . . The profusion of objects represented in the exhibit suggests the array of choices one makes while shopping, thus working in this sense to make even the activity an ethnic (but simultaneously very American) experience. While a relationship to an ethnic identity validates the consumerlike enjoyment of products, it is also the consumer's enjoyment of products that helps people to make a connection between themselves and these 'ethnic' objects/identities. (1991: 91f.)

The implication is of course that this representation of ethnicity is not authentic ('strong') ethnicity, indeed is inimical to it precisely because it has become infected by processes of commodification whereby objects appear to stand in relation to each other instead of through the human relations (of power and domination) which serve to create them.

But just because the attack on the commodity and exchange value is here articulated within a discourse of welfare and social justice, one should not assume that it is the sole property of the left wing populists, either now or in the past. There is instead another version of the narrative of demon commodity which has long been articulated on the political right, more often than not associated this time with a version of a past not so contaminated by the vulgar concerns of the market. And all too often in this version of the narrative, cultural otherness becomes something quite different. Now the other becomes he/she who, unlike the we whose culture aspires to higher values and ethical standards, is the bearer of a base culture that worships only commodities and money and who, when in our midst, poses a serious threat to our culture. Ideas about the Jews in Europe and, more recently, about Chinese culture have very often been informed by this version of the narrative of demon commodity.

Here then we have the outlines of that critical take on modernity that I have termed the narrative or trope of demon commodity; the view that buying and selling, what Marx called the formation of exchange value as opposed to use value, is at the heart of the destructive tendencies of modernity. According to this view we moderns apprehend a world in which distinctive objects and particular human beings are evaluated not for the practical uses to which we may put them or the individual ways in which we may relate to them, but also for a value which differs only quantitatively from the value of quite different objects and human beings. All particularity is reduced to mere quantitative difference. Moreover we take this world of exchange value to be in some sense natural instead of for what it 'really' is, namely an artificial way of arranging our social lives based on the dominance of the commodity form.

But because we have learned to take such an arrangement as natural we fail to see that such an arrangement is distinctly unnatural. It has the power to consume us and the bonds that unite us either as fellow humans or as members of cultures or communities. It is only in the state of cultural alterity that demon commodity is absent.

The demonisation of the commodity form amounts to a form of commodity fetishism itself, a fear and loathing produced by the very appearance of goods for sale on a market. Even looking at objects, as in a museum, seems to be enough to infect us all with profound alienation, or more accurately it seems to have this affect on others, for only we can see through the sham, see that those drawn into its web are lost for ever to seduction of modern capitalism. As bearers of alternative cultural values, and hence of different attitudes towards commodities, markets and money, peasants stand as supreme critics of demon commodity in much twentieth century peasantist discourse.

It is this rich amalgam of exoticism and universalism, translatability and untranslatability, otherness and sameness that begins to characterise the discourse of peasant alterity in the twentieth century, and that is at least occasionally still with us today as the reports on the Chiapas uprising suggest. But what are we to make of this blend of seemingly incompatible aims? Is Adorno right to imply that peasantism is a reactionary, because anti-modern, discourse, inevitably fascistic in implication? Is it, instead, emancipatory in the (Young) Hegelian sense – precisely because it goes straight to the heart of the alienating practices of modern society, as Lukács (and following him Taussig) appear to be arguing? Or rather is peasantism destabilising in a postmodern sense, not because it promises the universal emancipation of undifferentiated and autonomous human subjects, but precisely because it challenges all modernist metanarratives of emancipation which, by destroying particularism, are by definition hegemonising? Or does the fact of the generalisation of a European concept, even though it was originally embedded in a critique of modern universalising metanarratives provide yet another example of the way 'western' representational practices are implicated in the renewed western imperial project?

Why have these questions proved so difficult to answer? The reason for the intractability of the so-called 'peasant question', I would suggest, lies in the very ambiguity of the concept. All the above 'solutions' to the peasant question, it will be noted, depend rhetorically on the presumption of the radical *alterity* of the peasantry. For an Adorno peasantism is reactionary because peasants are themselves *pre*-modern – to turn to peasants is thus to turn back the clock. For a Lukács or a Taussig peasants are the true revolutionaries because, being located *outside* modern capitalism, they can see more clearly the unnaturalness of capitalist alienation. In the discourse of postmodernism as well, the 'otherness to modernity' of peasants – like the otherness of Lyotard's Cashinahua – shows us the violence of modern cosmopolitanism. And those who would argue that even the concept of peasantry itself is a western, hence imperial, construct, must presuppose a yet more radical state of alterity that the term 'peasant' misrepresents.

Yet if peasants are 'other than modern', then how is it that the *discourse* about them is modern? In none of the above examples do we hear the voice of a peasant other – that voice is at least mediated (at most constructed) by an author who is him/herself located firmly within the modern world. And it is here that the peasantist representations – of a Bartók, a Taussig, a Chayanov, a Traven, a Heyward, a Lukács, an Adorno – circulate, embedded in an ongoing modern argument about the merits and faults of techno-instrumental rationality, an argument in which the objects of these representations apparently do not take part. And just as the peasant is presumed not to be part of the world of the peasantist, so the latter, it is assumed, plays no part in peasant life. Our (modern) representations of the peasant world cannot by definition be implicated in the (non-modern) world of the peasantry.

What if it were otherwise? What if there were no inside and no outside in the relationship between our world and theirs? What if 'we' were as much a part of that alien world of the peasantry as 'they' were part of our own? An example serves to begin to break down the assumptions about identity and alterity that have always threatened to derail the debate over the 'peasant question'.

The Travels of a Concept

That a Soviet citizen in the 1920s would be concerned with the uniqueness of peasant existence would not have resulted solely from a need to develop a critique of the universalising metanarrative of neoclassical economic theory. Instead Chayanov was embroiled in a much more direct conflict with another form of universalising modernism, namely the official Marxism of a Soviet regime bent on collectivising peasant agriculture in as short a space of time as possible. This conflict brought together in violence both the advocates of Stalinism and the subjects of Chayanov's 'portraits' of peasant life. For the former this involved, among other things the need to eliminate rural 'capitalism', a policy pursued relentlessly at the expense of the so-called *kulaks*.

But in their pursuit of the kulaks, Stalin's forces cast their nets very wide, dispossessing, forcing into exile and imprisoning large numbers of rural landowners in the gulags. An argument that Russian agriculture was not to be so simply characterised as capitalist, that rural landowners were more often than not family farmers, and that in any case a viable agricultural system could be built on the backs of this class of peasants (what classical Marxists like Kautsky and Lenin called the 'middle peasantry') was, of course, a direct attack on the Stalinist programme – a fact that Chayanov himself learned to his cost when he too was apparently sent to a gulag (see Kerblay's introduction in Chayanov, 1966). Peasant, peasantist and collectiviser in the Soviet Union in the 1920s were not dwellers in alien worlds.

Nor was this conflict between a universalising instrumental modernism – represented in the Soviet Union by Stalinist Marxism – and a particularist peasantism a purely local or national one at the time.

One of the ironies of Soviet Marxism was the fact that it advocated very different policies at home and abroad, something which of course Trotsky pointed out for as long as he was allowed to do so by Soviet authorities. While relentlessly pursuing the path to communist agriculture and the elimination of the peasantry at home, the Comintern, the international arm of Soviet communism, advised members of communist parties in other parts of the world to await the arrival of truly capitalist agriculture, for only then would a communist revolution find support among the rural masses. As a result conflicts and debates over the peasant question emerged within the world's communist movements on a global scale.

Members of the Japanese Communist Party (JCP) (founded in 1922) early on came into conflict over the issue of whether, to paraphrase one commentator, they were witnessing the development of *Japanese* capitalism or a Japanese *capitalism*.[7] Those of the so-called Koza school – notably economists like Noro Eitaro (1900–34) and Yamadu Moritaro (1897–1980) – maintained that Japan's was a dual economy, with an advanced, capitalist industrial sector and a backward or pre-capitalist agricultural regime. In this model, the militarism of the Japanese state was thought to reflect the 'persistence' of feudal or semi-feudal relations in the countryside. In spite of rising levels of political repression during the 1920s, the JCP nonetheless advocated strategic alliances with liberals as the means of hastening the modernisation (proletarianisation) of a 'feudal' and, by implication 'reactionary' peasantry and, hence, laying the groundwork for a future socialist revolution.

In 1927, a group known as the Rono school broke away from the JCP. Criticising the JCP and the Koza school for its analysis of the peasant question, members of the Rono school argued that rural Japan was *already* capitalist, hence dismissing the possibility that farming life was in any way a unique form of modern existence. The debate took place in a series of rather abstruse articles on the question of whether ground rent was a manifestation of capitalist or feudal relations of production in agriculture. Based on their 'modernist' assessment of the state of Japanese agriculture, the breakaway Rono school argued for the need for a mass-based organisation of workers, peasants and others; criticised the JCP and the Koza school for its reformist tendencies; and advocated immediate revolution. As elsewhere, then, in Japan in the 1920s a debate over the 'agrarian question' emerged from within Japanese Marxism. On the one hand, there were those who argued that no uniquely peasant mode of existence existed in Japan since Japanese agriculture had already evolved along capitalist lines. According to this position, the 'peasant' economy could be understood using the same, universal categories of analysis employed in the analysis of modern economy and society as a whole. On the other hand were those who argued that the economic, social and/or cultural life of Japanese farming communities was not capitalist and hence not amenable to universalistic modes of description and analysis. It instead was structured by Japanese 'tradition' and hence constituted a unique form of rural existence.

The situation in the developing Chinese communist movement was somewhat different. In an interesting reinterpretation of the role of peasantism in the revolutionary ideology of the Chinese Communist Party in this period, Ralph Thaxton has argued convincingly that not only did Maoism successfully mobilise Chinese peasants, but that it did so by a substantial revision of communist ideology to take account of the peasantist, and not just a workerist, critique of capitalism (Thaxton, 1983). And in much the same period, the Indonesian Communist Party (PKI) experienced its greatest success in recruitment precisely in areas where at least a classically-conceived working class was least developed (see Schrieke, 1955; McVey, 1965; Williams, 1982). This was not because the PKI intelligentsia manipulated peasants for its own ends, but because at least some sections of it quite genuinely articulated a peasantist anti-capitalism, rather than a classical Marxist position. In contrast with Japan, this time it was the 'peasantists' who were more radical, calling for immediate revolution in spite of the absence of a developed proletariat, a revolution that would be carried forward by peasants in ways reminiscent of the classical Russian populists who modelled their socialist utopia on the unique and unalienated existence of the Russian peasantry.

But it was not just within the ideologies of revolutionary movements that the world was discovering peasants in this period. As the differences between Russian populists and German defenders of an *Agraarstaat* suggest, peasantism can just as well be articulated by the forces of law and order as by revolutionaries. Not surprisingly the European empires in this period provide examples of such bureaucratic peasantism. A particularly intriguing example is provided by the introduction of a peasantist discourse into colonial Indonesia by Dutch colonial officials during the period of the so-called Ethical Policy.

Chayanov comes to Java

Having begun to pursue a vigorously laissez-faire policy of capitalist modernisation after around 1870, within which its colonial subjects were always seen as profit-seeking utility maximisers, the Netherlands colonial government in Batavia began to revise its instrumental vision of development from the beginning of this century. Part and parcel of this shift was a changing image of Indonesian villagers; from a vision of a countryside populated by petty entrepreneurs, the Dutch rulers came instead to imagine a population in the grip of a uniquely eastern mentality. They were prompted towards this view in part by the discovery that policies that were supposed to lead to universal emancipation and wealth in fact appeared to be generating widespread misery among the rural poor, especially on the densely populated island of Java. But they were also clearly influenced by the threat to the stability of colonial rule posed by the spread of money, markets and modern ideologies, particularly socialism.

Echoing sentiments expressed in other places, an adviser to the colonial government wrote in 1926:

> Why should so much importance be attached to a strong peasant class in Java? . . . From a social point of view because here as everywhere else in the world, the best counter-weight against evolutionary currents is a calm, satisfied and steady nucleus of the population represented by a community of substantial, well-to-do farmers. For Java the importance of this factor is all the more accentuated, since the disturbing element of a too rapidly penetrating money economy in an agrarian community which until recently had been practically without it, causes a temporary lack of balance and discomfort, which makes the country people unsuited to their social task. (Kolff, 1926: 124f.)

That Javanese villagers were in fact peasants, however, was a conclusion reached only after considerable debate, particularly with the advocates of neoclassical economics and utilitarian evolutionism who held sway in the last decades of the nineteenth century. Perhaps the subsequently best-known participant in these debates was one Julius Herman Boeke who formulated later on the notion of a 'dual economy' to describe the peculiar combination of western and eastern economic mentalities found in the colonial situation. Boeke argued against the assumption that commodification was either a good thing in itself or the necessary expression of man's nature, maintaining that Indonesian villagers testified to the cultural/ historical specificity of *homo œconomicus*. But it took another group of colonial advisers and economists to come up with the view that the European notion of peasantry was also extendable to Java.

It is interesting to mark the arrival of the Indonesian peasant on the discursive map of at least some colonial scholars by noting the reception accorded the ideas of A.V. Chayanov when they were first made available to Dutch scholars in 1924. When Chayanov's 'On the Theory of Non-Capitalist Economic Systems' first appeared in German in 1924 it was immediately appropriated by a number of Dutch writers concerned with the organisation of agricultural production on Java (see also Aas, 1980). Although there were debates over both the general validity of Chayanov's theories, and the extent of their 'pertinence' in the Indonesian context, the almost immediate recognition of Chayanov's aims is striking. After all Chayanov was writing in circumstances which apparently differed in significant ways from those faced by these Dutch writers in the 1920s. And, in spite of some pretence to generality, Chayanov's theories were seemingly based on conditions totally foreign to them. In spite of this, it could be argued that, at least partly due to the stimulus provided by the publication of Chayanov's work, Dutch agronomists, agricultural economists and orientalists had constituted a category of peasant economy, society and culture striking in its similarity to Chayanov's, something that explains the enthusiasm with which Chayanov's own work was received in the Dutch colony.

A typical example of the Dutch treatment of Chayanov is found very early on, in an extended review by Van Doorn of Chayanov's 1924 essay (Van Doorn, 1924; see also Koens, 1926–7). In his paper, Van Doorn was concerned with the extent to which the theory of the family labour farm, designed to deal with the Russian case, could be made pertinent to Indonesia. Of its general usefulness Van Doorn was in no doubt. However it could not, he argued, be simply applied whole hog, prior to a thorough examination of the extent to which divergent socio-economic conditions on Java made modifications necessary. Among the differences cited by Van Doorn were: the significance of the 'joint families' in Indonesian societies as opposed to that of the nuclear family in the Russian case (Van Doorn, 1924: 288ff.); the significance of polygamy (polygyny) in parts of Indonesia (ibid.: 290); the ability of family heads to call on the labour of non-resident kin (ibid.); the suspicion that on Java it may be enterprise size which determines family size rather than vice versa, and that, therefore family size may vary with class (ibid.: 290ff.); the complicating effect of village and government institutions which allow those of higher political status to make demands on the labour of political subordinates (ibid.: 295); and, finally, the possibility that Indonesian land tenure systems do not permit the redistribution of land that, in Chayanov's case, allows farm size to adjust to demand (ibid.: 296). In spite of these potentially highly significant variables, Van Doorn does not seek either to question the general pertinence of Chayanov's work for Indonesia, or to criticise his basic arguments. The list of factors cited above are merely offered as suggestions for further research into the way Chayanov's theories might need to be modified to deal with specifically Indonesian conditions.

But Chayanov did not arrive out of the blue. In fact Dutchmen appropriated Chayanov's concept of a peasant mode of existence so readily because the groundwork had already been laid. It had been laid by, among others, those employed by the newly formed Department of Agriculture, Commerce and Industry who, in looking at problems to do with the 'development' of Indonesian agriculture were trying to come to grips with the nature of economic rationality in peasant enterprises, which a number of them approached from the perspective of accounting. In examining existing systems of accounting for agricultural enterprise, however, the authors of these articles were almost uniformly struck by the same thought, that is, that accounting systems developed for use on European farms were, by and large, unsuitable for the case of Indonesia. Why? Because there was a fundamental difference between most European agricultural enterprises, whether they were physically located in Europe or the colony, and the agricultural 'enterprises' of the indigenous Indonesian farmer.

This difference came to be perceived as a difference between modern 'enterprises' (*ondernemingen*) and peasant concerns (*bedrijven*) (see for example Koens, 1925; Scheltema, 1923). In most of these Dutch writings direct comparisons were made between Indonesian agriculture and European peasant farming systems. Partly as a result of their training in German economic theory, Dutch agricultural economists in the 1920s tended to view the 'facts' of Indonesian rural economy through the lens of German economic historicism. The emphasis was, then, less on the uniqueness of the East or of the colonial situation and more on the specific parallels (and differences) between Indonesia and non-capitalist Europe. However, economists like van Doorn, Scheltema, van der Kolff, Koens and even Boeke in this period differed somewhat from earlier generations of Dutch observers who favoured comparisons with the pre-capitalist German Mark or Russian mir. Instead comparisons were drawn more directly with contemporary European peasantries conceived of as manifesting only those features of pre-capitalism which have *survived* into the modern world. Once again, then, we have to do with a peasantist discourse which both stresses the particularities of the Indonesian situation, the uniqueness of the 'eastern mind', and yet does so quite explicitly by means of the more universal concept of peasantry. This particular combination of universalism and relativism arose only because of processes of globalisation – a cultural confrontation between West and East at a cultural level, but one which is here embedded in a relationship between West and East by which the representatives of the former are seeking to govern those self-same 'peasants' that they have discovered intellectually in their critique of instrumental modernism.

'Indigenous' Peasantisms

It can, of course, be argued that the spread of notions of a 'peasantry' within international communism, or through colonial regimes are clear examples of the imposition of alien western categories on non-western people, although it is somewhat misleading to treat Indonesian, Chinese or Japanese communists as though they were necessarily less 'indigenous' than non-communists. This is particularly so in the case of peasantist attempts to 'indigenise' Marxism in places like Japan, China and Indonesia. Moreover, for better or worse, Dutch colonial officials and their advisers were very much part of colonial society in Indonesia. The examples of Bartók and Chayanov demonstrate in any case the increasingly arbitrary nature of the distinction between western and non-western, indigenous and alien in the twentieth century.

But that peasantism was not produced solely out of the indigenisation of a European ideology (Marxism) or European governance of the non-West is demonstrated by the example of local Indonesian journalism in the 1920s. At much the same time as Dutch economists and colonial officials were discovering the particular virtues of the Indonesian peasantry, Indonesians were themselves developing concepts of village economy and the integrity of indigenous culture out of an encounter with self-proclaimed modernist discourse. By the 1920s, in the government of Sumatra's west coast, for example, a large number of Minangkabau themselves came to represent their own situation through the language of peasantism.

While the dominant concern of this discourse was with the nature and possible future of Minangkabau adat or custom, at least at the outset it was not adat but the 'traditional village economy' which was a central concern. And at least paralleling the developments in the discourse of their colonial masters, Minangkabau writers in the second decade of this century developed an understanding of this 'traditional village economy' while coming to grips with the implications of prevailing views of the benefits of economic modernisation.

While certain more or less uniform notions of the nature of the traditional village economy in Minangkabau were being developed by a variety of people in quite different contexts, nowhere is this particular modification of prevailing modernist discourse so clearly documented as in the pages of a newspaper called *Minangkabau* published in the coastal town of Pariaman in 1918. Like many other periodicals of the period, *Minangkabau* was seen as an advocate of progress or *kemadjoean*. Its editors, which included both Minangkabau and Dutchmen were, in this case, concerned particularly with the progressive development of agriculture. Indeed the paper was aimed particularly at the farming community.

The articles in *Minangkabau* cover a variety of topics, including the proper methods which farmers should employ in the paddy cultivation and, appropriately, a serialised translation of a short story by Tolstoy. But of particular interest from our point of view is an article written in instalments entitled 'Economie kampoeng' ('Village Economy'). The article is interesting both because in it its anonymous author lays out a description of what he/she calls progress in agriculture, at the same time describing that progress in terms which lead the reader inevitably to doubts about its benefits. In this sense the attitude towards village economy manifest in the pages of *Minangkabau* is an ambivalent one. The author of 'Economie kampoeng' is clearly in favour of progress, and yet the more its social and economic implications unfold, the more depressing the picture which emerges:

> Mutual cooperation is the basis of life in the village. Farmers need to assist each other at specific periods and particular seasons. That is why in early times right up to today the custom [adat] of mutual help has developed among farmers [*sipeladang*].
>
> Because farmers, unlike traders and artisans, depend on the produce of the soil, they do not get money every day. They produce clothes and tools in their own households. When they need money, they have none at all. Wealth for them is not money, but paddy in the granary, and livestock running loose in the forest.
>
> It then came to pass that people were no longer satisfied with the products of the soil, they wanted more. People then sought money by working for a wage. Then came roads and traders. The traders brought goods, which served to increase the desire [*hawa nafsu*] of the people, who wanted more. The farmers began to sell their crops for money to buy these goods. Then there were people who did not even want to be farmers at all, so they began to work as artisans or for a wage. In this way mutual help gave way to wage work. A new custom was introduced – of paying money to have someone plough the land, to hoe, to plant and to harvest.
>
> Now it does not matter where you work or what you do, as long as you can get money quickly, as long as you can get a wage working as a labourer there. You could work as a farmer, or on a plantation, or for the railroads, or whatever.
>
> But all this is a good thing. It is causing humans to progress. (*Minangkabau*, 1 (2), August 1918: 16ff.; my translation)

> Now with artisans and experts, the farmer can buy fertiliser, tools, buckets, clothing, thread, scissors, plates, kerosene, knives, files, saws. To get all this the farmer must sell a part of the paddy harvest.
>
> But the farmer, desperate for money, does not pay attention to markets. In fact the price will probably be low when it is harvest time. As a result the need for cash will exceed proceeds. The farmer will then have to borrow money. And misfortune befalls the farmer who borrows. There are many unscrupulous people, including people of our own race [Bumiputera as well as Chinese], who are prepared to lend money. They will even give money against a future harvest. In this way a farmer will become caught in a trap of indebtedness. But all this is a good thing. It represents progress. (ibid.: 34ff.)

As I have suggested, this myth of agrarian evolution, a short extract of which is summarised above, articulates an ambivalent attitude towards progress. On the one hand, the mythical past, when farming households were self-sufficient, when the desire for commodities was not present, when families helped each other, and when cooperation was facilitated by adat, is clearly presented in approving terms. On the other hand, the interjections about progress are genuine. The problem is, it seems, with the side effects of progress. The author of 'Ekonomie kampoeng' is not asking for the clock to be turned back. But neither is he/she arguing that progress is altogether desirable.

As in most contemporary accounts, this is where it is thought to be necessary to intervene in the evolutionary process, to preserve those aspects of the village economy worth preserving, to offset the damages wrought by progress. And typical of contemporary accounts, the saviour here is education. 'There are those', argues the author of 'Ekonomie kampoeng', 'who argue that the Minangkabau farmer is stupid or confused. The real problem is that there is no one to teach them. If Indies farmers were provided with teaching, they would quickly become knowledgeable [*berilmoe*], and we would no longer have to worry about the course of *kemadjoean*' (ibid.: 35).

Perhaps an even more sharply ambivalent attitude towards the traditional village economy is found in the pages of some of the local periodicals closely associated with the Indonesian Communist Party which appeared in the 1920s. One such was *Djago Djago* edited by Natar Zainoeddin. In an article entitled 'Moedoer dan Madjoe' ('Decline and Progress'), the author identifies progress capitalist-style as the destroyer of the 'traditional' features of peasant life:

> In the old days, before the capitalists came to the Indies, the people lived on simple earnings. But with the arrival of capitalists the lives of the people have become lives of misery, because their ways of earning an income were destroyed by the capitalists.
>
> In the old days, we transported heavy loads with carts pulled by buffalo, cows and horses, but these traditional modes of transport were destroyed by the capitalists, who replaced them with motor vehicles and trains.
>
> In the old days we used horse carts to travel from one place to another, but these were destroyed by the capitalists and replaced by cars and trams. . . .
>
> . . . Because of all these, the lives of we children of India become more and more miserable, so much so that we are now forced to work for a wage [*makan gadji*, literally eat a wage] just like them.
>
> Finally we, the children of India, will become nothing more than tools [*perkakas*] to be used by the capitalists. And when they design better tools and machines, we will be simply cast off. (*Djago Djago*, 30 October 1923: 2f.)

The above article, although it does not address the nature of the village economy directly, and while embedded clearly in a Marxist framework, nonetheless, like much Marxist populist writing, contains within it a notion of the simple yet desirable nature of economic life before capitalism. A particularly strong image is that of the wage worker being forced, literally, to eat money to survive, an expression which has now found its way into contemporary Indonesian (and Malay) to describe wage work. A strong contrast is drawn with economic life in the traditional village economy, where economic relations represented mutual association, cooperation and family ties. For many Minangkabau in this period, the wage labour relation was in fact the epitome of the evils of the kinds of progress and economic transformation being wrought under Dutch rule. It stood in sharp contrast to the relations of cooperation presumed to operate in the traditional village economy.

Another example of an 'indigenised' peasantism in this period is provided by Japanese agrarianism. Havens has argued convincingly that agrarianist discourse in Japan has developed in the context of attempts to indigenise Japanese modernity in the following terms:

... soon after the vogue of liberal western ideas in the 1870s had run its course, political and social writers began to search Japan's past for ways to disclose the secret of her national distinctiveness. A number of them found that agriculture provided the answer. ...

No longer a universalistic influence shaping the national consciousness, agriculture in the twentieth century has been specifically highlighted as one of a number of main influences affecting Japanese thinking. Japanese nationalists have clarified and trimmed, but few if any have tried to destroy, the imprint of the farm on the country's collective self-image. (Havens, 1974: 6)

The parallels between European peasantism and Japanese agrarianism are evident from Havens's description of the former:

The principal Nohonshugi [agrarianist] beliefs included a faith in agricultural economics, an affirmation of rural communalism, and a conviction that farming was indispensable to those qualities that made the nation unique. ... Not until a national policy of industrialization was implemented after 1868 did agrarianism arise as a conscious, if ill-defined, ideology that variously upheld farming on social, economic, political, and spiritual grounds. Only when people began to question seriously whether agriculture should continue to be the most economically productive and ethically approved occupation did its diverse partisans, for diverse reasons, begin to defend it. (1974: 8f.)

Havens divides agrarianism in Japan into two forms: bureaucratic and popular, the former strongest from the 1890s to the First World War, the latter in the 1920s. Both, he suggests, represented a revision of or a reaction to a more straightforward modernism established during the Meiji period. The rise of bureaucratic agrarianism is linked to: accelerated industrialisation, the Sino-Japanese War of 1894–5 and 'long-term forces such as inflation, the spread of technical education, peasant unrest, the concentration of landownership in fewer hands, and the failure of the government's large-scale farming program'(Havens, 1974: 57). The main policies advocated by these bureaucratic agrarianists involved support for a small-farm system, which involved 'protecting smaller landowners against both industrialism and the commercialization of large landlords' (ibid.: 64). While bureaucratic agrarianism did not necessarily translate directly into government policy, it did lead to continual government efforts to support credit associations. Bureaucratic agrarianism in Japan therefore emerged towards the end of the last century as a critique of techno-rational modernism, especially as it impinged on Japanese farm life: 'Here was an undeniably new emphasis in official agricultural thought in Japan: the specific acknowledgment, at the highest level of the national administration, that farming must be fortified against the spread of a commercial economy if it was to contribute to overall national development' (ibid.: 69). Its main spokesmen:'were modern men with modern assumptions, living in an industrializing age, who developed defensive, profarm doctrines that smacked romantically of traditional village life without recapturing the pre-modern ethos that encompassed it' (ibid.: 85).

A new generation of bureaucratic agrarianists emerged in the years between 1900 and the First World War, by which time Japanese industry had definitely overtaken agriculture as the main contributor to the national economy. Since agriculture could no longer be defended as main generator of national wealth 'a new justification appeared, stressing farming as the social, military, and ethical foundation of the country. Above all, it was the small cultivator, living in the classical farm village, who represented the ideal social type to twentieth century Nohonshugisha'(ibid.: 98).

The main spokesman for early twentieth century agrarianism was Yokoi Tokiyoshi, a professor of agricultural administration at the Tokyo Agricultural College. Early on, Yokoi was concerned with practical and technical issues in agricultural education, but he soon became interested in 'more abstract questions relating to the spirit and quality of farm life' (ibid.: 99). In 1897 Yokoi praised Japanese farmers in the following terms:

> In my opinion the vitality of a country is fostered by its middle class families; it is particularly well developed among farm families. Such qualities as innocence, sincerity, obedience, vigor, fortitude, trustworthiness, earnestness, and robust health are appropriate for soldiers and for defending the country. Don't farmers excel in these qualities above all? Although you cannot make a country out of land alone, the country must not be separated from the soil. Therefore the farmers, who have the closest connection to the land, love it the most and thus love the country the most. Likewise they are the people who feel the greatest loyalty for the ruler. If you accept the progressive doctrine that all men are brothers, it certainly is not necessary to define boundaries for countries using mountains, rivers, and lofty peaks, nor is it necessary to distinguish among peoples by means of ethnic differences. Therefore, to establish a country is an act of conservatism, and a country created by conservatism must initially be protected by conservative people. The only people who are particularly conservative are farmers. (cited in Havens, 1974: 101)

Contrasting urbanites and peasants in a 1907 article, Yokoi made that same link between money and the corrosive effects of modernity that peasantists have made in other places and times:

> City dwellers merely respect things in monetary terms, calculating everything on the basis of money and making profits without regard for their honour. Their conception of morality tends to be to sell land. . . . [Farmers instead are] the only class which does not take money as its standard. [They are] a class with integrity. (cited in Havens, 1974: 105)

> Agriculture is most honorable, profitable, and wholesome. Without yearning for money, it draws close to the land and takes mother nature as its friend. Being not covetous, it does not take impure persons as its partners. It is as free and independent as heaven. (ibid.: 108)

Yokoi saw city life as corrosive of proper social and cultural life, speaking of the danger of 'metropolitan fever' overwhelming the whole country. Related to this were dangerously subversive political ideas like socialism, which Yokoi argued are formed only in the urban environment.

As many critics of notions pertaining to the political virtues of agricultural life have maintained, the kinds of expressivist critique of industrialism and urban life articulated by polemicists like Yokoi align them with large landowners. But, as Havens points out, Yokoi's views transcended the interests of those large landowners who supported them. Instead, his 'ethical maxims and an antiprogressive outlook . . . appealed more to smaller, less imaginative landholders than to those large landlords who took a favorable view of technical development. . . . Yokoi's ideal type was the small village landowner who formed the same backbone of rural society that state officials had tried to strengthen in the 1890s' (ibid.: 109f.).

As far as the positive, anti-instrumental images of peasant life are concerned, there is not a large gap between the discourse of 'bureaucratic' agrarianists and 'popular agrarianists' in Japan, whose influence was strongest in the first two decades of this century. These included the famous Japanese anthropologist Yanagida Kunio, as well as novelists like Natsume Soskei (1867–1916) and Arishima Takeo (1878–1923), the latter of whom in one novel 'symbolically eradicated the landlord class by distributing his lands to tenants and taking his own life' (ibid.: 113). Mushakoji Saneatsu (1886–1976) was another populist novelist who founded a Utopian settlement in 1918, and who in 1928 wrote of the enterprise that 'What we are trying to do is to create a new society . . . and fulfil our destinies without need of money' (cited in Havens, 1974: 114).

Also influenced by Marxism, Mushakoji was in these early years nonetheless a great defender of the peasantry, arguing that agriculture could be defended on both economic grounds and in terms of its non-economic benefits for the nation. Like many peasantist critics of modernism Mushakoji made much of the superiority of non-modern rural 'values' – criticising capitalism's lust for profits, and arguing that the spirit of money-making was the epitome of selfishness and *contrary to human nature*. He insisted 'that the countryside was the repository of true values, such as frugality, harmony, altruism, and cooperation' (ibid.: 119).

An activist, and a central figure in the tenant movement that began during the First World War and continued throughout the 1920s, Mushakoji was somewhat different from other agrarianists because he laid great stress on class differences and class conflicts in the countryside. But like more recent writers on the peasantry such as Michael Taussig and James Scott, he argued that even rural class relations were distinctively pre-modern and moral. Arguing that traditional values still persisted in the countryside, he maintained that landlord–tenant disputes were resolved through 'exchanges of kindness' rather than through open confrontation. The disappearance of traditional rural life, he predicted, would lead to a very different situation, a total differentiation into large landlords and agricultural labourers 'clustered around them like ants' (in Havens, 1974: 126). Contrary to many socialists Mushakoji was alarmed by the 'demise of patriotism' and the 'advent of extreme individualistic thought'. Only the restoration of independent cultivation could stop this erosion of desirable non-modern values.

As the above suggests, Mushakoji's constructions of a moral peasant life in Japan make sense only in the context of a particular Japanese debate over the consequences of industrialism and the securing of bureaucratic control over the Japanese countryside in the early decades of this century. In this case we have a novelist who was at the same time an active participant in a particular populist response to these processes – the so-called tenancy movement.

Elsewhere, and at other times, 'indigenous' novelists also discovered the virtues of 'their' peasantries, thus in different ways working to indigenise both the European novel form and/or a 'modernist' vision of a backward and anachronistic countryside. An example is the Turkish novelist Mahmut Makal who established the Turkish genre of the 'village novel' in the early 1950s. But Turkish writers had begun to incorporate village themes into their novels from earlier on. As the study by Rathbun shows the Turkish village in fact became a central theme in many novels and short stories from around 1920. These novels generally introduced realist traditions and show the growth of writing in the Turkish vernacular. Among these novelists there was a conscious attempt to 'indigenise' the language of Turkish fiction by a diminution in the, previously, heavy use of foreign words, mainly from French, Arabic and Persian. The protagonists in these precursors to the Turkish village novel were generally urban/intellectuals, often motivated by the desire to improve the lot of the exploited villagers (see Rathbun, 1972).

While as we shall see in Mexico the turn to indigenous themes was probably strongest in the visual arts in which an attempt was made to draw on Mexico's pre-Columbian heritage, mention might also be made of the appearance of peasantist themes in Mexican novels in late interwar years. An example is Ermilo Abreu Gomez's popular 1940 novel *Canek: History and Legend of a Maya Hero*.

Malaysian novelists discovered 'their' peasants somewhat later. Early Malay nationalists, like their Turkish counterparts, tended to see rural dwellers as backward, ignorant, exploited, in need of education/modernisation. It was not until somewhat later on that the counter-modern virtues of the Malay village/Malay peasantry were discovered by Malay novelists (Banks, 1987). A good example of Malay peasantist fiction is an early novel by Malaysia's most prominent novelist, Shahnon Ahmad called *Kemulut* (Crisis). *Kemulut* tells the story of a peaceful and timeless Malay fishing village threatened by factories that pour out poisonous effluent into the river on which it is built, killing fish, plant life, animals and then a villager who dies graphically of mercury poisoning. In reprisal a group of village men first threaten to burn factories, and then approach (Malay) government officials to seek redress. Only when the story is leaked to the press does the federal government finally announce that factories will be closed until they clean up their waste disposal.

The events are narrated by, and portrayed through the eyes of, a senior village man and his teenage daughter. But the central 'character' of the novel is the peasant village – communalistic, egalitarian, consensual, non-competitive, culturally homogeneous and governed by standards of reciprocity, and morality that are clearly absent in the world outside, especially the industrial world of European-owned corporations and Chinese businessmen.[8]

In the Malaysian context, this traditionalist discourse has particular meanings and implications. For example, a central theme of *Kemulut*, as in other novels by Shahnon, is 'of the responsibility of Malay intellectuals for the advancement of Malay rural society which he had explored in his four political novels' (Banks, 1987: 126). This idea of the need for Malays as a group to confront the moral dilemmas of modernity by reasserting 'traditional' Malay standards of justice – standards moreover that have their origins in peasant villages – was implicated in the whole move towards a 'New Economic Policy' by which the Malaysian government (dominated by the Malay party, UMNO), sought not only to promote economic development, but to reassert what they took to be the rights of the 'indigenous' Malay inhabitants of the peninsula, particularly as against ethnic Chinese who were thought to dominate the economic life of the nation.

But Shahnon as an articulator of this Malay traditionalism is by no means the villager of his own novels. Born in Kedah, in 1933, the son of a postman, Shahnon worked first as a teacher in an English medium school, then as a military official, then again as a teacher until in 1968 he went to the Australian National University to do a degree in literature. He subsequently became lecturer and then Dean at the Science University in Penang. In 1982 he received Malaysia's highest literary award, the Anugerah Sastera Negara.

Shahnon Ahmad is, then, very much part of the Malaysian establishment, indeed his 'traditionalism' has recently come under the critical scrutiny of, among others, the more radical Islamic critics of the current government for being too 'westernised'.

As these examples of the constitution and consumption of the images of the peasantry show, the modern category of a uniquely peasant mode of existence emerged in different places and different contexts out of processes of modernisation that were occurring on a global landscape, processes that set off more general debates about culture and identity that were much more embedded in these processes than they were mere offstage reflections on them. If peasantisation implies a set of modern discourses about the unique virtues of peasant existence, then peasantism is by no mean external to the world of the peasantry, but very much part of it.

But does this now mean that we now are witnessing a non-western form of orientalism, whereby Hungarians, Russians, Indonesians, Chinese and Japanese intellectuals, activists, musicians and artists have been duped into accepting the identities previously thrust upon them by their imperial masters? Does the globalisation of a concept of a uniquely peasant mode of existence mean that non-westerners are themselves imposing a set of imperial categories and so distorting what is a genuine cultural alterity?[9] Perhaps paradoxically, given the tendency to equate the condition of the peasantry with that of radical alterity, has the attempt to articulate a peasantist critique of modernity failed because the discourse of peasantism is *too modern*? These are questions to which we shall now turn.

Notes

1 This account is derived largely from Antokoletz (1988).

2 Cited in *New Oxford History of Music*, vol. X, p. 275 (London: Oxford University Press, 1974).

3 Ibid.: 78.

4 This distinction has been made by Janós Breuer, among others. Ilona Fodor has argued, similarly, that Bartók was a 'progressive' rather than a 'reactionary' nationalist (see Antokoletz, 1988: 152f.,156).

5 This argument has been made by a number of Hungarian scholars, including Fodor, Markowski, Zoltai and even Lukács (cited in Antokoletz, 1988: 153ff.). Adorno's contention that the combination of 'folklorism' and 'modernism' in the work of composers such as Bartók is countered in a somewhat different way by the American composer Aaron Copeland who has argued that it was precisely out of the encounter with folk musics that truly modern music could break away from the tradition of German romanticism (see Copeland, 1968: 17ff.).

6 Chayanov has often been called a 'neo-populist' by those seeking to link his attitude to the peasantry to that of nineteenth century populists like Chernyshevskii, Mikhailovski and others, a tendency which stems from the definitions of populism offered by Lenin in particular and the Russian revolutionaries in general (cf. Walicki, 1969). However, what is often overlooked is the extent to which Chayanov was also intellectually indebted to the German economists. His own peasantism owes as much if not more to the latter's critiques of Austrian marginalism in particular and of the attempt by techno-rationalist thought to universalise instrumental rationalism by claiming that it was the defining characteristic of humanity.

7 A useful summary of developments in early twentieth century Japanese Marxism is found in Morris-Suzuki (1989). See also Hoster (1986).

8 Although relations with the Malay elites are organised by principles of morality and justice that were made famous in social scientific circles by James Scott in his study of the Malay peasantry (Scott, 1985).

9 See, for example, Chatterjee (1986), who points to the incorporation of 'orientalist' imagery within the discourse of Indian nationalism.

4

Alien Worlds: Representing Cultural Otherness

Where is the world? Where is the earth on which I used to live? Where
has mankind gone? I am alone. . . . I am on another planet, from which
I never can return to my own people. . . . I am with creatures I do not
know, who do not speak my language, and whose souls and minds I can
never fathom. (Traven [1929], 1980: 551)

Travellers to the world of the other for those in the grips of the ideology of
empire as often as not were seen, and saw themselves, as time travellers, a
common enough theme in nineteenth century literature, at least in Britain
and France. How many travellers are still called to far away places by the
promise of glimpses of life as it was in the stone age, or of peoples who
have remained unchanged for centuries if not millennia? And if writers like
Traven and especially Heyward retain this discourse of temporal alterity in
attempting to locate the 'Mexican Indian', the American 'Negro' somewhere far off in the past, they also employ the new metaphor of space
travel to describe their experiences. The European narrator of B. Traven's
The Bridge in the Jungle who ends up in an Indian community somewhere
in Mexico is struck by the thought that he is among alien beings, as though
he were on another planet.

A sympathetic reviewer of DuBose Heyward's novel about the people of
Catfish Row had the same thought, writing:

[T]he people of *Porgy* are savage aliens. . . . And in recognizing an alien quality
in the Negroes of his story, Mr Heyward takes a step forward beyond the usual
attitude of white writers of the South who deal with Negro life. [For Heyward it
is not a question of inferiority but of] strangeness. [Heyward makes] Negro life
more colorful and spirited and vital than that of the white community. . . . If the
two cultures don't readily mix, it may well be the Nordic who lags. (cited in
Alpert, 1990: 39f.)

And a member of the New York Theater Guild, who staged the play
enthused that it provided us with a window that 'opened to give us a peep
into an alien world' (ibid.: 48).

But if these alien beings were so genuinely different they would not have
been able to play so central a role in the novels. Yet they do. In Traven's
early novels we approach them through narrators and go-betweens. The
narrator of *The Bridge in the Jungle* himself needs a long-term American
resident of the village – a man who has married locally and 'gone native' –

gradually to help him understand what is going on. But in his later novels Traven and his readers were happy to part with this device, confident that they needed no interpreter to comprehend the lives of Traven's Mexicans. Heyward never felt the need for go-betweens – the white characters in *Porgy* are almost entirely peripheral to the story.

In this search for alien worlds and lives, these early students of culture had recourse to two avenues which served both to establish difference, yet at the same time to make these lives meaningful. These are the avenues of *language* and *medicine*.

Traven in the above extract makes a case for linguistic relativism directly. 'They' do not even speak his language, therefore he cannot fathom their 'souls and minds'. He/she who can truly learn their language will understand them. In John Huston's film version of *Treasure* the old man – the only one of the three prospectors who clearly knows the Indians – converses directly with them in 'their' language, an extremely rare occurrence in Hollywood films of the time. Never mind that all he is speaking is Spanish – that was exotic enough for the time. The old man's judgements of what the Indians want are clearly meant to be authoritative. Neither Curtin nor Dobbs have any doubt about it.

Heyward approaches this task differently – writing in what is meant to be, and what was certainly read as, the authentic argot of the 'gullah Negro'. Readers are now privileged to understand these exotic beings themselves without an interpreter. When writing about his Harlem 'street' characters, the white novelist Heyward's contemporary Carl van Vechten also sought to reproduce the language of urban African Americans of the 1920s. He is even obliging enough to supply his readers with a glossary of terms and phrases, which makes the task much easier.

But it is disease and its treatment that appears to present the greatest challenge to these translators of alien worlds. Can any sense at all be made of the fact that Mexicans, African Americans, Balinese do not know of, or even reject, the wisdom of western medicine? The fact that they rely on 'superstitions' , 'medicine men' and 'healers' is surely a sign of their primitive – hence temporally anterior – condition. But while for 'social Darwinism' witchcraft and healers are marks of a primitive condition, our twentieth century travellers are less certain. On closer inspection these phenomena make at least a kind of sense, more than that they even work, sometimes when 'western' medicine fails. Traven's Mexican novels are full of cures – the old man who knows nothing of medicine revives a drowning village boy, the chief's son is cured of blindness by a mestizo healer.

In *The Bridge*, the narrator witnesses the miracle of the floating board, performed by an ancient curer. But this miracle begins to make sense to him:

> No Indian can do anything more than we can do, and no Indian knows more than we. No coloured man, no man of any other race, no Chinese, no Hindu, no Tibetan can perform miracles we cannot perform. That's all nonsense, We think other races mysterious only because we don't understand their language well

enough and we don't understand their customs and their ways of living and doing things. It's because of this lack of understanding them that we believe them capable of performing all sorts of miracles and mysterious acts. (Traven, 1980: 576).

These are no miracles once we understand the *culture* of these alien beings – the beliefs and their effects make sense in the context of their language, customs and ways of living and doing things.

Walter Spies's Bali, like the Bali of Covarrubias, Mead and other contemporaries, is literally the 'island of demons', a place where illness and misfortune are caused by spiritual forces and cured by those who, through trance, can control them. Bali is no primitive throwback, no anachronism, no uncultured or uncultivated society. If anything, for observers like Walter Spies Bali is more civilised, has more culture, than the West.

And even DuBose Heyward who, perhaps more than the others, retains primitivist images of African Americans, nonetheless also sees in their apparently superstitious approach to illness a cultural logic that defies the primitivist label. When Bess returns from prison she falls gravely ill. What is Porgy to do?

> Now that all human companionship had been withdrawn, the watcher felt strangely alone, and smaller than the farthest star or most diminutive shell. Like a caged squirrel, his tired mind spun the rounds of his three alternatives: first, the white man's science, gaunt, clean, and mysterious, with the complete and awful magistracy which it assumed over the luckless bodies that fell into its possession. He knew that it returned some healed in body. He knew that others had passed into its portal, and had been obliterated utterly. Then his second alternative: the white man's God, vague and abstract as the wind that moved among the lichens, with his Jesus, who could stir him suddenly to his most beautiful songs and make his heart expand until, for a moment, it embraced all mankind with compassionate love, but who passed, as the wind passes, leaving him cold and disillusioned. One of these he must choose, or else turn his face back to the old blurred trail that receded, down, down, down to the beginning of things: to the symbols one might hold, tangible and terrifying; to the presciences that shuddered like dawn at the back of the brain and told one what to do without the process of thought. (Heyward, 1953 [1925]: 85f.)

Porgy opts for the latter, giving money to a boatman to give to an 'old conjer 'oman' to cast a spell. Bess is cured, although as it turns out the boatman spends the money on drink, and it never gets to the curer. Maria keeps him locked up and swears him to secrecy so Porgy and Bess will never know. The meaning Heyward wishes to convey is confused by his commitments to contradictory discourses – the one of primitivism ('down, down, down to the beginning of things'), the other of a cultural relativism. The cure is after all 'successful' which shows that the 'Negroes'' own ways of living and own culture are no mere feeble approximation of our own.

While British anthropology perpetually pays homage to Sir James Frazer, author of *The Golden Bough*, far more influential than this hodge-podge, sensationalist and primitivist compilation of myths, magical spells and superstitions has been a book that directly challenged the primitivist/ social Darwinist account of, in this case, indigenous African theodicy.

Evans-Pritchard's study of *Witchcraft, Oracles and Magic among the Azande*, first published in 1937 (Evans-Pritchard, 1965), not *The Golden Bough*, is the exemplary text for twentieth century anthropology.[1] And in the *Zande* monograph, as in *The Bridge*, *Porgy* and *Island of Demons*, the emphasis is on cultural relativism, on the internal logic of a theodicy within which witches are thought to cause most illness and misfortune. Not a primitive form of our own medical science, Zande witchcraft beliefs are, for Evans-Pritchard, a completely coherent *alternative* to science, maybe even a more powerful explanatory system than that provided by western medicine.

Such a vision of a culturally differentiated world represents an ambivalence to, if not an outright hostility towards, the civilisational narratives of empire. In his somewhat paternalistic style Heyward, as we have already seen, despaired at the 'civilisation' of the African American.

Typically of Heyward, indeed of other 'liberal' white writers on African Americans in this period, the language is a mixture of primitivism and culturalism. But it has moved away from certain of the prevailing primitivist assumptions about African Americans:

> The absence of atavistic motivation, the narrator's civilized view of the Row's failings, and the restraint and understatement in the treatment of primitivism indicate a notable movement toward genuine realism. Thus Heyward's primitivism – the 'woods' influence and the black man's sense of the rhythm of life – must be clearly distinguished from the pseudo-realism that Alain Locke called the 'last serious majority cliche, that of blood atavism and inherited Negro primitivism,' of which Locke began complaining in the year *Porgy* appeared. (Slavick, 1981: 66)

Even less are Traven's Mexican Indians a mere throwback to a primitive stage of human existence, ripe for the civilising mission of a more advanced culture. Traven's view of the transformations wrought by American imperialism are much more savage than are Heyward's. Anticipating more recent denunciations of American cultural imperialism in Latin America, Traven describes the effects of American culture on a Mexican funeral in uncompromising terms, writing for example with withering irony about the banality of American popular music – he describes it as the 'vomit of our civilization' – played at a Mexican funeral (1980: 610f.). For Traven Mexican indigenous culture can only provide the way forward rather than the way back to primitive roots.

Traven, Heyward and Margaret Mead may have intended to produce realist accounts of specific instances of cultural alterity. Yet in the public imagination the proliferation of images generated a merging or blurring of the particularities of Indian life in Mexico, African American culture in South America, Indonesian beliefs in Bali. Gershwin's production of the Porgy story allowed the denizens of Catfish Row to stand as bearers of African American culture in general, mixing, particularly in the music, the evolving spiritual musics of the South with the urban jazz rhythms of Harlem. It is not at all surprising that DuBose Heyward was considered the obvious choice to collaborate in the screenplay for Pearl Buck's *The Good Earth* – he had after all already established himself as an expert on non-western culture! The consequence was a new image of a world made up of a multitude of cultures.

The world as cultural mosaic, to repeat a by now somewhat hackneyed cliche is, as the examples of Traven and Heyward show, a twentieth century invention, one moreover that is still with us despite the theoretical sophistication of recent cultural theory. A recent example is provided by the so-called 'new historicism' of literary critic Stephen Greenblatt who, like many others before him, discovered a 'real' cultural otherness in Bali. Prefacing his account of the stimulus to the European imagination provided by the 'discovery' of the New World, Greenblatt gives us a more personal account of his own encounter with Bali: 'I reached a tiny village which in the darkness I identified less by the low, half-hidden huts and temples than by frenzied barking of the dogs at my approach. I saw a light from the *bale banjar*, the communal pavilion in which I knew – from having read Clifford Geertz and Miguel Covarrubias and Gregory Bateson and Margaret Mead – that the Balinese gathered in the evenings.' Greenblatt was at first distressed by the fact that the light was emanating from a VCR rather than from an oil lamp, testifying to 'the astonishing presence of capitalist markets and technology', but:

> [c]onquering my disappointment, I accepted the gestured invitation to climb onto the platform and see the show: on the communal VCR, they were watching a tape of an elaborate temple ceremony. Alerted by the excited comments and whoops of laughter, I recognized in the genial crowd of television watchers on the platform several of the ecstatic celebrants, dancing in trance states, whom I was seeing on the screen. (Greenblatt, 1991: 3)

This led him instead to conclude that instead of being destroyed, Balinese culture was being preserved due to 'the remarkable adaptive power of the local community'.

Bali for Greenblatt is, as it was for Walter Spies and earlier anthropologists like Margaret Mead, Gregory Bateson, and Miguel Covarrubias, and more recently Clifford Geertz, quite clearly an alien world which, even if tenuously connected to our own through technological transfers (and the presence of people like Greenblatt himself), is nonetheless present in its own right, independent of our own representations of it.

There are those who, committed to the notion that the modern sensibility is deeply stamped by racism and social Darwinism, choose imperial texts as exemplary twentieth century accounts of otherness. And these are not difficult to find. The popularity of an Edgar Rice Burroughs would seem to speak to a deep and enduring primitivism in the western African imaginary (see Torgovnick, 1990). But what all this conveniently ignores is that twentieth century modernist 'anthropology' at least from the 1920s was beginning to construct a new, if perhaps equally flawed, attitude towards the other. Rejecting the imperial discourse of racial/social hierarchy, professional anthropologists like Boas, Mead, Benedict, and Evans-

Pritchard articulated a new language of the relativity of culture, and of the world as a mosaic of cultures irreducible one to another in a civilisational or racial metanarrative. In so doing, these anthropologists constituted no intellectual vanguard – they were, instead, largely mirroring a changing public sensibility as the accounts of Traven, Heyward and Spies demonstrate. If anything, professional anthropology was riding rather than leading the trend.

The continuities between contemporary discourses on culture and identity and notions that appear in the interwar years is nicely manifest in what at first appears to be a very curious oversight in Edward Said's initial formulation of the critique of orientalism.

A Cultured Empire

I would not have undertaken a book of this sort if I did not also believe that there is scholarship that is not as corrupt, or at least as blind to human reality, as the kind I have been mainly depicting. Today there are many individual scholars working in such fields as Islamic history, religion, civilization, sociology and anthropology whose production is deeply valuable as scholarship. . . . An excellent recent instance is the anthropology of Clifford Geertz, whose interest in Islam is discrete and concrete enough to be animated by the specific societies and problems he studies and not by the rituals, preconceptions and doctrines of Orientalism. (Said, 1978: 326)

The astonishing realist assumptions behind this statement, together with the apparent exemption of Clifford Geertz from his 'broad and indiscriminate' attack on western representations of non-western societies has struck more than just this author as somewhat odd (see Marcus and Fischer, 1986: 1). For those who have traced the connections between Geertz's own account of Indonesian Islam, and Indonesian culture more broadly, to the images of Indonesia that circulate in colonial Dutch scholarship on Indonesia in the first few decades of this century this exemption appears even more paradoxical. It seems as though a classic case of colonial representation – Dutch orientalism – is being spared the orientalist label.

But this oversight on Said's part makes a good deal more sense to the extent that we are prepared to admit of continuities in imperial/counter-imperial discourse, continuities that become manifest when we consider an example of colonial debate over culture and difference that lies outside the nineteenth century, British–French nexus so central to postcolonial theorising.

A case in point is the changing images of Bali that began to emerge in the early part of this century, whose persistent qualities are so evident in the more recent accounts by, among others, the anthropologist Clifford Geertz and the literary critic Stephen Greenblatt.

A key figure in creating the images of Bali as Europe's other, as we have noted, was the German-born painter Walter Spies (1895–1942) who came to Bali in 1927 after acting as musician to the court of the Sultan of

Yogyakarta. Part of a circle of Europeans who set about capturing the unique culture of Balinese villagers in paintings, photographs, film, music and cultural performance[2], and whose presence stimulated the subsequent growth of the arts in Bali, Spies portrayed the Balinese as a kind of mirror image of westerners – highly cultured, artistic and contemplative as opposed to shallow and obsessed with technological mastery; feminine as opposed to masculine; enjoying free and non-hierarchical relations; spiritual as opposed to materialist. Linked to this Spies saw in Balinese society an escape from the sexual restrictions, particularly the restrictions on homosexuals, that operated in the west (see Rhodius and Darling, 1980; Vickers, 1989).

While Margaret Mead and her husband of the time, the British anthropologist Gregory Bateson, did not share Spies's view of Bali as a sexual paradise – they explicitly contrasted the sexual freedom of Samoa with the tight controls on sexuality in Bali (concluding that the Balinese were as a consequence culturally-constructed schizophrenics!) – they did do a great deal to perpetuate the images of a 'culturalised' Bali in which, in contrast to the West, everyone was an artist.[3]

This new image of a cultured empire also took root among Dutch academics and colonial officials in the 1920s. Modern anthropologists, ethnologists, legal scholars, and economists have constructed a number of concepts for the interpretation of the lives of the indigenous peoples of Indonesia, formerly the Netherlands East Indies. Notions like 'corporate village community' or the 'jural community', the 'kin-based' (as opposed to territorially-based) society, 'peasant economy', 'natural economy', 'non-capitalist calculation' and the like, first constructed in the discourse of a variety of Dutch writers in the colonial period continue to inform more recent scholarship on 'traditional' Indonesian cultures and societies.[4] Like more recent strands in postcolonial thinking, this historicisation and culturalisation of Dutch discourse on colonial Indonesia took place in the context of an explicit rejection of 'social Darwinism'.

In a collection of commentaries on policy in his country's most important colony compiled between 1868 and 1877, N. G. Pierson, a prominent Dutch liberal, put forward a strong case in defence of the liberal turn in colonial policy in the Netherlands East Indies in the 1860s. In contrast to the period of the so-called Cultivation System, when the Indies were treated as a vast state-controlled plantation, using forced labour and forced deliveries to extract a huge surplus to be used back home, the new policies would have the effect, argued Pierson, of generating a much to be desired modernising revolution within Indonesian society as a whole. In a precise echo of the manichean allegory that according to Said, JanMohammed, and other postcolonial theorists is such a central feature of imperial discourse, Pierson wrote: 'A German or English peasant of the fourteenth century who found himself in the Java of our times would very quickly feel at home' (1877: 270; my translation). Many of the preconditions for the successful development of European economy and society, he maintained, were present in the East Indies. It would take only the modernising effects of enlightened colonial government to produce that same development there.

Pierson's book was entitled *Koloniale Politiek* (Colonial Policy), but, as the colonial economist Boeke was to argue later, there was nothing particularly colonial about it.[5] Its prescriptions were those a Dutch liberal of the last quarter of the nineteenth century might advocate anywhere – free trade, free labour and freedom of operation for private capital. The difference between Pierson's liberalism, and that of earlier utilitarian theorists, was his evolutionism. Indonesia was *not yet* a liberal utopia, but could be made to become so under the civilising influence of Europeans. This was the best way to promote a modern society based on freedom, progress and the greatest happiness for the greatest number. While human societies might differ according to whether they were more or less advanced towards these goals, none were incapable of reaching them. Indeed the more backward would be aided by the actions of an enlightened colonial power. In this way Netherlands India too could achieve modernity, and an economy based on technological progress, commercial freedom (including the freedom to sell one's labour power to the highest bidder), and the general benefits of civilisation.

A clearer case of a colonialist discourse – turning otherness into anteriority, social Darwinist, contempt for difference, justificatory of the colonial white man's burden – could not be found. The logical goal towards which evolving societies were moving was one characterised, in Peel's terms, by a complete absence of 'sociological furniture' – no state, no families, no principle of social organisation beyond the individual acting out of rational self-interest (and, hence, respect for the interests of others) (see Peel, 1971).

As I have suggested, this particular variant of evolutionism characterised by a commitment to utilitarian ideals, was not the only variant in the late nineteenth century. Indeed others, while sharing the Spencerian belief in the fact of social evolution, adopted quite different positions on a number of questions. Within a developing European social theory, for example, Spencerian or 'social Darwinist' views were largely superseded among British liberals by those of the Fabians, who criticised Spencer on the grounds that in his schema the state could and would ultimately disappear. Durkheim, similarly, criticised the Spencerian schema in *The Division of Labour* when he argued that even under conditions of advanced organic solidarity (his equivalent of Spencer's differentiation), societies would require institutions to promote social integration, as well as collective representations/moral systems appropriate to a modern, differentiated society.[6] But let us examine the reactions to Dutch liberal scholarship in the colonial context, for here we see the beginnings of the kind of challenge to classical imperial ideology that have more recently been labelled 'postcolonial', although paradoxically here the challenge developed in the thinking of Europeans.

The kind of liberal discourse articulated by Pierson was, as I have suggested, quite clearly evolutionist. As the above shows, he tended to characterise Indonesian society as occupying a stage of evolutionary development through which England and Germany passed in the fourteenth century. But Indonesia was in no way incapable of advancing through the higher stages, indeed its advance could be accelerated by the actions of the colonial rulers. Subsequent Dutch critiques of these liberal assumptions took two forms. There were those who argued that non-western peoples were destined to remain stuck at lower evolutionary stages, hence being incapable of reaching the same levels of civilisation as were western people. While no doubt certain Dutch scholars would have accepted such racialist assumptions, more interesting from our point of view is the development of a second set of critiques of liberal evolutionism which derived from an expressivist critique of utilitarianism, for these laid the groundwork for some of the best-known works by Dutch scholars on Indonesia in the modern period, and hence for modern ways of conceptualising Indonesian otherness.

The emerging critique of the position adopted by Pierson exists in weak and strong form. The weak form questions the capacity of Indonesian society to move along the evolutionary track laid down by European societies at a pace which makes it practicable to think of liberal policies having any marked effect in the short or even the long run. The hard version questions whether Indonesian societies could or should be on the same track as the west at all. According to this latter view, Indonesian societies are seen as developing according to their own logics, their own cultural dynamics, their own unique *Volksgeist*, to use Herder's term.[7] The Dutch critics of liberal evolutionism developed very specific kinds of analyses of Indonesian culture and society, developing new languages of cultural alterity and identity to do so.

Probably the best-known critics of Dutch liberalism in the period under consideration were those associated with the so-called Leiden School. Pierson, like many of our contemporary economists of development, saw Indonesian custom (adat) as part of an undesirable tradition, a tradition which would only act as an obstacle to the modernisation of colonial society. This view contrasts sharply with that developed by the highly influential members of what came to be called the Leiden School, whose major work was the voluminous codification of indigenous adat published between 1911 and 1955 (Dutch East Indies, Commissie voor het adatrecht).

Their leading spokesperson, Cornelius Van Vollenhoven, according to one recent commentator 'believed in the possibility of merging existing traditions with western modernism by fostering respect for traditional Indonesian laws and customs (the so-called adat) and wished to leave tradition respectable and intact, particularly on the local and regional level, so that society could cope with modernizing influences in its own specific Indonesian ways' (Schöffer, 1978: 90).[8]

Hooker has characterised the school as a whole by their attitude towards westernisation:

> Members of the school disapproved strongly of rapid Westernization of Indonesia, especially where this was to be accompanied by the introduction of a codified Western legal system. They warned against a forced pace of Westernization and advocated a gradual social evolution through the growth of stable adat communities especially in the Outer Provinces. This resulted in the formation of a school of jurisprudence whose whole philosophy came to rest upon a distinction between the laws of various races. (Hooker, 1978:15)

The emergence of the Leiden School in the early decades of this century, with its particular brand of legal historicism, marks a sharp break with the liberal ideals of the 1860s and 1870s. The ideas themselves had an important effect on colonial policies, not least because Leiden became the training ground for a whole new generation of colonial officials who took up their posts in the East Indies strongly influenced by the new images of the strength and integrity of indigenous cultural traditions, and hence the inappropriateness of 'western' notions of progress and modernity in the Indonesian context.

While for the genuinely conservative critics of liberalism Javanese cultivators might be seen to be stuck at an original primitive stage of cultural and economic evolution, for others the difficulty might be seen to lie either with the speed at which liberals expected Indonesians to advance along the European path of modernisation, or the assumption that they should advance along the same path at all. The debate gave rise, for example, to a number of attempts to characterise Indonesian land rights which were not strictly speaking conservative (a reversion to views prevalent under the Cultivation System), but which were, at the same time, not in accord with those advocated by liberal scholars like Pierson and the authors of the documented results of this research known as the *Eindresumé*.

This debate, to which the *Eindresumé* represents a contribution, was increasingly characterised by two features. First, and somewhat paradoxically, most of the participants, whether leaning towards the communal or the individual characterisation of traditional tenurial patterns drew heavily, and often explicitly, on models of cultural and economic evolution developed in Europe to deal with the evolution of European societies. Moreover the models, as well as the comparisons, most in favour were drawn from writings either dealing with Germany or drawing their inspiration from the work of those associated with the German Historical School of Economists. It is significant in this respect that the only British evolutionary writer who appealed to Dutch writers on Indonesia in this period was Henry Sumner Maine, rather than more positivistically-inclined evolutionists like Spencer and Tylor.

A second feature of these writings is that even those relatively sympathetic to the findings in the *Eindresumé* tended to temper their liberal sympathies with an emphasis on the historicity of concepts of property.

The developing debate over the characterisation of Indonesian land rights was only seen to have been resolved by many Dutch Indonesianists with the publication of two influential pieces by Van Vollenhoven: *Miskenningen van het Adatrecht* (1909), and *De Indonezier en zijn Grond* (1919). In these articles Van Vollenhoven offered a resolution of the issue of the nature of Indonesian land rights that continues to inform our understanding of Indonesian cultures (see, for example, Aas, 1980: 229ff.).

In these articles Van Vollenhoven argued that both individual and communal tenure were western legal concepts which made little sense in Indonesian adat. Instead patterns of land use in Indonesia were firmly embedded within existing jural communities (*rechtsgemeenschappen*). While individual cultivation or other use of land may be found in Indonesia, 'nowhere in Indonesian adat law does the individual household appear to have the status of an autonomous jural community' ([1907] in Holleman, 1981: 45). Instead individual use of land is always subject to the rights of disposal or rights of avail (*beschikkingsrecht*) of the jural community as a whole. What did Van Vollenhoven mean by this term?

> In Van Vollenhoven's conception it is the fundamental right of a jural community freely to avail itself of and administer all land, water and other resources within its territorial province . . . for the benefit of its members, and to the exclusion of outsiders, except those to whom it has extended certain limited, and essentially temporary, privileges. The right of avail is thus conceived also as the basic communal source of a whole range of discrete and more or less individualised user rights, which are vested in persons or groups by virtue of their membership of the community. (Holleman, 1981: 43ff.; see Van Vollenhoven, 1909, 1919).

Van Vollenhoven then provided a way of conceptualising a system of land rights which was neither individual nor communal, a system which he insisted was uniquely non-western. In so doing he provided a way of conceptualising Indonesian communities in general, and those of individual Indonesian societies in particular which continues to influence modern anthropological discourse. And like both more recent cultural anthropologists and postcolonial theorists, he seriously questioned the 'social Darwinism' of nineteenth century colonial ideologues like Pierson.

If Van Vollenhoven and the Leiden School represented Indonesian communities as distinctively 'non-western' (rather than 'pre-western'), thereby also questioning both the possibility and the desirability of classical colonialism's 'civilising' project, J.H. Boeke is best known for the development of concepts of distinctive forms of economic rationality in colonial societies in opposition to what he took to be the existing universalisation of western forms of economic behaviour. One consequence of this development was a discourse which sought to characterise Indonesian villagers as peasants, as we have seen. But a more general outcome of Dutch economic historicism was an image of a distinctly non-western Indonesian economy that escapes the principles of bourgeois economic rationalism, and shows the workings of a distinctly different 'Eastern Mind', thus paving the way for recent anti-instrumentalist characterisations of Indonesian economic organisation (see for example Geertz, 1963, 1984).

Julius Herman Boeke, the Dutch economist best known for his concept of economic dualism (a term he did not actually use until 1930), was perhaps the clearest exponent of this view. Boeke began his studies in the field of Dutch literature at the University of Amsterdam before changing to political science (*Staatswetenschap*). He moved to Leiden to study for a doctorate under Van Vollenhoven where he wrote a dissertation on 'Tropical-Colonial Political Economy' which was submitted in 1910 (Boeke, 1910). It was here that Boeke formulated some of his views on the uniqueness of economic conditions in a colonial situation not, as has been frequently pointed out, as a result of personal experience of Indonesia, but as a consequence of his readings in economic theory, on the one hand, and colonial publications (notably the available publications of the Diminishing Welfare Commission), on the other.

Only after having submitted his dissertation did Boeke then go to the colony to take up a position, first with the Education Department in Batavia and, later the Popular Credit Service. While doing government work, Boeke also taught government and economics and, from 1924 to 1928, he served as a Professor of Economics at the Batavia Law School. Boeke returned to the Netherlands in 1929 to take up a new chair in Tropical-Colonial Economics at Leiden, and did not return to Indonesia until after the war, during which time he was imprisoned by the German occupying forces. During the revolutionary period he served again with the Dutch, assisting in their attempt to reconstruct the system of higher education in a colony now fighting for its independence.

Two quotes from his dissertation serve to illustrate Boeke's critique of liberal and 'social Darwinist' discourse on Indonesia, from the standpoint of the economy:

> [T]he deductive[9] method derives its value from the fact that it isolates a property which it presupposes as present in every individual; from the intellectual and moral properties with which it is integrated in the actual lives of individuals, in order to lay a general basis for the clarification of economic phenomena in actual life by indicating the acts and considerations to which that property must lead under various circumstances. Now what do the practitioners of the deductive method understand by the term *homo œconomicus*? With it they indicate first of all that this being attempts to reach the aim of all acts, the gratification of needs, by applying the hedonistic or economic principle, which principle is: maximum satisfaction with a minimum of effort. Thus it is assumed that an act is performed on a strictly 'rational' basis, 'as if it had taken place under the guidance of commercial calculations from start to finish'. In positing the *homo œconomicus*, however, a second principle is tacitly assumed, namely that the economic act will be performed as soon as there is an opportunity for it, that a motive for action is constantly present, and that there are always ungratified economic needs. As soon as reality fails to meet this second premise the deductive method loses its value for explaining that reality, and so proves to have given too much credence to its assumption that the economic urge is universally human. (1910; quoted in Boeke et al., 1966: 10f.).

Western economic theory is, however, not applicable in colonial societies, because here:

> there is not one homogeneous society but a Native society side by side with a society of foreigners, not one people but a multiplicity of peoples, not one course of development but a clash between two heterogeneous stages of development, not a sense of solidarity but one of ruling and being ruled. And finally, there is . . . a group which is interested primarily in the products of the soil and asks no more of its people than a certain amount of labour of a quality that does not necessarily entail their advancement.
> The problems facing colonial economics are consequently of an entirely different kind from those with which 'general' economics occupies itself, and by no means different only in a gradual sense.
> Hence we come to the conclusion that from the point of view of theoretical economics we may – and must – speak of a separate discipline of colonial economics:
>
> 1 because much that is axiomatic in the abstract-theoretical or deductive method must be recognised as non-existent in the economic mentality of the Natives;
> 2 because even in case it might be possible to accept a certain measure of economic inclination, the economic problems coming to the fore in a colonial society are so specific in nature that there is little scope for applying the principles derived from Western conditions to any great extent. (1910; quoted in Boeke et al., 1966: 11).

Central to Boeke's attempt to characterise economic behaviour in a non-capitalist society was the distinction between 'economic' and 'social' needs, a distinction which in his dissertation Boeke derives largely from the writings of German economists, especially Bücher; Gurewitsch, a student of Schmoller (see Bücher, 1901; Gurewitsch, n.d.: 23ff.); and the ethnographer Schurtz. Western economic theory, by which Boeke refers both to classical political economy and the economics of the Austrian School, is based on the central stimulus of economic needs. Since Indonesians are in general motivated primarily by social needs, this theory is of little use in the Indonesian context.

Social needs are those which derive from a sense of dependence on the norms which society imposes on its members, and are of two types: the urge to imitate and to adapt to the social pattern and the urge for distinction or prestige. Economic needs, on the other hand, are not felt by man as member of a collectivity, but by individuals. The goods which gratify such needs must therefore meet man's individual requirements.

The distinction between economic and social needs, Boeke maintained, is not an absolute one. The value of something may be determined by both types of needs acting in conjunction. It is, however, important to separate them since for Boeke the development of western economic rationality involved the increased importance of the economic determinant of values. The fact that social needs are predominant in non-western society is manifest in forms of entrepreneurial organisation markedly different from those prevailing under capitalism.

What is significant from our point of view is that Boeke, as early as 1910 brought the issue of non-economic calculation to the forefront in the analysis of the Indonesian economy, hence calling into question both the wisdom and the supposed economic benefits of the colonial civilising mission. In so doing he created a vision of a radically different form of society, culture and 'mind' in the East. Though he may have initially been searching for a developmental trajectory suitable to the colonial context, he was clearly highly pessimistic about the developmentalist projects of Dutch liberals like Ham. The influence of Van Vollenhoven is evident here, although, unlike his teacher, Boeke perhaps never sufficiently stressed the positive aspects of the non-western condition.

Another colonial scholar whose work has had a significant influence on more recent writings on Indonesia was the Dutch Islamicist Christian Snouck Hurgronje, who acted as an adviser to the colonial government during the period of the Aceh Wars. The resistance to Dutch colonisation of the Aceh region of northern Sumatra was led, from the late nineteenth century, by Islamic leaders, the *ulama*. It was Snouck Hurgronje's view, however, that Aceh was far from being an Islamic society, but was instead governed by the principles of adat, or local custom. In other words Hurgronje rejected the attempt to read off Acehnese society from the pages of the Koran, as it were, instead manifesting, in Said's later description of Geertz, an interest in Islam 'discrete and concrete enough to be animated by the specific societies and problems he studies' (1978: 326). Of course here the context was somewhat different – Snouck Hurgronje was arguing against a vision of a generalised 'Islamic society' propounded, not just by an earlier generation of European orientalists, but now by the Islamic leaders of an anti-colonial struggle.[10]

Dutch colonial discourse on Indonesia was thus radically transformed in the early decades of this century. If nineteenth century colonial ideology had come to be informed by a view of a passive, backward, even decadent Indonesia ripe for the civilising and developmental influence of the more advanced European power that ruled it, this gave way to very different images of uniquely Indonesian (or Javanese, Balinese, Minangkabau, etc.) forms of cultural, social and economic organisation and developmental trajectories. Many Dutch colonial officials and scholars therefore, came to reject to varying degrees those variants of 'social Darwinism' which, in any case, had achieved only a tenuous hold on the thinking of colonial rulers even in the nineteenth century. The weakness and then rejection of the kinds of civilising ideologies that were, at least according to postcolonial theory, so entrenched in French and British imperial discourse makes the case of colonial Indonesia an extremely suggestive one. Indeed knowledge of this case leads one to suggest that some of the criticisms of imperial ideology offered by postcolonial theory were anticipated, not by Indonesian nationalists, but by Dutch colonial officials and scholars in the 1910s and 1920s, a fact that gives further support to the suggestion that there have in this century been significant continuities in the languages of empire and counter-empire.

Yet the case of colonial Indonesia is not all that unusual. While not repeated in all its detail elsewhere in the world at this time, nonetheless the changes in the discourses of governance and ideas about citizenship that were taking place in many parts of the world at much the same time, like those in colonial Indonesia, depended increasingly on ideas of inherent difference or otherness – cultural and/or racial – instead of earlier 'social Darwinist' assumptions about a universal endpoint of social evolution that would ultimately produce a homogenised humanity. This was the case even within the colonial systems of Britain and France where previously utilitarian evolutionism and civilising ideologies had reigned supreme.

Morocco, for example, the last of the French colonies, was made a protectorate in 1912, long after the nineteenth century height of empire. And like Dutch colonial rulers and orientalists, French planners in Morocco were highly critical of their predecessors in Indochina, Madagascar and Algeria. The head of the colonial educational mission in Morocco, for example, was quick to contrast his own philosophy with that of the nineteenth century advocates of the 'mission civilisatrice', while French planners wished to distinguish themselves clearly from an earlier generation of 'expropriateurs' and 'convertisseurs' (Rabinow, 1992: 172). When it came to drawing up a plan for the city of Casablanca, the colonial planner Prost took as his counter-model the city of Algiers, a city which had been completely re-made in an earlier period. Like Haussmann in Paris, the French planners in Algiers almost completely destroyed the old city in an effort to open it up by means of broad avenues and grand public spaces, so much so that travellers to Algiers complained that, coming to experience the exotic, all they saw was French (ibid.: 174).

In Casablanca, 'tradition' was, instead, to be preserved rather than destroyed. The new approach, in Rabinow's words, was one in which 'difference', no longer seen as an anachronism to be swept aside by a superior European style, was, instead 'directly thematised'. If civilising intent there was, it was the French settlers rather than the Moroccans, who were the target. The preservation of tradition was to be for their benefit.[11] This new approach, according to Rabinow, saw as its central task 'how to conceive and build cities where different races . . . with different customs and practices could cohabit' (1992: 178f.).

The concern with culture and difference in French imperial circles finds its parallel in the recognition by British colonial governments that in spite of long periods of colonial rule based on the two 'basic principles of . . . the rule of [universal] law and economic freedom [laissez-faire]', rather than leading to the gradual evolution of a universal society colonialism had produced economic, political and cultural pluralism. J.S. Furnivall, an officer with the government of Burma, and commissioned by the British to see if 'features of colonial rule in Netherlands India might suitably be adopted in Burma', was led to remark that contra the assumptions of the nineteenth century, 'social Darwinist' advocates of colonialism's civilising mission '[t]he obvious and outstanding result of contact between East and West' has been the evolution of 'not a homogeneous but a plural society', that is of a 'society with different sections of the community living side by side, within the same political unit. Even in the economic sphere there is a division of labour along racial lines' (Furnivall, 1956 [1948]: 304f.).

A similar transformation was taking place in southern Africa, this time with different consequences. The doctrine of apartheid or separateness, formally recognised in law in 1948, was in part the outgrowth of a critique of liberal theology deriving from the work of the Dutch philosopher Abraham Kuyper, an important figure in the Dutch Reform Church in Holland, and subsequently Prime Minister of the Netherlands. Kuyper resurrected an earlier polygenetic thread in Christian theology to argue for what he called the 'pluriformity' of creation, hence providing a religious justification for the insistence by advocates of apartheid on the necessary separation of European and African in South Africa (Hoernlé, 1939; Thompson, 1985).

At the same time there developed in South Africa an Afrikaner anthropology. While the history of South African social anthropology is closely intertwined with its history in Britain, itself a twentieth century outgrowth of Spencerian and Durkheimian positivism, this Afrikaner anthropology drew instead from the German *Volkenkunde* tradition, and hence drew sharp 'cultural' boundaries between Africans, Europeans and 'Coloureds'. Here it was not the 'social Darwinist' heritage, but an anthropology of culture and difference that shaped the twentieth century version of empire in South Africa characterised, as it was, by the apartheid system (see Sharp, 1981; Kuper, 1988; Dobow, 1989).[12]

But the 'discovery' of culture and difference in the early decades of this century was not restricted to the architects of empire. Indeed during this period it seems that advocates of empire and counter-empire alike shared in a new and more generalised discourse about culture, difference and identity. The case of the early twentieth century renaissance in Mexican art shows this clearly. At precisely the time Walter Spies was representing Bali as uniquely non-western cultural paradise, so in a different context Mexican artists were discovering the power of indigenous Mexican themes. The best known of these was Diego Rivera who, rejecting his commitment to European Analytic and then Synthetic Cubism, discovered the integrity and the vitality of indigenous aesthetic traditions in the Americas. At first integrating Mexican themes into his cubist paintings, on his return to Mexico Rivera abandoned cubism altogether and returned to a realistic style to represent Mexico's history.[13] But while Spies sought in the Balinese other an escape from western techno-modernism and sexual authoritarianism, Rivera saw in Mexico's pre-Columbian past a populist heritage that could be harnessed to socialist transformation. Like B. Traven, whom Rivera may very well have known in Mexico, Rivera's art contrasted authentic people's culture with the universalising and hence imperialising imagery of high modernism. This connection between in-digenism and revolution is nicely outlined by Traven who in *Government* sharply contrasts life in Indian and mestizo communities, the latter contaminated by the forces of capitalism and United States imperialism. Liberation is, however, promised not by the direct actions of the indigenes, but by those living in a third type of community, that of the Bachahontes or rebels. These latter have also been caught up in the world of capitalist modernity, but can succeed in opposing it because of their roots that are more ancient than capitalism. They have a chance of withstanding modernity because 'they are rooted in an organic relationship with the land that forms their culture and determines their character (see Murphy, 1987).

Rivera's interests were in archaeology, anthropology and Indian folk art. As one critic has written: 'He glorifies the pre-Columbian world as a lost paradise, as an advanced civilization whose medicine, art and social order rank among mankind's greatest achievements'.[14] Thus Rivera's Mexican murals are testimony to the beauty of Indian peoples, festivals, and dances. On the other hand, in his murals Indians are always portrayed as being of lower social status to be integrated into society by literacy and education. The liberator thus plays a superior role, lending to Rivera's imagery a certain paternalism. The work of the other Mexican muralists demon-strates a parallel attempt to come to grips with the significance of indigenous cultural traditions for a modern Mexico. But unlike Rivera's which draws on images of an Aztec and Mayan past, Orozco's work contains almost no pre-Columbian imagery whatsoever. Orozco, instead, represents modern Mexico as a mestizo amalgamation of the culture of conquerors and conquered, a painful part of the birth of a modern and distinctly Mexican nation. Siqueiros introduced the Indian heroes directly into the present, as in the painting of the return of Cuauhtemoc who thus becomes a symbol of a contemporary protest.

Less overtly political, but equally concerned with themes of culture, difference and identity, was the painting of Wifredo Lam. Of Chinese, indigenous, Spanish and African descent, Wifredo Oscar de la Concepción Lam was born in the Cuban village of Sagua la Grande in 1902. He studied first law and then painting in Havana and then Madrid where he studied painting and was caught up in the Republican cause. In the 1930s he was in Paris where he began a long friendship with Pablo Picasso, and met the pantheon of European modern art – Léger, Matisse, Braque, Chagall, Le Corbusier and Miró. On the subject of Picasso Lam said: 'What made me feel such empathy with his painting, more than anything else, was the presence of African art and the African spirit I discovered in it' (quoted in Fouchet, 1976: 137). This empathy Lam traced back to his own childhood among Afro-Cubans. And while Picasso had by this time left his African period behind him: 'Lam could at least follow up its lessons on his own account', producing paintings like 'Maternity' that is influenced by the work of the sculptors of the Ivory Coast (Fouchet, 1976: 126). During the

Second World War, Lam fled the Vichy government. In Marseilles he came into close contact with orthodox Surrealists – Chagall, Ernst, Dominguez and Brauner – as well as surrealism's chief theorist André Breton who, in spite of the fact that he did not see Lam's work as surrealistic according to its own exacting standards, was nonetheless an admirer of Lam's Paris paintings. 'From then on', writes Lam's biographer, 'Surrealists recognized him as one of their own' (Fouchet, 1976: 159). As targets of fascist hatred, the Marxist, Jewish and surrealist intellectuals of Marseilles were anxious to escape France, and Lam managed to escape with many of them on a ship that left Marseilles in 1941 bound for Martinique where most of the passengers including Lam were interned in the local leper hospital[15]. In Martinique many of the surrealists, Lam among them, became caught up in the *negritude* movement which, locally in any case, considered the surrealists to be important allies.

Finally, Lam was permitted to leave Martinique, from whence he returned to Cuba after an absence of seventeen years. Back in Cuba, he was horrified by the depredations of the Batista regime, determined once again through art to join the political struggle against racism and dictatorship. But unlike a Rivera, Lam did not choose realist modes of representing the suffering of Cubans:

> painting the drama of Cuba 'objectively' did not suit Lam's temperament, driven by intense subjective forces. He had to interpret the encounter of reality with the energies so long stifled of a race cut off from its original mythology. Lam had no intention of painting the black slave under the slave-driver's lash, or the Cuban proletariat equally enslaved by the capitalist. He preferred to entrust his message to great avenging figures, rising out of the country's unhappy subconscious and imposing their presence like spectres in order to work on the demolition of the prisons and the hovels of contempt. (Fouchet, 1976: 193)

This work, then, contains references to African art, but like Bartók's use of Hungarian peasant musics, Lam's use of African artistic themes does not attempt an authentic reproduction. Lam's is instead a language of 'changes, fusions and avatars' (ibid.: 198). Seen by many as his masterpiece, the 1942–4 painting 'The Jungle' is done in this style. Surreal rather than realist in its use of African motifs, it nonetheless is completely given over to representing 'the spirit of the negroes'.

Much postcolonial representation therefore does not in any simple sense transcend the concepts and categories of the cultured empire, still speaking of 'the spirit of the negro', the uniqueness of Indonesian custom, the (musical) alterity of the Hungarian peasantry. Instead it developed these images in a challenge to the rights of colonial or national elites to speak indigenous culture. Therefore what the languages of both advocates of empire and counter-empire shared in this period was an antipathy towards techno-instrumental modernism and a vision of a terrain of radical cultural alterity where these forces of modernity were inoperative.

To quote one prominent nationalist intellectual in Indonesia looking back on this period in colonial history:

[the] partisans of [the] historical school of law looked for the permanent and official establishment in Indonesia of a traditional and largely unwritten customary law. . . . By using ethnological concepts and comparing the existing customary law in the various regions of Indonesia, van Vollenhoven demonstrated with great skill that there were certain common elements in all. He found, *inter alia*, a preponderance of communal over individual interests, a close relationship between man and the soil, an all-pervasive 'magical' and religious pattern of thought, and a strongly family-oriented atmosphere in which every effort was made to compose disputes through conciliation and mutual consideration. . . .

In the broadest sense . . . van Vollenhoven . . . found in Indonesia only what he, as a European reacting against the individualism and formalism of European law . . . was looking for. . . . In this light we can see that the exaggerations in his analysis and picture of Indonesian customary law were the results of his own personal ideals and sentiments; and that these ideals and sentiments were in their turn simply the manifestations of certain currents within one legal school flourishing in Europe at that time. . . .

But the attempts to put this theory into practice . . . revealed the paradoxical dualistic quality of colonial society. . . . In the general framework of colonial relationships it was inevitable that the final word in the form and context of customary law would be with van Vollenhoven and other jurists of similar views. This meant, essentially, that customary law could only be applied where it did not conflict with the interests and policies of the colonial system. (S. Takdir Alisjahbana, 1966: 72)

But if Van Vollenhoven, Boeke, Snouck Hurgronje and others gave the classically orientalist impression that they knew better than Indonesians what Indonesian culture was all about it is equally clear that, while the Indonesian voice might have been absent from the representations of Dutch rulers, it was not silent in Indonesia itself. Indeed one wonders whether it were not ever thus with orientalist discourse, since why ever would colonialists even feel the need to 'justify' colonisation if nobody was resisting it?

As I have suggested, this discourse of resistance – a postcolonial discourse to the extent that it envisages the end of a situation in which Indonesian identity is being determined by Dutchmen – partook of much the same language of culture and identity, the uniqueness of Indonesian conditions, and so on, as did that of foreigners in the Dutch colony. Indeed in some cases apart from the fact that it was mobilised by Indonesians, it was indistinguishable from the Dutch language of cultured empire.

As we have seen many Indonesians in the 1920s were coming to form an image of a traditional village economy governed by principles of mutual respect and cooperation in opposition to the contemporary development of a money economy dominated by base desire (*hawa nafsu*) and the dominance of money (people even being forced to 'eat money'). It is not surprising that for many a cure to the problems wrought by economic modernisation rested in indigenous customs (adat) and the modes of social organisation to which they gave rise. Unlike the Dutch writers on the peasantry, whose primary concerns were with what was seen to be the preservation of elements of traditional economic organisation, more significant for Indonesians were the cultural values which underpinned traditional economic life. The discursive construction of Minangkabau adat in West Sumatra was thus a task which was of greater interest than economic values alone.

The vehicles for the constitution of Minangkabau adat were the large numbers of voluntary organisations which mushroomed towards the end of the second decade of this century. The first of these was the Sarekat Adat Alam Minangkabau (or SAAM, Adat Association of the Minangkabau World) established by Datuk Sutan Maharadja in 1916 'to counteract the Kaum Muda education and political movements'. First set up in Padang, SAAM branches were soon established in a number of towns in the highlands (Taufik, 1971: 17, 28f.). SAAM was a conservative organisation, its membership drawn largely from among coastal aristocrats and *panghulu* loyal to the Dutch. And clearly as the political atmosphere in the region hotted up, first as a consequence of the activities of Sarekat Islam, the radical nationalist organisation which established a branch in Padang in 1916, and later when the Indonesian Communist Party (PKI) established a foothold through its first local branch in 1923 a number of colonial loyalists saw in Minangkabau adat an alternative to political radicalism of all types. In their hands, the construction of Minangkabau adat was born out of conservative reaction.

One organisation devoted both to the construction of an adat system and to conservative ideals was the *Perkeompoelan Minangkabau* (PM: Minangkabau Association) founded in Bukit Tinggi on 20 February 1926. The stated aims at least of the leaders of the PM were, first, to carry out research on Minangkabau adat; second, to publicise the results of that research among its membership and beyond; third, to engage in discussion with adat experts and others in order to decide how best to resurrect a social life governed by adat (or at least those aspects of adat suitable in contemporary conditions); and, finally, thereby to prevent the penetration of Minangkabau by what were apparently seen to be alien ideologies and social movements. Specifically, although it was a largely hidden agenda (at least in the official publication) PM leaders were concerned with countering the effects of communist propaganda in Minangkabau. PM, then, seems to have been one of those adat organisations which began to spring up in mid-1925, with or without the backing of the colonial government, which had as their aim the combating of communist influence in the Minangkabau heartland (see Taufik, 1971: 41).

Like other conservative groups in the 1920s PM became involved in the construction of a particular discourse on Minangkabau adat and tradition, in ways which also parallel interestingly enough the transformation of the discourse of certain Dutch agricultural economists and students of Indonesian jurisprudence in much the same period.

But, while Taufik Abdullah is clearly right when he suggests that organisations like PM were involved in the construction of an adat-oriented discourse in the 1920s within an inherently conservative and pro-colonial politics, with the aim of turning back the clock advanced by Islamic modernism, creating a system of 'traditional' government which would have no place for modernist reformers or PKI revolutionaries, and, at the same time restoring a 'traditional' colonial order (see Taufik, 1971), he is wrong to suggest that this was true in all cases.

Quite different from the Minangkabau Association, in both its membership and aims, was the so-called Boedi Tjaniago Association (Vereeniging Boedi Tjaniago, VBT). The VBT was originally based on a village association in Bukit Sarungan near Padang Panjang. In 1919 members of the association brought out the first number of what was to become a monthly circular, called *Surat Edaran Boedi Tjaniago*. For a number of reasons, however, the initial venture was unsuccessful, and it was not until the beginning of January 1922 that further issues were published. From then at least until the end of September of that year the association, renamed Perserikatan Anak Negeri Padang Pandjang (PANPP, Organisation of Villagers of Padang Pandjang), was able to bring out a twice-monthly journal, now called just *Boedi Tjaniago*.[16]

The stated aims of PANPP and the journal, *Boedi Tjaniago* were the promotion of knowledge and learning, their motto being: 'for learning, knowledge of adat and skill'. This is spelled out in the following, a translation of an extract from the first issue:

> A lack of learning is what causes us to lose in the race of life. So that we can lead a happy life and acquire intelligence, we must have education. Then we will slowly progress, and we will not be left behind in the race of life. (*Boedi Tjaniago*, No. 1, January 1922)

Three themes dominate the pages of *Boedi Tjaniago*. These are adat, progress (*kemadjuan*) and freedom (*merdeka, kemerdekaan*). Like their more conservative contemporaries, members of the PANPP were concerned to argue that Minangkabau society in the future should continue to be governed by the principles of Minangkabau adat. We live in a world, one contributor maintains, organised according to three sets of regulations: religious, legal and those deriving from adat. Religious rules are oriented to the afterlife (*achirat*), adat regulations are for the organisation of our daily lives, while laws function to ensure our security. The Minangkabau religious rules come from Islam, and that is right and proper since for historical reasons the religion in West Sumatra is Islam. But, the author points out again, religion is properly to do only with the afterlife.[17]

But what is adat? According to our anonymous writer, adat is no more than custom (*kebiasaan*). All countries have their own distinctive customs, indeed even in the Indies there are a variety of adats. Each people should live according to their own individual customs.

The contrast between this and the more conservative constructions of adat available at the time lies in what might be termed the essence of adat. As we have seen, for contributors to *Berito Minangkabau* the essence of adat seems to be correct behaviour within the context of a clearly defined adat hierarchy. For contributors on adat issues to *Boedi Tjaniago* on the other hand, the essence of adat might be described as democracy. What emerges in the pages of *Boedi Tjaniago* as the most significant element of adat organisation is the extent to which it promotes cooperation and encourages each individual to play a role in decision-making. Identifying democracy as the key element of adat involves a selection from a range of custom, a selection which is quite explicit:

> Adatnja sama rata [democratie], tak ada bertinggi berendah, hanjalah jang diradjakan kata moefakat [republiek]. (*Boedi Tjaniago*, 1 April 1922: 7; parenthetical remarks in the original)

> Its [Boedi-Tjaniago's] adat is egalitarian (democracy). There are no higher ups or lower downs. The only things that are considered important are those which have been decided according to consensus (republic).

The insertion of the Dutch terms makes the comparison between adat and European notions of democracy explicit. Indeed a direct comparison between the principles of Boedi Tjaniago adat and European social democracy is a theme which crops up over and over again in the pages of *Boedi Tjaniago*.[18]

The people associated with the journal *Boedi Tjaniago* were therefore, like their near contemporaries in the Minangkabau Association, directly concerned with the preservation of an adat-oriented society in Minangkabau. As a consequence both groups became involved in the construction of a discourse on adat in which were embedded images of the nature of traditional Minangkabau. However, the resultant conceptualisations of adat and tradition differ significantly.

For example, the lead article in the first issue of the new journal which appeared on the first day of 1922, entitled 'Hindia Merdehka (Zelf Bestuur)' uses an image which appears time and time again in the pages of Indonesian periodicals in the early 1920s, a comparison between the situation of the people of the Indies and that of a bird in a cage which, although it may be well treated by its owner, nonetheless will always choose freedom if it is given the opportunity (*Boedi Tjaniago*, 1 January 1922: 3–6). 'Hindia Merdehka' establishes the agenda for subsequent contributions on adat, education and other subjects. Although these articles never take up the notion of *merdeka* (freedom) in detail, all are in one way or another concerned with the nature of society once the freedom of the peoples of the Indies has been achieved.

Journals like *Boedi Tjaniago* presented strong arguments in favour of independence for the Indies as a whole. Unlike nationalist publications of the 1930s, here there is little interest in the notion of an Indonesian nation, understood as a single social-cultural unit. Instead an independent Indies would, it seems, be composed of a variety of what we might now term separate ethnic groups, each governed according to local adat principles.

While as we have seen Muslim reformers in West Sumatra in the early decades of this century claimed to be the foremost advocates of 'modernism' and, hence, of progress (*kemadjuan*), it would be a mistake to assume that the defenders of adat were in some way less whole-hearted in their advocacy of progress. In the case of progressive adat organisations, such as the one which published *Boedi Tjaniago*, progress was very much something to be desired and promoted. Here the themes of freedom and democracy (based on Minangkabau adat) are brought together. The ultimate justification for both of these things is that together they, and they alone, would bring progress to all areas of the lives of the people of West Sumatra. As numerous contributors to the pages of the journal are keen to argue, the ultimate goal of the organisation is to search for the path which will ensure *kemadjuan* in the fields of education, agriculture, industry, trade, and financial matters. But progress was not considered simply a desirable development of human productive powers. It was instead viewed as the unfolding of the human spirit towards a more desirable state, a state of greater knowledge (*pengetahoean*), and a state characterised by greater love of one's country. It was, in short, viewed as a condition of altogether finer human feelings (*perasaan jang haloes*) (*Boedi Tjaniago*, 1 May 1922: 3–6) [19].

The case of the Boedi Tjaniago association of Padang Pandjang, therefore, demonstrates clearly that the construction of Minangkabau adat in the early 1920s took place not just in the discourse of Dutch colonialists or pro-colonial Indonesian conservatives, but also among highly progressive groups dedicated to freedom, progress and the full democratisation of life. By the middle of the 1920s, at least some Minangkabau were constructing images of a traditional village economy and a traditional culture which, it was thought, could form the basis for a future society in West Sumatra. Not only did this particular form of populist anti-colonialism play a significant role in the debates of the 1920s, but at least some of them appeared to be setting the nationalist agenda as well.

At much the same time as early Indonesian nationalists were debating the validity of their, different, cultural heritages, Béla Bartók as we have seen was swept up in a nationalist movement against a Germanised culture and a Germanised Austro-Hungarian ruling class that involved once again an indigenous reclamation of Hungarian culture. And like the Indonesian intellectuals in Sumatra and Bartók in Hungary, Haitian intellectuals in the interwar years were also coming to grips with the vagaries of colonial oppression, in the form of the United States occupation, and their own racial/cultural traditions. Haiti is an interesting case because it was the site of one of the earliest movements for national emancipation based on the principles of the French Revolution to develop outside the western world, a movement, moreover, that captured the imagination of many European intellectuals, among them Kleist and Heine as we have seen. Ideas about the special values and characteristics of indigeneity that were articulated in Haiti from the 1920s are, therefore, quite clearly understandable only in the context of a debate with 'western' universalism – first of the classic French variety, and then of the United States which occupied the country from 1915 and 1946 and which practised a colonial racism while espousing universal democratic principles in ways long familiar in the history of European empire:

> The pre-1915 Haitian elites had never held to any ideological proposition with fanatical conviction – except perhaps the association of the 1804 revolution with the regeneration of the black race. Ambiguity was their forte. But by undermining many tenets of the elites' vision of themselves and others, the occupation revealed inconsistencies inherent in that vision that they had conveniently ignored. More important – in questioning political independence . . . the occupation undermined the basis of the delicate edifice that these contradictory propositions constituted. The times called for a redefinition, or at least a reshaping, of the old categories. (Trouillot, 1990: 131)

That redefinition took the form, first, of the *mouvement indigeniste* launched by the publication in 1928 of a book by Jean Price-Mars. The result was:

> A series of attempts by *noir* and *clair* intellectuals to mount a wide-ranging reevaluation of the national culture. . . . These writers criticized the elites' tendency to imitate the West and to ignore peasant culture. They emphasized the need to study the peasantry, to make an inventory of its practices, and to take into account the African roots of Haitian culture. The *indigenistes*' critique suggested that the elites' political failure stemmed in part from their contempt of Haitian popular culture. (ibid.)

The development of Haitian indigenism was contemporary with, but distinct from both *noirisme* and the notion of *negritude*. Indigenism, for example, did not constitute a political movement per se. That was the province of the more narrowly circumscribed movement for *noirisme*: 'a strictly political ideology rooted in claims of "natural" legitimacy and calling for a color quota within the state apparatus'. *Negritude*, also articulated in Haiti at the time, most notably or perhaps notoriously by François Duvalier who was a young man during the American occupation, carries these ideas onto a global stage, arguing for a global reversal of the 'unequal evaluation of peoples, religions, and cultures' (ibid.).

In the interwar years, then, the world discovered what I have called the cultured empire – artists, colonial rulers, academics, nationalists and populist Marxists all in different ways rejected the 'social Darwinism' of nineteenth century western thought, and the techno-instrumental modernism of the early twentieth century, and set off on a discovery of cultural uniqueness, identity and alternative paths of development.

What they offered instead was not so much a more accurate reflection of the world, but a new way of constructing that world, this time as the site of a diversity of cultures. The discourse of cultural alterity that developed from the 1920s is therefore a particular construction of the world as cultural mosaic. Since quite clearly such a broad discursive or cultural movement, manifest in such a tremendous variety of political viewpoints (as well as discourses that were only very tenuously addressed to political issues) cannot be merely reduced to a conflict over colonialism, the question becomes why should such a globalised discourse of difference have emerged where and when it did. To some extent Anthony King is correct to draw our attention to development in the imperial centres, for it is from here that the new concern with global difference probably first spread, not just recently, but in the 1920s as well. The Dutch introduced both modernism and its critique into their Indonesian colony, Diego Rivera brought a despair of European modernist aesthetics to Mexico, Walter Spies sought his escape from Europe in Bali, B. Traven left because he might otherwise have been arrested. But why should Europeans be seeking an escape in the first place, why should a western public be so eager to consume these new images of cultural difference and plurality, and why should Mexicans and Indonesians seek to articulate their anti-colonial passions through images of the integrity of indigenous culture, rather than in other ways?

Perhaps, as King suggests in the passage cited earlier, the answers to these questions are not to be found in the context of empires, if by that term we understand the rather specific arrangements whereby Europeans exploited and dominated peoples in the remotest corners of the globe during the heyday of British and French colonialism in the nineteenth century. Perhaps instead it has, as Rabinow remarks, less to do with empire and more to do with modernity itself, at least as that project has unfolded since the beginning of the end of nineteenth century colonialism, and the emergence both of new forms of power, and new kinds of resistance to it, in the early decades of this century. If this is the case, then the phenomena we have been investigating in colonial contexts are also taking place in the heartlands of modernism.

Notes

1 Marcus and Fischer too have commented on the centrality of Evans-Pritchard's text for an understanding of the myths of twentieth century as opposed to nineteenth century anthropology (1986).

2 Spies in fact played an important role in the creation of the modern version of the famous *kecak* or 'monkey dance', still considered a must for all western tourists interested in Balinese culture. It would be ironic if this were the performance Greenblatt watched on the VCR that night! Spies was also close to Margaret Mead and Gregory Bateson who came to Bali to do research in the 1930s, and who themselves of course did much to shape current representations of Bali.

3 See Bateson and Mead (1942). Besides the account by Vickers, those of Pollman (1990) and Picard (1990) deal with the issue of construction of a twentieth century Balinese imaginary.

4 A clear illustration of this is found in the debate over Geertz's notion of agricultural involution. Most contributors to the debate, whether pro- or anti-Geertz, accept the validity of a model of Indonesian society in the 'traditional' period which draws heavily on the work of writers like Boeke and Van Vollenhoven. The debt of Geertz and other recent writers to the earlier generation of Dutch scholars is not always made as explicit as it is, for example, by Aas (1980), who relies directly on Van Vollenhoven's account to characterise the 'traditional' system. But a cursory reading of early twentieth century Dutch ethnology is sufficient to draw our attention to the striking parallels between recent attempts to characterise Indonesian tradition and those of colonial scholars.

5 Boeke's critique of Pierson is found in Boeke et al. (1966).

6 For general accounts of Spencerian evolutionism see Burrow (1966) and Peel (1971). For a discussion of the developing critique of Spencer in Britain see Hawthorn (1976), especially chapters 5 and 6.

7 The influence of German social theory on Dutch writers was marked in this period (see Kahn, 1993).

8 The compilation of writings on Indonesian adat is contained in: Dutch East Indies, Commissie voor het adatrecht, 1911–55. For more detailed discussion of Van Vollenhoven see Holleman (1981); H.L.T. de Beaufort (1954); and F.D.E. van Ossenbruggen (1976).

9 In Boeke's writings, as in the work of the German Historical School of Economics on which he drew, 'deductive' economics refers both to the classical political economy of the Scottish Enlightenment, and to neoclassical economics. The historicist critique of deductive economics maintained that it falsely universalised what was in fact a historically unique notion of the autonomous, maximising individual economic subject, viz. *homo œconomicus*.

10 For a discussion, and critique, of Snouck Hurgronje's role during the Aceh War, see Siegel (1969).

11 As Rabinow points out, the desire to preserve tradition did not necessarily benefit the Moroccans, indeed it was rarely even defended in such terms.

12 I am grateful to Paul Cocks for drawing these developments to my attention.

13 For discussions of Rivera's wedding of Marxism and indigenism in his murals see various contributions in Cynthia Newman Helms (1985).

14 See Hans Haufe, 'Indian Heritage in Modern Mexican Painting' in Billeter (1987: 81).

15 This journey was made famous by Claude Lévi-Strauss who describes it in *Tristes Tropiques*.

16 The National Library in Jakarta has a copy of the first number of *Surat Edaran* (as far as can be established the only number which appeared), together with six of the twelve issues of *Boedi Tjaniago*. The last of these is dated 30 September 1922. There is no record of any further issues being published, and hence it is not possible to establish whether further publications appeared after that time.

17 The article referred to here is entitled 'Hindia Merdehka' (A Free Indies), and appears in the first issue of *Boedi Tjaniago* dated 1 January 1922. The significance of this discussion of the proper function of religion is obvious. It represents a far from subtle critique of those who would argue that Islam should play a role in the organisation of social and political life in the here and now.

18 A long article comparing adat Boedi Tjaniago and European social democracy appears in *Boedi Tjaniago*, 1 May 1922.

19 To understand more clearly the images being constructed here it is important to note the significance of the two sets of oppositions being employed. First there is the distinction between *akal* (reason, intellect) and *hawa nafsu* (desire, physical need), a distinction particularly important in Muslim thought at least in Indonesia. Second, there is an opposition between *halus* (refined) and *kasar* (coarse). Without wishing to argue that these oppositions have at all times and in all places between central to Indonesian cultures, it is nonetheless interesting to note that these themes also ran through Acehnese cultural beliefs at much the same time (see Siegel, 1969).

5

Culture, Multiculturalism and the (Post)Modern City

> Los Angeles, like all cities, is unique, but in one way it may typify the world city of the future: there are only minorities. No single ethnic group, nor way of life, nor industrial sector dominates the scene. Pluralism has gone further here than in any other city in the world and for this reason it may well characterize the global megalopolis of the future. (Jencks, 1993: 7)

> Nowhere are the issues dividing America more pronounced: the imperative of the nation as a whole culture set against the desire for subcultures to flourish. *E pluribus unum* (out of many, one) is a formulation no longer adequate to that duality which many want: a dialogue between the one and the many, the center and the peripheries, with both sides equally acknowledged and allowed to talk. (ibid.: 8)

At some point in the 1980s Los Angeles, and to an only somewhat lesser extent Miami and Houston, became the cities of a new future – not the modernist future of a Le Corbusier, for whom careful planning, and the harnessing of modern technique to urban architecture would ensure a bright future of orderly, architecturally-unified 'radiant' cities; not the traditionalist future of a Lewis Mumford for whom regional planning, decentralisation and scaling-down would produce the kinds of livable 'garden cities' away from the dirt and danger of industrial centres that Ebenezer Howard had envisaged; not an urban future built around the lively and interactive, and therefore secure, urban neighbourhoods of a Jane Jacobs. The sense was that these earlier critiques of the modern city were inappropriate to the unique conditions of Los Angeles and Miami. Los Angeles and Miami – not London, Paris, New York or Chicago – were the exemplary cities of our time. These were the first inherently multicultural, global, postmodern cities. If solutions there were to the problems of contemporary urbanism, then they would have to emerge in and work for places like Los Angeles, Houston and Miami.

An earlier generation of observers, wedded to the high modernism of Europe and the East Coast, had failed to appreciate the significance of places like Los Angeles. With their elitist aesthetic traditions, they could only scorn a popular culture that revolved around freeways, Disney theme parks, the popular media, and the information industries. Only Baudrillard had seen through the false nostalgia of the modernist avant-garde. Those with an appreciation of 'popular culture' could see what these old world intellectuals could not. Here the variegated images of the postmodern city circulated freely, challenging and changing our modernist urban imaginary in the city streets of Ridley Scott's *Blade Runner*, the corporate offices of *LA Law*, the parade of changing 'identities' in *Miami Vice*, James Elroy's cynical and amoral Los Angeles policemen. Even Elmore Leonard had moved his band of authentic, if still endearing, street people from the dead centre of Fordism in Detroit to the post-fordist landscapes of Florida.

A central theme of this postmodern urban imaginary is the theme of difference. A 'Latin' character in a novel by the Florida-based crime writer John Walter Putre sees it this way:

> 'It's a very strange place, here,' Secassa replied mildly, . . .'Always, maybe, places are strange where some portion of a people live somewhere apart from their natural home. There are Latins in this town who are doctors, men of learning, Señor Doll. And others who make what livings they do by stealing the stereophonic tape decks out of cars. Normally the two would meet each other only when the one had the bad luck to get caught in the process of ripping off the other's Mercedes . . . but here those thieves and doctors find they have something else besides being on opposite sides of a theft in common. They are Latins, and, by that standard alone, they are at once together and apart from everyone else.'

After hearing Secassa's description of the Florida town, our hero muses:

> A strange place, Secassa had called the town, a strangeness he's set forth in terms of two rival cultures – one Anglo, the other Hispanic – forced by circumstances to live in apposition [sic], but neither with any more desire to integrate with the other than the minimum their physical proximity required. It was, Doll conceded, the understandable, perhaps even inevitable, perception of a man who regarded himself as an exile, accurate so far as it went – but incomplete. . . . The town had once been as Secassa believed it still to be, a place where a commonly held white consensus prevailed. (Putre, 1991: 42f.).

It is no accident that this should be perceived most strongly in a place like Florida. Florida is clearly one of those 'new spaces', like Houston, of which Michael Fischer writes:

> Multiculturalism takes on a new form in these spaces, both like and unlike the older urban immigrant entrepots of New York and Chicago. What fascinates me in these spaces, places and passages are the cultural translations. We need a new map of America that begins to envision the pilgrimage sites that Indians are establishing among the Hindu temples of North America, the establishment of a little Tehran in Los Angeles. . . . Above all, we need attention to the discourses immigrants use in making sense of their own lives, in comparing their own value systems with their new settings, or in forging philosophically resonant frames that draw on the genres, tropes, metaphors and imagery of both old and new cultural settings. . . . Descendants in the future may retell these stories differently and in more seamless, less discordant forms; for the moment they serve as birth pangs of something new. (1992: 36f.)

A profound difference, previously submerged, now emerges because the old 'liberal' (for which read Anglo) consensus has collapsed. Those of us privileged to escape that oppressive or hegemonic metanarrative are now free to consume the city with a postmodern sensibility. Carl Hiassen, now Florida's pre-eminent crime writer, in one of his early books saw the *barrios* of Miami through an appreciative Anglo eye once he realised that traffic laws are themselves culturally-relative:

> Meadows drove up Twenty-seventh Avenue, his attention only partly on what he was doing. Paint stores, drugstores, a muffler shop flashed by in the night, all shrouded and locked tight. The only life in the streets came, as it always did, in the *barrio*. Traffic picked up there, and many cars brandished red, white and blue Cuban flag decals on a bumper or back window. Swarthy men in guayabera shirts clustered in gesticulating knots before shops that dispensed cigars, *cafecitos* and memories. A black and gold Trans Am cut Meadows off near the Flagler street intersection. He took no affront. *El barrio* had its own unwritten traffic rules, and no prudent man drove there without anticipating some spontaneous display of *brio*. A red light that stopped traffic dead in staid Coral Gables was only a *gringo* challenge to *machismo* here. (Hiassen and Montalbano, 1981: 87)

No metanarratives, no consensus even about traffic rules, only the pure enjoyment of difference. In the words of Iris Marion Young:

> City life . . . instantiates difference as the erotic, in the wide sense of an attraction to the other, the pleasure and excitement of being drawn out of one's secure routine to encounter the novel, strange and surprising. . . . The erotic dimension of the city has always been an aspect of its fearfulness, for it holds out the possibility that one will lose one's identity, will fall. But we also take pleasure in being open to and interested in people we experience as different. We spend a Sunday afternoon walking through Chinatown, or checking out this week's eccentric players in the park. We look for restaurants, stores, and clubs with something new for us, a new ethnic food, a different atmosphere, a different crowd of people. We walk through sections of the city that we experience as having unique characters which are not ours, where people from diverse places mingle and then go home. (Young, 1990: 239)

If the postmodern city is a new kind of urban space, then its problems are not amenable to modernist solutions. In other words the 'problems' of the urban are now differently perceived – the chaos against which Le Corbusier struggled, the dirt and decline of community that Mumford decried, even the threat to the body against which Jacobs railed now seem in some way to contribute to the eroticisation of city life, the celebration, particularly in American popular culture, of the authentic life of the street.

In a book entitled *Into the Badlands: Travels Through Urban America*, the English journalist John Williams seems particularly drawn to the urban sleaze he finds depicted by the authors of the detective fiction he has set out to interview. Towards the end of the book he writes of a final encounter with the New York streets:

> At this point I begin to feel, not afraid precisely, but sick maybe. Sick of all the baseball caps that say, 'Shit happens' and of the gun shop and the sex shop and the bad beer and sick reality of all the evil that people do, all the viciousness, and sick at last of being fascinated by it and, worst, of seeing bad things not as bad but as research, as material. (Williams, 1991: 238)

But why should urban sleaze come to be so avidly consumed, so much a feature of the current voyeurism of people like Williams and the middle classes in general? The answer to the question is that the achievement of street cred aspired to by Williams, and its passive achievement by his readership comes to be seen as an act of rebellion, since street cred has itself come to be seen as a culture that grows up in the shadow of, and then directly challenges, the hypocritical liberalism of a hegemonic discourse:

> *street culture* has evolved what may be called a code of the streets, which amounts to a set of informal rules governing interpersonal behavior, including violence. . . .
> The code of the streets is actually a cultural adaptation to a profound lack of faith in the police and the judicial system. The police are most often seen as representing the *dominant white society* and not caring to protect inner city residents. (Anderson, 1994: 82; emphasis added) [1]

Jencks's book, written in the aftermath of the Los Angeles riots, is more than an exploration of the newness of a city that is made up entirely of (cultural) 'minorities'. It is also meant to be a response to the 'problems' as he sees them. The problem, however, is not a problem of disorder, chaos, or even violence. It is 'the dilemma of multiculturalism at its most acute' that is posed by Los Angeles, and hence by all cities of the future, the justifiable need for all 'voices' to be heard, for all identities to be affirmed. It is this problem to which Jencks's 'solutions' are directed, solutions that are absent in earlier American liberal ideas about assimilation and the melting pot. Given Jencks's particular and long-standing interest in the built environment, not surprisingly he focuses on architectural solutions. Specifically the book represents a defence of what Jencks calls Hetero-architecture – defined as an architecture of variety as a sequence of opposed historical types or of an eclectic mixture of styles.

But the analysis of a hetero-architecture is explicitly linked to a more encompassing search for a new politics of pluralism. 'I am,' Jencks writes, 'like many of the architects discussed here and many post-modern philosophers who will not be mentioned except in passing, a believer in pluralism, variety and difference as positive ends in themselves' (1993: 9).

This has implications not only for the architecture Jencks espouses, but also for the way he writes about it: 'Several kinds of architecture will be illustrated in this text and, following post-modern poetics, I will *switch voices* suddenly depending on which tone is more suitable for a particular context' (ibid.; emphasis added).

And this postmodern poetics is also linked explicitly to a political project, one Jencks describes as an end of modern liberalism – the liberalism of the individual – and the rise of a 'postmodern liberalism' by means of which groups and subcultures turn themselves into legal individuals (ibid.: 10). This too is the 'politics of difference' of which Young writes – not a politics informed by an abstract (and hence ultimately monocultural) notion of justice, but a genuinely multicultural politics within which alternative notions of justice can be brought into play.[2]

Modern or Postmodern?

Let us first consider more closely Jencks's claim that the cultural diversity of which he speaks is indeed something new. Is Los Angeles *historically* unique? Is, in other words, Los Angeles the first city of 'only minorities', a place where 'pluralism has gone further . . . than in any other city in the world'? Is Los Angeles as a consequence the first postmodern or global city? There are at least superficial reasons to be sceptical. For example in 'New York City in 1920 over half the males over twenty-one were of foreign birth. By 1940, when New York City's total population was about 7.5 million, 5 million of those reported being "of foreign stock" in that year's census. Two million of New York's residents at that time were Jews' (Kahn, 1987: 197f.). Would not a city two thirds of whose residents identified themselves as 'foreign' be potentially at least as 'multicultural' as Los Angeles in the 1980s, particularly given that those not of 'foreign stock' would have included a large number of recent African American immigrants from the South?

Perhaps the cultural diversity of a Los Angeles, Miami or Houston is not such a recent development. Perhaps what is new is the politics of pluralism advocated by Jencks. *E pluribus unum* is, Jencks says, *no longer* adequate; the old metanarratives of justice, argues Iris Marion Young, must now be dispensed with because they flow inevitably from the cultural presuppositions of only one of the many cultural groups inhabiting the American city. We have here to do with the assertion that a multicultural politics is a new invention, one that has only recently replaced a cultural politics of assimilationism, a common enough assertion in places like the United States, Canada and Australia – societies which over the last ten years or so have chosen to represent themselves as multicultural.

At least in the American context such a claim is at best debatable. In the United States perhaps the nearest equivalent to 'assimilationism' was the policy of 'Americanization' by which various levels of the US government, employers and an array of voluntary organisations, sought to introduce immigrants to the benefits of American culture, persuading them at the same time to jettison their old-world loyalties and cultural attachments. One European immigrant writing as an 'unassimilated foreigner' in the 1920s described his 'first acquaintance' with this process of 'civic teaching' in the following terms:

> A young lady had been appointed as our instructor in English, American history, and civics. Economics was not included in this curriculum. Her method was rather mechanical and lacked conviction. The only time she warmed up to her subject was when she indulged in some bitter criticism of government ownership, with occasional reference to socialism, the whole of it coupled with a clumsy eulogy of the company's resident stockholder. Americanism, according to her definition, meant the perpetuation, as permanent and immutable national traits, of the various characteristics distinctive of the pioneers during the period of individual competition and colonization from the shores of the Atlantic in the general direction of the Northwest. These traits she enumerated as follows:

private property, parliamentary democracy, evangelical Christianity, and the monogamic [sic] home. She dwelt at length on the ethical side of Americanism, but I was considerably amazed that most of those ethical percepts [sic] were summarized in the language of the poker table. Still, at closer inspection, the different principles mentioned constituted a fairly good epitome of Americanism. . . .

These fundamental American traits may have had a certain positive value in pioneering days. Today, with the free land all gone and the leading economic force in the nation shifted from extensive agriculture to mechanized industrial production, the maintenance of the morals of an elapsed economic period as permanent national traits can only have a negative purpose of social discipline, and is no longer conducive to national progress. (Anon, 1920)

All this was linked, of course, to nineteenth century ideas of America as a cultural 'melting pot', and specifically to an image prevalent in the late nineteenth century of urban society as a racial hierarchy, headed by a white Anglo-Saxon majority in which racial inferiors had as their only option conforming to the values of that majority (see Kornbluh, 1987).

As the tone of the above quote suggests, certainly by the 1920s there was a good deal of opposition to this ideology of the melting pot. Konrad Berkovici, for example, author of a popular 1924 'guidebook' to New York City maintained that taken together the culturally-distinctive groups that lived together in New York were producing a new civilisation, not homogeneous or 'Americanised', but one in which each group has a full awareness of its own culture.[3] It was these separate cultural traditions and institutions that held the whole together, ensuring its continued stability. The real danger to social integration was not the absence of a common culture, an overarching consensus, but that these distinct cultures would break down either because people crossed the line (for example, Negroes trying to live white) or because groups lost coherence without a permanent locale or geographical focus (like the Gypsies). Robert Park and Louis Wirth also saw the problem, rather than the solution, in the breakdown of migrant cultures – something they feared would occur among second generation immigrants.

The Los Angeles of the 1980s is certainly not identical to the New York of the 1920s. Yet the difficulties in locating either an urban social pattern or a form of urban politics that comes somehow *after* modernity suggest that the continuities cannot be ignored, and that taking them on board might change our perspective on contemporary urbanism in potentially significant ways. At the very least these continuities suggest a different approach to both Jencks's text and the architecture in whose defence it is written.

The text Jencks maintains is written with an eye to a new postmodern poetics which, recognising diversity, no longer represents the world in one voice. It instead speaks to us in what Jencks at one point calls different 'voices'. And just as the text 'switches voices', so the hetero-architecture which constitutes Jencks's subject matter is also an architecture that switches voices because it:

may represent variety as a sequence of opposed historical types, as Disneyland has done on a populist level, or the architect Jon Jerde has done on a commercial plane; or it may be an eclectic mixture of styles as in Charles Moore's work; or a set of different metaphors and contrasting materials as in Frank Gehry's. (Jencks, 1993: 7)

But how can Jencks's text speak different voices when it is the work of only Jencks himself? How can a building designed by Jon Jerde, Charles Moore or Frank Gehry combine genuinely different architectural visions? Elsewhere, instead of describing his style as the result of different voices, Jencks more honestly writes of different 'tones' – tones, presumably, of a single authorial voice. If we cut away the pretence that Jencks's post-modern poetics, or the designs of the Los Angeles School of Architects, or the fragmented discourse of justice of an Iris Marion Young, are any more multi-authored than were earlier accounts of the multi-ethnic city, then the issue appears in a very different light. We can now see clearly that what we are dealing with is a particular *representation* of the city, an *image* of a culturally diverse rather than a culturally homogeneous city. And contrary to the impression generated by talk of 'diversity', the plethora of urban voices, and so on, what we have here is more accurately seen as a representation from a singular vantage point, a vantage point that appears to exist *outside* the hurly-burly of the diversity of lives that it claims to represent. Rather than being located *within* any single urban voice, what we have here is the bird's eye view of someone privileged to see all that diversity without actually being part of it. In the case of hetero-architecture we can quite literally look down and around us, and in so doing see a new kind of homogeneity – not of a mass of individuals striving after a single civilisational goal, but of a mass of cultures, different yet each curiously the same since each has its own language, voice, set of customs and beliefs and identities.

Where does this multicultural imaginary come from? How has the inherent diversity of modern urban life been fitted into a representational grid known as multiculturalism? What has provided that privileged vantage point from which intellectuals, popular writers, journalists, architects and musicians have been able to gaze upon an urban landscape of cultural diversity?

Contrary to much of the current multicultural rhetoric, the image of urbanism as diversity has a respectable genealogy at least in the American imagination. For example, mouthing what was probably already a cliche, the author of a series of articles on ethnic groups in New York wrote in 1921 that 'New York is: The largest Negro city; the largest Jewish city, the largest Italian city, the largest Irish city, the third largest German city in the world' (Hartt, 1921).

Or consider the popular travel book by the Romanian Konrad Berkovici first published in 1924. Like no other city, New York, Berkovici wrote, 'offers the best study of the nations of the world, samples of each being centered in different sections within easy reach of one another' (cited in

Kornbluh, 1987: 50). Berkovici proceeded to catalogue each groups' languages, foods, smells, theatres, libraries, clothing, housing, music, newspapers, coffee houses and political participation.

That cultural pluralism rather than unity or homogeneity was a key feature of the American city was also a central tenet of the Chicago School writers like Robert Park and, especially, Louis Wirth (see Kornbluh, 1987: 50; Miller, 1992), as it was for their contemporary Randolphe Bourne who argued that America's national character lay not in the legacy of Anglo-Saxon institutions, but in the future creation of a multicultural society (in Kornbluh, 1987).

In a recent re-reading of American culture between the wars, based on the content of the large number of 'little magazines' that appeared in the interwar years, the American literary critic Walter Kalaidjian has argued that our blindness to the 'multicultural' nature of an earlier phase of the American cultural renaissance has been the result of the appropriation of the history of cultural modernism by a literary elite. In fact, the concern with cultural alterity and hegemony, the search for other voices, the internationalisation of the cultural field that we commonly associate with postmodernism are all present in this earlier period in a form Kalaidjian terms 'revisionary modernism' (see Kalaidjian, 1993).[4]

Harlem in a 'Multicultural' New York

Just such a revisionary modernist was the New York-based American writer Carl Van Vechten whose novel on New York's Harlem, controversially titled *Nigger Heaven*, and which first appeared in 1926, probably more than any other book, including those by the leading African American writers of the Harlem Renaissance, shaped the public perceptions of the 'lifeways' of urban African Americans at the beginning of the period that, I want to argue, marks the formation of our current discourse on the culture of American urbanism.

If literary critics can read anthropological monographs for their literary qualities, then anthropologists can surely read novels for their anthropological messages. It seems the critics' consensus is that *Nigger Heaven* failed as a novel. But this makes it no less interesting to the anthropologist, for two main reasons. First, it was clearly a very popular novel; it sold out its first printing of 100,000 copies almost immediately. It therefore should tell us something about American culture in the 1920s. Second, like contemporary anthropological monographs such as Margaret Mead's *Coming of Age in Samoa*, it seeks to represent the culture of a particular exotic people – the residents of New York's Harlem. Since Van Vechten had plenty of direct experience of Harlem, it can therefore also be read as ethnographic monograph.

There is, however, a degree of tension between these two dimensions of the text. It is clear that the 'ethnographic' message that we may take from the novel – that Harlem is made up of a great diversity of peoples and

cultural attitudes; that many of the 'natives' are highly-educated, cultivated, open-minded, hard-working, in short 'civilised' – appears to largely
contradict the message taken away by its many avid consumers, particularly outside the African American community, namely that Harlem is a
privileged site of exoticism, primitivism and behavioural licence.

The main characters of the novel – Mary Love and Byron Kasson – are
both examples of Alain Locke's 'New Negro'. Locke, Professor of
Philosophy at Howard University, was probably the most successful
articulator of the general ideas of the post-First World War Harlem
Renaissance, arguing that the African American was now ready to take a
central role in American life. Unlike the 'Old Negroes', stereotyped in
literature and music as unsophisticated, rural, members of homogeneous
farming communities, dependent on white patronage, and passively
accepting of their fate, the New Negro was sophisticated, city-based and
hence a member of a heterogeneous urban community, an active participant in the shaping of Negro culture, proud of his/her race, independent,
and prepared now, in the words of the Jamaican socialist W.A. Domingo,
to insist on 'absolute and unequivocal *social equality*' (cited in Huggins,
1971: 53). A central figure in Locke's vision of the New Negro was the
creative artist – writer, painter, sculptor. He placed great stress on the way
African Americans could come to be released from the 'arid fields of
controversy and debate to the productive fields of creative expression'
(ibid.: 59). Success in the creative arts was seen as a significant goal in
itself, perhaps because these fields were held out by white society as the
crowning achievements of European civilisation, and hence proof of its
superiority.

As Huggins, author of one of the definitive studies of the Harlem
Renaissance points out, this ideal of cultural renewal or renaissance was
not restricted to the African American community. Indeed in some sense
Locke's 'New Negro' was part of a general postwar movement in the
United States to create a culture to rival that of Europe, and was informed
by similar 'very traditional [American] values of self-sufficiency and
self-help. . . . Whatever else he was then, as Locke explained him, the
New Negro was an assertion of America' (ibid.: 59).

Mary Love and Byron Kasson – she a highly literate and aesthetically-
sensitive librarian, he a graduate of the University of Pennsylvania and
aspiring writer – are both stereotypical 'New Negroes', in their sophistication and levels of education, in their desired occupations, in the fact that
they live in Harlem, widely recognised at the time as the cultural capital of
the Negro world. They both strive to achieve genuine excellence. Early on
Byron tells Mary how his University teachers recognised his talent, but he
suspects it was only because of his race:

> Oh, I haven't published much. I've had a piece or two in Opportunity, but that
> won't keep me alive. At college they said I had promise. I know what they
> meant, he added, 'pretty good for a coloured man.' That doesn't satisfy me. I
> want to be as good as anyone. (Van Vechten, 1926: 36)

Both are frustrated by white racism. Mary is angry that while she is as good if not better at her job than most white librarians, she is paid less than they are and constantly overlooked when it comes to promotion. But Mary and Byron are also proud to be black. Not for them the strategy of 'passing' which is, instead, used by some of their friends to overcome this glass ceiling.

As bad, if not worse, than the whites sometimes are fellow blacks. Byron is told by Howard – Olive's fiancé – that it is tough in New York. Whites won't give you any proper work, and 'You'll have to fight your own race harder than you do the other . . . every step of the way. They're full of envy for every Negro that makes a success . . . Why, more of us get on through the ofays than through the shines' (ibid.: 108).

In a controversial study of early African American residents of Washington, Philadelphia and Chicago, E. Franklin Frazier (1962) argued that they constituted a 'black bourgeoisie', recreating the feudal relations of dependence that existed between whites and blacks in the South and hostile to the creative and egalitarian aspirations of the more recent migrants. *Nigger Heaven* is filled with members of this 'black bourgeoisie', including Byron's own family who refuse to help him because he will not compromise with white society and take a job as an elevator boy. The Bronx family whom Mary visits for an elegant dinner are horrified by the exhibition of African sculpture that she has organised at the library.

While certainly proud to be black, and far less judgemental than the black aristocracy of the foibles of their fellow Harlemites, Mary and Byron too aspire to greater things. But this produces feelings of intense alienation. Civilisation also implies a loss. Mary is worried, for example, that she is missing out on the positive features of her race – the African beat – 'This love of drums, of exciting rhythms, this naive delight in glowing colour'. The problem is that she can achieve it only through 'mental understanding', rather than instinctively as do so many of her race. In fact 'this primitive birthright which was so valuable and important an asset, a birthright that all the civilized races were struggling to get back to – this fact explained the art of a Picasso or a Stravinksky' (ibid.: 82).

And this brings us back to the 'anthropological' reading of the novel in both senses. Huggins praises *Nigger Heaven* for producing the first 'generally read novel [that] had chosen the Negro as its subject and abandoned the stereotype' (Huggins, 1971: 103) in producing an image of Harlem, not as homogeneous, but as 'a social microcosm of New York City. The reader had to reject definitions of the Negro as a type. There was a wide variety of characters, tastes, and values . . . Harlem was no monolith, and the Negro fit no stereotype' (ibid.: 102). The contrast is explicitly drawn with contemporary novels like DuBose Heyward's *Porgy* which, while attempting to present the Negro with dignity, nonetheless retained a degree of stereotyping.

And yet, even if only as a rhetorical device (a less charitable view would be in order to ensure financial success) precisely to avoid stereotyping, Van

Vechten has, as the above quote suggests, written an ethnography in which all the characters of Harlem put in an appearance. And, Huggins is undoubtedly correct when he maintains that it was less for the rather preachy and boring sections about Mary and Byron, and more for its portraits of the more colourful and exotic residents of Harlem that a white audience consumed the novel so avidly. Ethnography had a (white) market, philosophical writings on the New Negro did not.[5]

Numerous examples could be given, but one will suffice. I refer to the character of Anatole Longfellow, alias the Scarlet Creeper, who puts in only a very brief appearance in the prologue, and again in the last few pages. We first meet him strutting 'aimfully down the east side of Seventh Avenue' wearing:

> a tight-fitting suit of shepherd's plaid which thoroughly revealed his lithe, sinewy figure to all who gazed upon him, and all gazed. A great diamond, or some less valuable stone which aped a diamond, glistened in his fuchsia cravat. The uppers of his highly polished tan boots were dove-coloured suede and the buttons were pale blue. His black hair was sleek under his straw hat, set at a jaunty angle. When he saluted a friend – and his acquaintanceship seemed to be wide – two rows of pearly teeth gleamed from his seal-brown countenance. (Van Vechten, 1926: Prologue)

In the short prologue, a beautiful young woman, apparently a prostitute, approaches the Creeper and offers him money to take her dancing and, apparently, to have sex. This the Creeper accepts nonchalantly, as if it were merely his due. If sex is there, so is jazz, and probably drugs, and certainly violence (the Creeper returns at the end only to despatch Byron's enemy Randolph Pettijohn). It is presumably glimpses such as these of an 'authentic' Harlem (authenticity is guaranteed by the language, the Creeper speaks the language of the streets)[6] which contributed to the book's commercial success.

What is the contextual significance of such a discourse of difference within the modern city and how is cultural pluralism then constructed as a consequence? Quite clearly texts like those of Van Vechten, and subsequently of Jencks and Young, are *representations* rather than reflections in thought of some pre-given cultural reality. But we need to go further than merely stating that obvious fact. Representations, including our own, are not off-stage reflections on the processes under investigation, they are part of them. As I have already argued these representational practices are *part of* a modern imaginary, however much it might be assumed that they have reference to a culture exterior to it. But more than this, they are implicated in, and implied by, political and economic practices that are themselves part of particular 'modernising' trajectories. It is not particularly helpful merely to dismiss the variety of such practices as 'imperial' or 'hegemonic'. Van Vechten's representation of a 'multiracial' New York in the 1920s, for example, did not go unchallenged by 'indigenous' critics. Moreover, it is interesting to note that African American criticisms of *Nigger Heaven* did not take the form of an argument that Van Vechten had denied the uniqueness of African American culture. Indeed many of Van Vechten's African American critics gave voice to the kinds of 'civilisational' ideas that are more commonly associated with imperial discourse. The problem with recent cultural theory is that its simplistic contrasts between 'social Darwinism' and 'cultural identity' fail to capture what is in fact a far more complex set of cultural debates.

While, as we have seen, Van Vechten's novel proved very popular among whites, it was criticised by many blacks, including some, but not all, close friends of Van Vechten who were leading writers of the Harlem Renaissance in the 1920s. The remark made by Duke Ellington about George Gershwin's 'folk opera' *Porgy and Bess* when it was first performed a decade later – 'this portrays my people in a bad light' – was commonly made about *Nigger Heaven* as well. Not surprisingly, a good deal of criticism focused on the title. But it is interesting to note the tone of the more detailed criticism. While, as we have seen, Van Vechten obviously made an effort to portray Harlem intellectuals in a sympathetic light, while the novel contains a detailed attack on the racism of white society, while he tried hard to avoid a general, stereotyped representation of the people of Harlem, Harlem intellectuals found fault with precisely those parts of Van Vechten's novel which represented a Harlem outside the confines of (white) civilisation. While, as we have seen, contemporary multiculturalism may find a cultural integrity in African American street life, critics took issue with Van Vechten's portrayal of the underside of Harlem through street characters like the Scarlet Creeper.

The other face of Harlem is certainly manifest in its sexual licence, the drinking and drugs. While sensationalist, however, Van Vechten's accounts of these things are not intended as condemnatory. On the contrary they are represented as part of a culture that provides an alternative to the straight-laced, hypocritical culture of white society, and of the society of Harlem's 'black bourgeoisie'. They are not a vehicle to attack Negro life, but on the contrary for a critique of 'traditional American values'. For many white Americans 'Harlem seemed a cultural enclave that had magically survived the psychic fetters of Puritanism' (Huggins, 1971: 89). That Van Vechten's Harlem was seen as an antidote to dominant American values, rather than merely a civilisational grid against which African Americans would always be found wanting, is further evidenced by the presence of Harlemites just as exotic as the Scarlet Creeper, but less likely to be seen as inferior. The self-confident and cosmopolitan Lasca Sartoris, for example, with whom Byron becomes infatuated, is no low-life street person. The former wife of an African prince who had lived for a long time in Paris, she is an image of a strong, un-Americanised African American woman. And consider the following description of Mary's friend Adora, the widow of a wealthy real estate agent, and herself a former star of the Harlem music halls:

She *was* beautiful, of that there could be no question, beautiful and regal. Her skin was almost black; her nose broad, her lips thick. Her ears were set well on her head; her head was set well on her shoulders. She was a type of pure African majesty. (Van Vechten, 1926: 28)

This celebration of the beauty of otherness is a long way from an imperial discourse that seeks always to measure the other according to the yardstick of the self.

If such an authoritative modernist voice there was in the Harlem of the 1920s, then it was the voice, not of the (white) Van Vechten but of the black artists, writers, politicians and philosophers of the Harlem Renaissance itself. For them public images of Harlem life needed to conform to the parameters of Alain Locke's New Negro. The central concern was to avoid making the Negro appear ridiculous to whites, which meant avoiding elements of Negro life that did not conform to the civilisational values that an uneasy white America was itself attempting to assert – an attitude informed by what Australians call cultural cringe. This contrast between Van Vechten's exoticising tendencies and the 'civilising' tendencies of the Harlem intellectuals is nicely illustrated by the very different photographic style of Van Vechten himself, and Harlem's leading black photographer of the 1920s, James van der Zee. Van Vechten's photographs of Harlem personalities like William 'Bojangles' Robinson, Bessie Smith and Zora Neale Hurston are all self-consciously exoticised. Robinson, for example, appears naked from the waist up, Thurston against a jarring geometrically-patterned background. All have enigmatic expressions on their faces, deliberately unreadable. In sharp contrast James van der Zee's carefully-posed portraits are all of people dressed impeccably in suits and 'American-style' dresses. Some sit around elegantly laid out tables, others pose in or near conservative but expensive cars. They all look directly and openly into the camera. They are, in short, all clearly 'civilised' people, normal (well-off) Americans.[7]

But there is a tension between this – let us call it, cosmopolitanism and particularism – a tension that was an important feature of the project of the Harlem Renaissance. For this was not just the case of a people seeking to conform to white values, who had uncritically accepted the civilisational ideology of a racial/cultural hierarchy. This was also the voice of a militant generation proud to be black. We cannot, I think, see here a simple opposition between assimilationism and identity politics, for both are present. The real question seemed to be, what does it mean to be black, what are the sources of blackness? Here, different possibilities presented themselves.

One, of course, was 'ethnographic' – that is it lay in the everyday lives of the people of Harlem and their culture. In spite of the ambiguities and contradictions in his novel, it is precisely such an identity that is constructed by Van Vechten. And while this may have proved to be the enduring image, *at the time* such a source was not favoured by African American intellectuals. Indeed it has been pointed out that the one feature of contemporary urban culture in Harlem that had attained international recognition, that is jazz, was largely ignored by Harlem intellectuals in the

1920s apparently because it was too closely associated with 'the streets'. Instead two other sources were drawn upon, although by their very nature they always posed problems. First there was 'folklore' – that is the stories, music and other cultural forms developed in the American South during the period of slavery. These demonstrated the tremendous creativity of African Americans even in appalling circumstances. Southern folklore fired the imagination of Harlem intellectuals in different ways – we might here only mention the very popular and influential studies by anthropologist Zora Neale Hurston,[8] and the spiritual music of Southern black Christianity. While jazz was not an important theme in the discourse of the Harlem Renaissance, because of its folkloric significance great praise was lavished on the tradition of the spiritual.[9]

The second source of a Negro identity was, of course, diasporic. The discovery of African artistic traditions, the use of African settings and so on, became very important to cultural production in Harlem in the 1920s. One need only mention here the importance of Africa to the otherwise quite different political philosophies of W.E.B. Du Bois and, slightly later, Marcus Garvey, and the prevalence of African imagery in a good deal of the work of Harlem painters and sculptors in the 1920s (see The Studio Museum, 1987).

But, as I have suggested, the Southern folklore traditions and Africa posed real problems for Harlem intellectuals in search of sources of what was called at the time 'race pride'. The former, for example, brought with it the baggage of Southern subservience, Uncle Tomism – the Old Negro not the New (one suspects, for example, there was an element of this in the critical reaction to *Porgy and Bess*, because it was based in the South and not Harlem which, of course, Gershwin knew better, and because of its use of spirituals). Africa, however, was equally problematic – this time perhaps because it was already so strongly associated with primitivism that Harlem intellectuals had difficulty ridding it of primitivist connotations.

It is clearly the case that Africa-America constitutes a unique case in the context of American urban culture, a consequence generally of the unique history by which Africans came to America, but more directly of the primitivist representations that dogged them from the start and which early on took such firm root in the American imagination, both black and white. Other groups have had less difficulty in finding sources of cultural identity less tinged by social Darwinist assumptions of racial/cultural inferiority.

But in spite of the unique position of urban African Americans in the 1920s, and the ways in which Harlem intellectuals attempted to address issues of racism, in the longer run it seems that it was the ethnographic/cultural/'ethnic' construction of African Americans that prevailed. Thus, for example, by 1980 the consensus among American liberals was that all groups, including the American 'Negroes' (as well as whites) constituted, not 'races' nor 'civilisations', but so many different 'ethnic groups', all different and yet also more or less the same, since each had to be forced into the single category – 'ethnic group'.[10] And as our opening discussion suggests, for many intellectuals in the 1980s, the African Americans constitute just one of the tiles of that cultural mosaic that is the postmodern, multicultural city.

In the popular imagination too there is a very real sense in which the image of African Americans, for both blacks and whites, now draws on ethnographic sources (street cred, rap, ghetto dress, violence, basketball). This, as the above discussion suggests, has its origins in the 1920s, and it has involved a range of producers and consumers of images, black and white, such as those discussed above. People like Van Vechten, for a variety of reasons, played an important part in that process, both as patrons of Harlem artists and intellectuals and as representatives of that 'American culture' that most writers of the Harlem Renaissance saw as external to their own.

To paraphrase Sportin' Life, it need not necessarily have been so. What are for Huggins the 'failures' of the Harlem Renaissance are perhaps better seen as the failure of Americans in general to recognise the interior rather than the 'multicultural' relationship between African Americans and American culture. On this point Huggins is extremely eloquent:

> But the positive implications of American nativity have never been fully appreciated by Afro-Americans. It seems too simple: the Afro-American's history and culture *is* American, more completely so than most others in this country. . . . Negroes . . . have voiced a strange alienation from that culture. They wrote about it as if they were not a part of it, or it a part of them. . . . Sometimes black intellectuals made claims for the Negro contribution to *it*. Sometimes they tried to fashion their work in *its* image. Occasionally they attempted to deny *it* and to adopt some other culture and tradition to work within. Whatever, it was something that was not them. What a perverse conception! The truth was (and is) that black men and American culture have been one – such a seamless web that it is impossible to calibrate the Negro within it or to ravel him from it. . . . The lesson it leaves us is that the true Negro renaissance awaits Afro-Americans' claiming their *patria*, their nativity. (Huggins, 1971: 308f.)

Were African Americans solely responsible for this state of affairs? Or is this notion of a distinctive African American *culture*, a notion perhaps first clearly formulated by Carl Van Vechten, and since perpetuated by liberals, postmodernists and multiculturalists alike, the real problem. It is interesting in this regard to contrast the history of African American identity politics with that of American Jews.

Jewish Postmoderns Avant La Lettre?

If the discourse of multiculturalism has transformed race into culture in the case of African Americans, in the case of American Jews religion has also become a cultural identity. In the *Harvard Encyclopedia of American Ethnic Groups* Jews and 'Afro-Americans' constitute two of the 101 groups it constitutes as 'ethnic'.[11] The article on the Jews concludes with the following statement: 'Having achieved prosperity and social integration as a result of a set of historical conditions, Jews now have the option of identifying with, or ignoring, the ethnic community nurtured by their collective experience' (Thernstrom, 1980: 597).

If modern African American identity owes a great deal to the Harlem experience, then modern Jewish identity is intimately bound up with the experience of Jewish migrants to New York's Lower East Side. As poor, recently arrived immigrants to New York – African Americans from the West Indies and the American South, Jews from central and eastern Europe – the two groups had a good deal in common. Both, moreover, had come from places where they had experienced the full force of racism and, during the interwar years, both witnessed renewed racist violence in their places of origin. The revitalised anti-Semitism of postwar Europe; the renewed racism and racial violence in a South racked by the Ku-Klux-Klan, Christian fundamentalism, lynchings and massacres, were excellent antidotes to any nostalgia for their homelands among the residents of Harlem and the Lower East Side. That common experience probably explains both the parallels in the way the two communities forged their identities in subsequent years, as well as the rather close political links between them. The significant role played by Jews in the early years of the NAACP (National Association for the Advancement of Colored People) is a case in point, as are the sympathies that developed between prominent African American and Jewish intellectuals. Of the latter mention must be made of the alliance between W.E.B. Du Bois – the radical African American intellectual and politician – and Franz Boas – Jewish immigrant, nephew of Moses Hess and 'father' of American anthropology. Already by the 1890s Boas was doing his best to combat racism and social Darwinism in the scientific community, writing articles attacking the theories of leading 'social Darwinists'[12] and lending his support, sometimes unwittingly, to Du Bois in the latter's struggle for leadership of the African American community with the conservative, but considerably more powerful, Booker T. Washington.[13]

But while the similarities of the Jewish and African American experience in northern cities in general and New York in particular are marked, there are also significant differences which belie the attempt to subsume both into an ethnic or multicultural grid. Moreover, in spite of the blandness of documents like the *Harvard Encyclopedia*, it does not seem as though Jews and African Americans in the 1980s related to each other as fellow 'ethnics' within a multicultural America. Instead we are bombarded with images of conflict and significant hostility between these two 'ethnic groups'. This appears to be recognised in more recent, radical multicultural discourse, in which Jewishness is rarely accepted as a valid 'postcolonial' or 'multicultural identity' for a variety of reasons, including, presumably, the perception of a generalised Jewish 'prosperity' (of which the *Harvard Encyclopedia* speaks) and the role played by American Jews in prompting American support for Israel.

These kinds of conflicts between 'ethnic groups' have led recent observers, as we have had occasion to note, to a critique of the cultural essentialism upon which notions of multiculturalism are built. The processes by which Jews on the one hand, African Americans on the other, are defined and define themselves as unique cultural groups, and the related processes by which individuals form their own identities by 'identifying' with one or other of the array of such groups have come to be seen as highly problematic given the apparently arbitrary ways in which these identities have emerged and the violence of the conflicts they appear to generate. Are 'Jews', 'African Americans' and the other 108 ethnic groups listed in the *Harvard Encyclopedia* really the discrete cultural groups they appear to be? Is it not possible to combine them, to live in their interstices, to change one's identity from one day to the next, even to create a new cultural identity? The language of hybridisation, of marginality and borderlands, of the free play of identity and the invention of tradition characterises a good deal of avowedly postmodern commentary on issues of culture and identity.[14]

It is interesting to note, however, that many of these issues are already implied in the processes of identity formation in an earlier period and that, moreover, some of the differences between the Jewish and African American experiences may be traceable to the different ways in which these two groups negotiated them. Summing up the African American dilemma in *The Souls of Blackfolk*, W.E.B. Du Bois wrote:

> .It is a peculiar sensation, this double-consciousness, this sense of always looking at one's self through the eyes of others. . . . One ever feels his twoness – an American, a Negro; two souls, two thoughts, two unreconciled strivings; two warring ideals in one dark body, whose dogged strength alone keeps it from being torn asunder. (cited in Chametzky, 1986: 104)

This 'double-consciousness' seems to have been at the heart of the dilemma to which the writers of the Harlem Renaissance addressed themselves. And, perhaps largely because of the persistence of the primitivist tag, it is a problem that seemed to be without solution. In the current language of postmodern identity formation, the dilemma was caused by the essentialisation of the categories 'Negro' and 'American', denying as Huggins has argued, the former any stake in the latter.

Quite clearly for many Jews today this essentialised distinction between 'Jew' and 'American' also exists. One need look no farther than Crown Heights in Brooklyn to realise that. But to read the Lubbavitcher Hassidim as though they represented all American Jews would be a grave mistake. For, I want to suggest, the 'postmodern' strategies of marginalisation, hybridisation and the 'free' play of identity have for some time also been a significant part of the identities of at least some groups of American Jews from quite early on in this century. This is manifest in the role played at least by certain Jewish writers, artists, musicians and intellectuals in American culture at least from the early years of the twentieth century. These appear to stem in the first instance from the way in which, from a strong base within New York's Jewish community, Jewish artists and intellectuals have managed, probably more successfully than African

Americans, to have Jewishness recognised as part of mainstream American culture. While, as Huggins has suggested, African Americans have always had difficulty in claiming their American 'nativity', Jews have been more successful in this regard. In other words, at least in the interwar years Jewish writers and intellectuals have been able to negotiate the relationship between 'American culture' and 'other cultures' (including of course 'Jewish culture', but also that of other groups) more successfully than have other American 'ethnics'. Why this should have been the case is not a question easily answered. To some extent clearly the differential success of African American and Jewish intellectuals in negotiating the boundaries imposed by the discourse of culture and ethnicity has been due to the greater strength of American racism than of American anti-Semitism. To some extent, too, these differences are entwined with the greater economic strength of the Jewish community, although in the early decades of this century these differences were far less marked than they were to become.[15] But there is also a sense as we shall see in which these differences stem from what, following Louis Wirth we might call the strength of a 'duplex' culture – and what might now be called a self-consciously hybridised and marginal culture – among European, and then American Jews, and its relative weakness in African American communities, itself a result of the differing historical experiences of the two groups.

The contrasting fortunes of Jews and African Americans in the entertainment industry is an interesting case in point, not because, as some anti-Semitic African American leaders argue today, it has been dominated by Jews, but because Jewish musicians and entertainers have exhibited their 'postmodern' talents rather successfully there. The contrasts are evident from very early on, when both Jews and African Americans in New York played significant roles in theatre and the music business. But from the early days of the New York entertainment industry, there was an important difference in the experience of Jewish and African American entertainers. For the former there was a highly developed and lively vernacular tradition – the tradition of Yiddish theatre, where Jewish comics, musicians and actors could and did perform in Yiddish in front of a local audience. African Americans, by contrast, depended to a much greater extent on white audiences, white-owned theatres and clubs, and so on. Gershwin's *Porgy and Bess*, for example, was in one sense part of a long line of 'Negro' shows that featured Harlem actors and musicians playing to white audiences, either in the jazz clubs of Harlem (the best-known of which, like the Cotton Club, did not even have blacks in the audience) or the theatres of Broadway. Inevitably, this meant that the entertainers of Harlem were more likely to see themselves through white eyes, and to mould their (public) personae according to the tastes of their, predominantly white, audiences, while Jewish entertainers were much more likely to mould their personae to the tastes of their fellow Jews.[16]

It does not follow from this, however, that as a result Jewish entertainment was somehow more purely Jewish. Quite the contrary in fact.

Perhaps because of the self-confidence that came from the strength of a vernacular theatre and entertainment industry, it seems that Jewish entertainers became, paradoxically, less culturally pure than their African American counterparts. While, for example, African Americans agonised over whether or not a Carl Van Vechten or a George Gershwin was, or was not, presenting an accurate picture of African American life, Jewish entertainers and musicians appeared to be far happier with eclectic and hybridised styles.

As cultural producers operating between different traditions in the fields of the arts and entertainment Jews played a significant role. A case in point is the part played by Jews in the very early stages of the modern music business. The song writers, musicians and those who turned sheet music into big business who together constituted the cultural phenomenon known as Tin Pan Alley were overwhelmingly Jews from New York's Lower East Side. Borrowing from a variety of musical traditions – including those of the Yiddish theatres and music halls, and African American ragtime – the musicians of Tin Pan Alley created a highly eclectic style that appealed to an extremely broad audience:

> Popular music after 1910 . . . was the single most important ethnic group contribution to the city's commercial culture. It was the almost exclusive creation of the European Jews who had settled on the Lower East Side. . . . What began on the Lower East Side, the Tenderloin, and Harlem became a national phenomenon. (Taylor, 1988: 128)

Another example has been the 'success' of prominent Jewish novelists from Cahan to Saul Bellow in achieving recognition as significant figures in the American, rather than simply the Jewish, literary scene. In a recent study of Jewish and Southern writers, the critic Jules Chametzky argued persuasively, contra the assertions of high modernism, that 'good' American literature always starts from unique experience – ethnic, regional or gendered – and can be said to have 'succeeded' when it then becomes accepted as part of American culture. Jewish and Southern novelists, particularly in the postwar period, have in this way succeeded both in writing novels that are now considered part of the American literary canon, but also in so doing they have established a tradition of placing recognisably Jewish or Southern characters into the narratives of popular culture. This is another way in which Jews have proven successful in negotiating the spaces *between* what are, in the discourse of multiculturalism, seen as separate and discrete cultural identities. The situation of African Americans not recognising, or not being permitted to recognise, their nativity in American culture could not be said about Jews. A consumer of popular American culture today would be hard put not to assume that Jewishness was not in some very real sense an American phenomenon.

There is yet a third sense in which American 'Jewish culture' contains within it the kinds of hybridising and syncretising forces that have recently been labelled postmodern, and this concerns the extent to which Jewish writers, musicians and artists have not simply negotiated the spaces between 'American' and 'Jewish' cultures, they have also generally operated across most of America's ethnic and cultural boundaries. While perhaps of somewhat minor significance, an extremely intriguing example is of the way in which Chinese food could be said to have become a significant part of Jewish culinary culture in New York City (see Tuchman and Levine, 1993). Cuisine is generally taken to be a highly visible mark of cultural distinctiveness. That eating out in Chinese restaurants should become so integrated into Jewish cuisine is a mark of the ways in which Jewish culture particularly in New York, while at one level inward looking, at another level should be so happily syncretic/eclectic.

More generally this example points to the ways in which Jews, particularly in New York in the interwar years, negotiated the spaces between the cultures of the different immigrant groups, the culture of Harlem and that of the American mainstream. The relationship between Jews and Poles in Chicago as described by the Chicago sociologist, and student of Jewish culture in both the Old and the New Worlds, is particularly intriguing in this respect. Commenting on Thomas and Zianecki's acclaimed study of Polish migrants, Wirth wrote:

> The relationship between the Poles and the Jews in Chicago is of especial interest. The two groups detest each other thoroughly, but they live side by side on the West Side, and even more generally on the North-west side. They have a profound feeling of disrespect and contempt for each other, bred by their contiguity and by historical friction in the past; but they trade with each other on Milwaukee Avenue and on Maxwell Street. A study of numerous cases shows that not only do many Jews open their businesses on Milwaukee Street and Division Street because they know that the Poles are the predominant population in these neighborhoods, but the Poles come from all over the city to trade on Maxwell Street because they know that there they can find the familiar street-stands owned by Jews. These two immigrant groups, having lived side by side in Poland and Galicia, are used to each other's business methods. They have accommodated themselves one to another, and this accommodation persists in America. The Pole is not accustomed to a 'one-price store'. When he goes shopping it is not a satisfactory experience unless he can haggle with the seller and 'Jew him down' on prices. (Wirth, 1928, cited in Smith, 1988: 155)

There is no overarching metanarrative of justice here. Instead both Pole and Jew have developed a highly pragmatic cross-cultural discourse in a situation that at other places and other times has been fraught with danger.

The role played by Boas and other radical Jewish intellectuals in the early years of the African American struggle is a further case in point. And it goes without saying that the spaces between African American and Jew were not the only ones negotiated by Boas. As the founder of cultural anthropology in America, Boas in fact made the role of synthesiser, intercultural communicator and translator a professional one.

The relationship between the songwriters of Tin Pan Alley and African American ragtime musicians is a further example of Jews as marginal/interstitial and hybridisers. George Gershwin, who himself got his start on Tin Pan Alley, developed a similar relationship with both jazz musicians and the spiritual choirs – integrating these musics into new musical forms that were neither authentically African American, nor merely a repetition of earlier white musical styles, but which ultimately found an audience far greater than the audience for any particular 'ethnic' music – whether that be Yiddish, African American or European.

There is a general tendency in the literature on Jewish identity to draw hard and fast distinctions between those who have retained that identity – the conservative and the orthodox – and the 'assimilated' Jews. As we have seen, studies of nineteenth century Judaism tend to distinguish between those who followed Moses Mendelssohn and embraced the Enlightenment, hence turning their backs on their unique heritage, and those who for various reasons resisted. We have already had occasion to question this distinction for the nineteenth century, by drawing attention to the creation of a distinctive Jewish subculture precisely among those 'German Jews' who were supposedly the most assimilated. In the case of American Jews, as the above account suggests, the contrast between assimilated and unassimilated must similarly be questioned. For as I have suggested it could be argued that supposedly assimilated Jews – like Franz Boas, Louis Wirth or George Gershwin to name just three – were in fact developing a new kind of relationship to Jewish culture – one that was often quite self-consciously both marginal, but also hybridising and synthesising. Were such Jewish artists, musicians and intellectuals of the interwar years in fact postmodernists *avant la lettre*?

Culturalism, multiculturalism and even a postculturalist discourse of cultural synthesis and hybridity were then, contrary to the impression given by recent writings on the postmodern city, all part of a debate in the United States in the interwar years over the nature and future of major American cities. Paralleling the re-emergence of an expressivist critique of social Darwinism, articulated now within a language of a global cultural mosaic, some American writers, artists and intellectuals were increasingly disinclined to go along with the homogenising implications of programmes aimed at 'Americanising' the large number of urban immigrants – whether from Europe or the American South, instead choosing in one way or another to celebrate their cultural diversity and even in some cases to reconceptualise 'American culture' as a synthesis of many cultures rather than an expression of traditional, pioneer values.

We can then, I think, speak in this period of a genuinely global discourse on culture and difference, one which finds a home for exotic other cultures whether they be located in far-off Bali, nearer home in the American neo-colony of Mexico, or even closer to home in places like Charleston, South Carolina or even in the heartland of modernism, New York City.

Notes

1 In far-off Australia, even middle class school children listen to rap, and favour clothing styles that have their origins in American urban ghettos. National outrage greeted the results

of a newspaper poll of school kids that showed Michael Jordan to be far and away their most popular sporting figure – this in a country where cricket, rugby and Australian rules football are supposed to be the 'national' sports.

2 For a critical discussion of Young's vision of a justice without metanarratives see Harvey (1992).

3 Berkovici's guide is discussed in Kornbluh (1987).

4 A somewhat similar revision of the history of American and European modernism that demonstrates, among other things, the significance both of mainstream culture's concern with cultural otherness both at home and abroad, and of non-Anglo cultural voices has been performed by Peter Woolen (1993).

5 One wonders how many teenagers like myself read *Coming of Age in Samoa* for its message about the cultural contingency of adolescence and how many hoping for some juicy bits.

6 Carl Van Vechten was widely known to be a local 'expert' on Harlem. Like Walter Spies in Bali, Van Vechten was *the* person to be approached by foreign travellers for a tour of Harlem nightspots, or to arrange a party where Harlem's leading characters would be present (see Huggins, 1971: 91ff.).

7 These photographs are reproduced in The Studio Museum in Harlem (1987).

8 As an African American, a woman, and an anthropologist (Hurston was a student of Boas and contemporary of Margaret Mead) Hurston has recently attracted a good deal of attention in anthropology. A recent account of her career by an anthropologist is the one by Deborah Gordon (1990).

9 In the importance they attach to the Southern spiritual both DuBose Heyward and George Gershwin were probably closer to the ideas of the Harlem Renaissance than was Van Vechten whose exotic side of Harlem is defined musically instead by jazz. Ironically it is Byron and Mary, those who have moved furthest from their urban cultural milieu who are the ones interested in spirituals and Africanism.

10 M.G. Smith (1982) in a critical review of *The Harvard Encyclopedia of American Ethnic Groups* shows clearly the kinds of mental contortions that were required to fit both black and white into a single grid of ethnic differentiation.

11 Their significance is marked by the number of pages devoted to each group – twenty-four pages for Afro-Americans, twenty-eight pages for Jews.

12 These early writings are discussed by Baker (1994). Boas's strategy of combating racism in the more popular media continued through the 1920s. See, for example, Boas (1925a, 1925b, 1927).

13 The intellectual and political relationship between Boas and Du Bois is documented in a recent article by Lee Baker (1994)

14 See, for example, Kellner (1992) for a discussion of the construction of postmodern identities. Jencks, too, finds the notion of hybridisation an attractive metaphor when talking about culture and identity in the 1980s (1993: 112ff.).

15 According to a study done in New York in 1920, the average income of Jews on the Lower East Side was, if anything, lower than average incomes in Harlem (see Phillips and Howell, 1920).

16 Huggins too has made a good deal of this distinction (see Huggins, 1971: 286ff.). Much the same can be said about a number of the Harlem Renaissance writers and artists. Rudolph Fisher's *Walls of Jericho* and Claude McKay's *Home to Harlem*, both published in 1928, were both made possible by white patronage, something which, Huggins argues, affected the characterisation and narratives in significant ways. Even Zora Neale Hurston's folklore research was carried out with the support of an influential white patron of Harlem intellectuals, Mrs Rufus Osgood Mason who, it is said, had very firm ideas on the subject of the 'exotic'. The book, significantly, is also dedicated to Carl Van Vechten (see Gordon, 1990).

6

A World System of Culture?

In early 1994 a dress designed for supermodel Claudia Schiffer by Chanel designer Karl Lagerfeld provoked an immediate hostile reaction by a leading Indonesian *ulama*. Lagerfeld, it seems, had based his design on what he took to be the calligraphic notation of a Persian love poem, learning only later that what he had in fact borrowed was a Koranic verse. At pains to defuse the situation Chanel's chief executive immediately apologised to the director of the Grand Mosque of Paris, who in turn professed himself happy with the apology and the promise that the design would be withdrawn.

*

New Zealand Pakeha (white) artist Dick Frizzell attracted the ire of Maori artists after an exhibition at Auckland's Gow Langsford Gallery in 1992 of a series of 'irreverent' works that re-presented Maori motifs through a variety of western artistic styles. (Leonard and McCormack, 1993)

*

'I should charge for being a psychiatrist. They [employers] tickle me; sometimes they come and ask me questions and talk to me about their problems like I'm a doctor. They tell me *I'm* the only one they can talk to. They even ask me to pray for them; they act like black folks' prayers are different or like I have a direct line to the Lord'. (African American domestic quoted in Mary Romero, 1992: 112)

*

Recently at the conclusion of an Australian football match, a tremendously skilful Aboriginal player, provoked by the racist taunts of opposing fans, bared his chest to the crowd and proclaimed his pride in his blackness and Aboriginality. The incident received wide press coverage and gave rise to a good deal of very public soul searching about the extent of racism in sport – almost all of it very sympathetic to the player. All might have returned to normal had it not been for a press conference held by the Chairman of the club whose fans had instigated the incident who offered the view that as long as Aborigines adhered to 'conventional' behavioural standards, then they could be expected to be treated with the dignity they deserved. Problems arose, he said, when they did not behave like white people. These remarks led to widespread public furore – the Chairman was himself attacked for giving voice to racist sentiments, he was forced into an inarticulate apology and, on his subsequent visit to the Northern Territory – whose local aboriginal football teams have provided the Australian league with some of its finest players – was plagued by boycotts. One ex-footballer even painted up and placed a supposedly traditional tribal curse on him at a dinner given in his honour.

*

In one of his many speeches in which he has largely succeeded in turning himself into one of that select band of 'elder statesmen' Lee Kuan Yew, formerly Prime Minister of Singapore, told his audience: 'If you bring a child into the world in the West, the state cares for him. If you bring a child into Asia, that's your personal responsibility. . . . As long as our society remains in this traditional way, we will be different. We will not allow muggers to clonk you on the head and grab your belongings and leave you dying or dead on the streets' (cited in Jasper, 1994: 34f.)

We live in a world characterised not just by difference, but by a consuming and erotic passion for it. Gone are the metanarratives by which modernist thinkers sought to interpret the world through simplistic Enlightenment universalisms. But gone too are the forces of modernism and cultural imperialism that have operated in the past to constitute a homogeneous world after images constructed in eighteenth century European bourgeois thought, hence making it possible for those of postmodern sensitivity at the same time to fear and marvel at that difference which is thereby revealed to them.

And because our economy can satisfy a multiplicity of consumer niches, so there is a form of difference to suit every taste. The would-be dictator prefers the taste of 'traditionally' Asian forms of 'strong leadership' provided by the real-life dictators of Asia; middle class parents look to 'ethnic' maids to provide their domestic life with cultural meanings absent outside it; the postmodern *flaneur* indulges a kind of fearful exultation in urban ethnicity. We are, in short, now free to consume difference and to consume it publicly, wherever we find it. We no longer need feel guilty at our desire to avoid the canonical pronouncements of those arbiters of good taste, the aesthetic avant-garde. Are we not told on the contrary that that modernist aesthetic was stultifying, even fascistic? Moreover, we need no longer fear that our experiences of difference will be denounced as inauthentic. We exalt in our ability to confound the high priests of modernity by changing our identities on a whim precisely by changing the forms of difference we consume, even by playfully consuming more than one identity at any one time. Recognising difference is, in short, an exhilaration, indeed a liberation, allowing us to expose the false universalism of the Enlightenment utopia.

There is, at the same time, a dark side to all this. The process by which human beings are differentiated in the contemporary world has consequences which, if not intended, are nonetheless a logical outgrowth of the ways in which that difference has come to be conceived. Observing the European scene, Pierre Taguieff has written of what he calls a new 'cultural racism' which inscribes the discourse of cultural difference into projects that were previously grounded in a biological fragmentation of the human species:

> il est temps que le mouvement antiraciste . . . prenne conscience de la rupture qui s'est opérée dans les représentations et les argumentations racistes elaborées, à savoir le *déplacement de l'inégalité biologique vers l'absolutisation de la différence culturelle*, et en tire les conséquences pour le type ou le style du combat à venir.' (Taguieff, 1992: 15)

And no one needs reminding of the horrors of events in Rwanda and the former Yugoslavia where difference is once again proving reason enough for genocide.

Yet what does it mean to say that cultural difference has become global? Consider the current popularity of the idea of a global culture. For students of the global condition it has become almost an article of faith to maintain, against those who earlier suggested that the global reach of modernism would ultimately produce a more homogeneous world culture, that the world has become increasingly interconnected – economically, politically, but just as importantly culturally – and increasingly culturally differentiated at the same time. Echoing this sentiment a leading spokesperson for the school argues that the current 'process of globalization', contrary to earlier expectations of an increasingly homogeneous world, 'leads to an increasing sensitivity to differences', a 'paradoxical consequence' of the fact that:

> the flows of information, knowledge, money, commodities, people and images have intensified to the extent that the sense of spatial distances which separated and insulated people from the need to take into account all the other people which make up what has become known as humanity has become eroded. In effect, we are all in each other's backyard. (Featherstone, 1993: 169f.)

Surely recent cultural theorists have been correct to point to the shortcomings of earlier theories of global cultural homogeneity. As Stephen Greenblatt's discussion of the way the Balinese put 'imperial' technologies like VCRs to their own cultural use cited earlier shows, commodities do not necessarily carry the cultures of their place of manufacture with them, and 'other cultures' are perfectly capable, indeed frequently do read them in ways very different from the way they are read in the imperial cores of the world economy. Nor is it any longer the case that cultural flows are entirely one way – the disjunctures between the global flows of peoples, commodities, money and cultures ensure an increasingly differentiated global landscape of culture (see Appadurai, 1990).

But is it really this simple? Does the concept of an internally heterogeneous global culture really capture what is going on? First, if symbols/images/commodities are read so differently from one culture to another, what is really global about global culture? Do we not have to do here once again with a classical anthropological view of a world made up of a plurality of largely unrelated systems of cultural meaning only superficially connected by signs or material objects? How then does the current age of communications revolution really differ from earlier periods when cultural contact was similarly intensive?

Second, in spite of all their talk about the need to take cultural factors seriously, many students of the global condition fall into the trap of assuming that 'global culture' is somehow an objective rather than an interpretive reality. In fact, of course, it is not and we are entitled to wonder whose interpretive reality it is. Are we to understand that 'global culture' is a shared, that is homogeneous, meaning or is it too subject to different readings depending on where one stands within it? Clearly, for example, an Asian mapping of the globe would depart significantly from the maps drawn by western intellectuals. What are we to make of *this* disjuncture?

Third, globalisation theorists, with some notable exceptions, do not seem to know whether the diversity they have discovered is external or internal to the processes of global capitalist development, the global spread of the modern nation state, and so on. Do we have here to do with a homogeneous 'western' culture superficially imposed upon a pre-existing and still vital cultural diversity? Or is the diversity of local situations constituted out of the expansion of the West?[1] And if the latter, is this differentiation of cultural meanings something that is relatively recent, a consequence as Featherstone suggests of recent changes in the techniques of communication? Or did it happen some time earlier, with the European voyages of the sixteenth century, or the free trade imperialism of the early nineteenth, or the period of classical colonialism after the middle of the last century?[2]

The problems raised for globalisation theory by questions such as these can it seems be more effectively addressed when we recognise that many globalisation theorists share with earlier writers on the cultural homogenisation of the world the misleading assumption that only with 'globalisation', that is only with the expansion of the West beyond its cultural boundaries, does the issue of cultural diversity arise. It might be better to see current patterns of cultural diversification as in some sense a continuation on a global level of processes that were built into modernisation from the very start. And if so can one perhaps speak of both universalising and particularising threads in the processes of cultural globalisation, either contemporary or at different times in the past? And if the latter then what are the factors that account for culturally differentiating processes within what is now a globalised modern condition?

There is clearly something rather specific about the current discourse of a culturally differentiated world. Many are coming to see the current 'taste' for difference as a very recent phenomenon. Here I want to suggest that in fact our current concerns about multiculturalism, postcolonialism, the validity of the 'anthropological' project, and so on are a part of a particular phase in the history of modernity and globalisation – one that has its origins in a specific period, namely the interwar years, one that may now be drawing to an end with the apparent decline of American hegemony in the global system. Yet at the same time the notion of a 'world of difference', so central to the images of the globe that circulate in current cultural theory is, far from being objective fact, instead only a particular take on the world, one that originates particularly in the United States. Here too we may speak of a 'cultural globalisation', that is a process by which people throughout the world come to employ a discourse of culture and difference, using the same or similar categories that developed in the American context, but articulated this time more often in very different projects.

I have stressed at the outset that I am interested primarily in cultural difference as an important signifier in the discourse of modernity, rather than in other cultures out there in the world. As many others have also argued, notions like culture, other cultures, cultural difference and so on, are cognitive structures with a significance which is more or less independent of the world they seek to represent. Put most simply, I assume that 'culture' is a cultural construction.

'Culture' as Cultural Construction

There are, in fact, two problems with the image of a culturally diverse world that lead us to its discursive dimensions. The first, on which most attention has focused, arises from the fact that the project of, variously, describing, translating or interpreting 'other cultures' contains a fatal flaw in so far as it can never genuinely succeed in locating these cultures except in relation to, and hence within the culture of, the person doing the interpreting. The argument that the western texts that purport to describe the 'culture' of this or that group of people are cultural artefacts of 'the West' and hence have little to do with otherness at all is by now, a relatively standard one – in part a consequence of a poststructuralist revolution in the treatment of anthropological texts, and in part the result of a postcolonial critique of western discourses. The problem is clearly evident in the 'poetics' of Jencks's representation of a multicultural Los Angeles characterised by, in his terms, a 'switching of voices'. This is reminiscent of the claim of 'dialogical' ethnography – textual accounts of other cultures which give a place to the voice of the other – so effectively criticised by Stephen Tyler when he wrote:

> Those who would make . . . dialogue the focus of ethnography are in a sense correct, for dialogue *is* the source of text, but dialogue rendered as text, which must be the consequence, is no longer dialogue, but a text masquerading as a dialogue, a mere monologue about a dialogue since the informant's appearances in the dialogue are at best mediated through the ethnographer's authorial role. While it is laudable to include the native, his position is not thereby improved, for his words are still only instruments of the ethnographer's will. And if dialogue is intended to protect the ethnographer's authority by shifting the burden of truth from the ethnographer's words to the natives' it is even more reprehensible for no amount of invoking the 'other' can establish him as the agent of the words and deeds attributed to him . . . unless he, too, is free to reinterpret it and flesh it out with caveats, apologies, footnotes, and explanatory

detail . . . These, then, are not dialogues, but sophistic texts like those pretences at dialogue perpetuated by Plato. (Quoted in Marcus and Cushman, 1982: 44)

The point is that the voice is not the voice of the other, it is the voice of the author, simply spoken in different tones. Does not the same apply to 'hetero-architecture' – does it really speak different voices, or is it a single architectural subject speaking different tones of his own architectural voice?

But there is here a second problem, less often discussed in current debates over who is and should be authorised to speak about other cultures, for it will be noted that the conclusion about postmodern poetics does little to undermine the assumption that these other cultures are still 'out there', that the modern world is still a cultural mosaic – it is only that now individuals can never hope to escape the boundaries of their own particular corner of it.

But regardless of who is permitted to speak it, this language of cultural differentiation is artificial. A child examining a television screen through a magnifying glass is surprised to find that the images constructed by the brain bear an imperfect relationship to that collection of separate coloured dots that make up the television image. The cultural imaginary takes the dots for something more than technique, as though the dots of colour represented reality itself. But of course the procedure of drawing discrete circles in cultural space is quite clearly an arbitrary one, or shall we say is possible only by reference to things external to that space – from the realms of geography, governance, politics and the like. Otherwise cultures can be seen to merge one into another (as do the dots in television pictures).

It is intriguing to note that many have been quite prepared to abandon the concept of race on precisely these grounds, namely that it is impossible to centre discrete and unchanging human groups on the phenotypic features for so long considered the defining characteristics of races – skin colour, facial features, hair quality, and so on. But is this flaw specific to the idea of *a* race? Is not the notion of *a* culture formally identical? Those markers used to assign people to one or other of the world's cultures are equally ambiguous, and are far from enabling us to demarcate discrete, to say nothing of unchanging cultural groups – the Balinese, the Indians of Chiapas, the 'gullah Negroes' of South Carolina – except by reference to a necessarily arbitrary enclosed space.

This can be illustrated with regard to any of those other cultures beloved of classical anthropology – that locating them requires a spatial centring that cannot be easily justified by reference to 'cultural traits' alone. Take, for example, the account of Bali offered by the Norwegian anthropologist Frederick Barth. 'Observe the litany' he writes, 'of authorities within the tradition that make conflicting claims to be heard in Bali-Hinduism's variously instituted liturgies and priesthoods', among whom he lists the Sanskrit manuscripts, the highest-ranking priests, the main body of temple priests, the family and descent group priests, the deceased ancestors and the gods. Add to Barth's own list Indonesian government officials,

Balinese politicians and aspiring politicians, people promoting Bali as a tourist destination, the cultural performers, musicians and dancers. Add further to Barth's list the voices of non-Balinese also seeking to represent 'Balinese culture' – the artist Walter Spies, the anthropologists Gregory Bateson and Margaret Mead, the anthropologist cum cartoonist cum travel writer Miguel Covarrubias, contemporary observers like Clifford Geertz and Stephen Greenblatt, and Barth himself. 'To approach such a raucous cacophony of authoritative voices with the expectations that their messages and their teaching will be coherent', and hence to hope to put together a single authentic account of 'Balinese culture' on the basis of consistent patterns which run through the accounts of all these authorities would, says Barth, require a very 'dogmatic anthropologist' (Barth, 1989: 127f.).

Of course anthropologists and others are increasingly coming to recognise the indistinctiveness of the intellectual operations involved in producing this spatial imaginary of cultures, a fact manifest in the contemporary romancing of what are currently called 'borderlands', that is areas between cultures where diverse cultural influences produce ambiguity, paradox and cultural pastiche (see for example Fischer, 1992); or the discovery/ construction of diasporas which also point to the difficulty of the spatial metaphor in the cultural imaginary (see for example Appadurai, 1993). But in challenging the fixity of cultural boundaries, these discoveries in fact serve to preserve the myth of the cultural centre – since cultural impurities are seen to exist only when one moves away from the purity of the centre. Borderlands acquire their distinctiveness, their capacity to fascinate, only because they stand in contrast to the idea of a pure cultural centre. But now that the colours on our map are merging one to another, centres, like boundaries, become arbitrary points in cultural space, acquiring their significance only when something outside that infinite variation is imposed, thus defining this or that point on the map as the focus of cultural purity. Cultures, like races, 'no longer exist'.

But what possible good can it do to assert that – at least twentieth century – 'cultural pluralism' is a language or a discourse, that is to put it bluntly that 'cultures' are a cultural construct? I would want to argue that a strategy that seeks to subvert identity politics by engaging in free identity play is, at least on its own, relatively unhelpful. The charge of racial or cultural essentialism is all too often used as a stick with which to beat movements and discourses seeking to challenge the hegemony of western universalising practices. We are very quick to speak of creolisation, imaginary or invented traditions, or cultural inauthenticity when we are talking of discourses with which we are out of sympathy. But such denunciations can only be legitimised by a hidden appeal to pure, real and/ or authentic cultural traditions, notably western ones. And is it not equally impossible to define a purely western or European culture without recourse to culturally-arbitrary signifiers – notably those manipulated by western state apparatuses which manipulate symbols of cultural purity in order to bring them into line with already-existing political boundaries? No matter how carefully one works to define the uniqueness of western cultures one will also find difference lurking not just in their borderlands but at their cores.

Instead of continually pointing to the 'constructedness' of culture, the concept of cultural pluralism might be added to the concepts of race, gender and nation discussed by the anthropologist Michael Taussig who maintains that:

> When it was enthusiastically pointed out within memory of our present Academy that race or gender or nation . . . were so many social constructions, inventions and representations, a window was opened, an invitation to begin the critical project of analysis and cultural reconstruction was offered. And one still feels its power even though what was nothing more than an invitation, a preamble to investigation has, by and large, been converted instead into a conclusion – eg. 'sex is a social construction', 'race is a social construction' , 'the nation is an invention', and so forth, the tradition of invention. The brilliance of this pronouncement was blinding. Nobody was asking what's the next step? What do we do with this old insight? If life is constructed how come it appears so immutable? How come culture appears so natural? . . .
>
> No matter how sophisticated we may be as to the constructed and arbitrary character of our practices, including our practices of representation, our practice of practices is one of actively forgetting such mischief each time we open our mouths to ask for something or make a statement. Try to imagine what would happen if we didn't in daily practice thus conspire to actively forget what Saussure called 'the arbitrariness of the sign'? Or . . . [t]ry to imagine living in a world whose signs were indeed 'natural'. (1993: xvi–xviii)

Cultural pluralism indeed appears natural. To play on an old anthropological distinction, it is or has become, like race, a very powerful 'folk concept'. But this must be qualified. In their time-worn contrast between 'folk' and observers' models – between what many are accustomed to terming the 'emic' and 'etic' – anthropologists have generally assumed that 'folk models' were just that – the cultural constructs of the other. In fact, if nothing else, the above discussion of the development of a discourse of cultural difference demonstrates that it has been intellectuals more than any other group who have proven most committed to this particular 'folk model'. 'Cultures', as we have come to understand them, are part of the languages of a Traven and a Heyward, a Bartók and a Spies, a Van Vechten and a Diego Rivera, an Edward Said, a Stephen Greenblatt, a Clifford Geertz and a Lyotard. As the above examples show, cultural otherness is also part of the discourse of French fashion designers and Islamic intellectuals; New Zealand artists both *pakeha* and Maori, as well as of the editors of upmarket art magazines who are happy to represent both; professional football players and their employers, as well as the Australian media now sensitised to the racism they used unthinkingly to articulate, and prepared to speak sympathetically of the cultural integrity of Australia's indigenous inhabitants; Anglo employers of African American domestics as well as the academic authors of 'radical' accounts of Anglo-racism. We may be none the wiser about the world views of the typical Balinese, Native American, African American or Hungarian,

Muslim or New Zealander, Aborigine or white Australian. But of the cultural vision of the world's intellectuals, we now know a good deal. 'Culture' is a cultural construct of the intellectuals.

But as the above quote from Taussig suggests such a statement when continuously repeated confuses the purpose of cultural critique with its starting point. The next step involves asking why it is that even having recognised its conceptual status, cultural otherness should seem to have a life of its own. The preliminary answer given in this case is that the discourse of cultural difference is more than the endpoint of a process of purely academic reflection. Like other such concepts – such as class, race, nation, gender, and so on – it is also a mode of being. Those who believe the world is made up of a diversity of cultures are also impelled to act singularly and collectively in ways which, as it were, make it so. As a consequence, not only is the discourse of cultural difference an important part of the culture of modernism in different parts of the world in so far as it is part of a process of the production and reproduction of modern social life, so cultural difference too is part of the modern condition not just in the West, but now throughout the globe as well.

How, then, can we account for the development of the modern language of cultural difference, a language that as we have seen achieved genuinely global reach at least by the time of the interwar years, when it appears sometimes to have replaced, or at least constituted a significant challenge to, the 'social Darwinist' discourse of nineteenth century Britain, France and the United States? Sometimes drawing explicitly on concepts and categories that were first clearly articulated in the thought of German intellectuals in the nineteenth century, sometimes reinventing them altogether, culturalism took hold of artists, musicians, novelists and intellectuals in central and eastern Europe, Africa and Asia, and in the Americas, North and South.

A common explanation, as we have seen, accounts for the current state of global culture to the development of new communication technologies. But as I have pointed out, the modern discourse of cultural pluralism in fact has its origins in the interwar years, not in the much more recent 'information age'. In any event it must be asked why an increase in information should lead us to construct humanity as a fragmented rather than a unitary category, since in other places and other times such encounters have had just the opposite effect, that is the subsumption of the other within a general understanding of what it is to be human.[3] Surely, therefore, we need to explain under what circumstances 'knowledge' of humanity is integrated into a particular discourse of cultural difference, and the notion of globality on its own cannot do so.

Of course globalism in the particular form of the globalisation of European polity, economy and culture *is* one context within which concern with human difference did arise, something that goes some way towards explaining the language of cultural and racial difference in nineteenth century imperial ideology in general, and 'social Darwinism' in particular.

But, as we have suggested, while the language of empire is still with us, since the first few years of this century it has had to compete with an equally, if not more powerful, culturalist language explicitly opposed to it, a language that came to characterise the discourse of both colonialist and counter-colonialist alike. To also characterise this new ideology as imperial would be to so generalise the concept of empire as to explain everything and nothing at the same time. If there is indeed something specific about the nature and role of representations of other cultures in classical colonial contexts, then surely there will be differences between these and, say, the representation of India in the writings of nineteenth century German writers or of Japan in twentieth century America, neither of which arise in a colonial context *sensu stricto*; or in twentieth century colonial contexts which differ significantly from those of the nineteenth. And without subscribing to the myth of intellectual objectivity, is it sensible to assume that intellectuals are inevitably captive of ruling colonial discourses? Even a crude class theory would need to take account of the rather particular class location of intellectuals before linking their discourse on cultural difference directly to the interests of 'capital', 'the state', or 'empire' Once again our explanations are too simplistic and generalised to be of much use in exploring the patently different ways in which cultural otherness has been represented, even in the modern West.

Perhaps it is, then, the rise of postmodernism, that incredulity towards the metanarratives of (western) modernity that accounts for a renewed interest in alternative languages and voices? In one sense this explanation makes a good deal of sense – a postmodern sensibility is almost co-terminous with an interest in cultural difference/otherness. And yet the circumstances that permit the postmodern escape from modernity them-selves need to be explained. And in any case, as much of the previous discussion has suggested, we need at the very least to examine more closely the roots of postmodernism within the history of modernism (while at most we might question the extent to which postmodernism genuinely super-sedes modernism). For example, in the previous chapter, it was argued that the rather particular circumstances of Jewish American intellectuals, writers and musicians in the interwar years contributed to their identity as cultural synthesisers and hybridisers. And surely one reason why contem-porary cultural theorists began to abandon western metanarratives when and where they did was precisely because the 'other' now had a voice, and used it to deny westerners the right to speak it as they had in the past (see Said, 1989). Postmodernism seems effect rather than cause in the produc-tion of a world obsessed by cultural difference and identity.

This leads, of course, to the postcolonial alternative – that it is not the postmodern critique, or globalisation per se, that has led to the current state of affairs. It is instead the 'voice' of the 'subaltern' other finally breaking through. Culture and identity are on the cultural agenda in New Zealand precisely because Maori artists are now empowered to publicly denounce the way they are represented by a Pakeha artist like Frizzell.

Chanel must now be sensitive to cultural otherness because Islamic voices previously silenced by orientalism can now speak back.

Surely this is once again too simplistic to account for the variety and different uses of images of cultural difference that circulate and have circulated in the modern world. Can all discourse on cultural otherness really be so easily categorised as either colonial or post(or anti-)colonial? Take once again the case of the New Zealand artist discussed here. At first sight this would appear to be a case of a simple clash between a colonial discourse (articulated by Frizzell) and a postcolonial one (articulated by his Maori critics). But what should we make of the fact that both these voices in fact appear *in the same text*, an article in a mainstream arts magazine? Or of the fact that Frizzell has made a conscious intervention in a debate over the use of Maori images in the iconography of New Zealand identity that has been going on for at least twenty years? Does the text cited here, written by a non-Maori, because it mobilises the views of certain Maori artists really speak the authentic voice of Maoriness? And, to be more controversial, do the Maori artists quoted therein themselves speak directly the voice of a Maori culture suppressed for centuries by European representations? Does the subaltern remain a subaltern when he/she speaks in the academy?[4]

Much the same could be said of the case of Chanel. Whose voice is the colonial one and whose the postcolonial: the designer, the Indonesian *ulama*, the chief executive of Chanel, the director of the Paris mosque, the author of the newspaper article, or its readership? Yes, clearly the sudden clamour of 'other voices' is important, but why it should be that such other voices are being heard now, and whether they were always silent in the past, needs further investigation. The articulation of the voices of the subalternist intellectual and that of the hegemonised voice that he/she claims to speak needs to be more carefully examined.

Such paradoxes have led some to argue that the postcolonial and postmodern critiques of canonical texts that are so closely linked to the current project of cultural differentiation have been the instrumentalist project of certain intellectuals seeking the material/cultural rewards offered by the Academy (see for example Sangren, 1988). Modern intellectuals have been integrally involved in the articulation of cultural identities (see for example Smith, 1983). Indeed defining cultural identity is by definition part of the modern intellectual project. But this kind of instrumentalist critique is inadequate partly because it fails to establish that the rewards are really all that great, and partly because of its staggering sociological naivety in treating intellectual culture (or more accurately the intellectual culture of those with whom one disagrees) as though it could be entirely explained by self-interest. In offering the above analysis of the rise of 'postmodern anthropology', Sangren makes no attempt to explain his own, hostile, position in similar terms. In short one cannot speak of genuine reflexivity unless one is reflexive about one's own position as well ⌐at of others.

This leads us finally to the somewhat apocalyptic vision of the decline of western civilisation that has been provoked by the recent celebrations of multiculturalism. At one level such a vision is extremely naive to the extent that it rests on an essentialised view of western culture. Despair at the cultural disintegration of the West derives its legitimacy from a hidden appeal to pure, real and/or authentic western cultural traditions, something it would be impossible to specify without recourse to culturally-arbitrary signifiers – notably those provided by western state apparatuses which manipulate symbols of cultural purity in order to bring them into line with already-existing political boundaries.[5]

And yet there is clearly a link between prevailing patterns of global political and economic hegemony and the processes of cultural globalisation, although not the one articulated by those who bemoan the erosion of 'traditional western values'. As we shall see the rise of the model of a global multiculturalism is embedded in the processes through which the United States rose to pre-eminence in the global system. And the evidence of its decline may well be a consequence of the demise of the political and economic hegemony of the United States qua nation state.

Most of these accounts of cultural difference have, therefore, proved inadequate to the task of evaluating the role played by the discourse of cultural difference in the culture of late modernity, its ethical and political ramification and its implications for what is usually presumed to be its opposite, supposedly universalistic discourses of freedom and emancipation. And as the above suggests one reason for this lack is our inability to see the idea of cultural difference in anything but black and white terms – it is either embraced as liberating or denounced as threat, it is always either imperial or counter-imperial – and the project of constructing it is inevitably treated as a monolithic one. In fact as we have seen constructing humanity as a culturally fragmented category has been associated with political projects of both the left and the right, with regimes of domination as well as with movements for liberation, with a politics of identity but also of cosmopolitanism.

Moreover, there have been and continue to be very different conceptions of culture and difference in modern discourse – culture is sometimes seen as immutable, sometimes as infinitely manipulable, differences sometimes taken to be insuperable and at other times translatable. In particular, an important distinction must be made between what might be termed anthropological and hermeneutic languages of difference.

Anthropology versus Hermeneutics

A curious presupposition appears to derail much of the current debate on culture and difference. The curious presupposition to which I refer is that in spite of the fact that modern society has been, from its very inception, both discursively and sociologically 'multicultural', despite the fact in other words that what we have in the late twentieth century come to call multiculturalism could be said to have been constitutive of both modernism and modernisation, many continue to think of cultural difference as though it somehow lay outside modernity.

This presupposition is evident, for example, in the assertions of a Jean-François Lyotard about the alterity-to-modernity of both the Cashinahua (who are *non*-modern) and of himself (who is *post*-modern), or of a Stephen Greenblatt who argues for the radical alterity of the 'Balinese'. In their assertions about the radical alterity of 'other cultures', these contemporary writers are articulating a classical anthropological notion of cultural otherness, producing in their texts an unmediated account of these other cultures as though they were external to the author and the society from which he/she comes. As often expressivist critiques of modernism as they are modern justifications of empire, such anthropological texts appear to advocate an escape from modernity predicated upon the existence of other worlds. As such these texts construct a Bali, an Indian village, even a quarter of a modern city as an alien world – mysterious, free of modern contamination, a world into which only the author can escape, and from which he/she can launch a critique of modernity.

Contemporary anthropology frequently retains this rhetoric of an alien world, something which it achieves by writing out of ethnographic texts all evidence of the encounter between the society from which the ethnographer comes and the world into which he/she has disappeared, and reporting back an account of life 'over there' as though it were completely unmediated either by the ethnographer or his/her predecessors.

The image of otherness, of culture and difference, that emerges from this *anthropological* language of difference is an image of a world of discrete and bounded cultures (our own just one of the many) – providing for the scientist so many separate laboratories to test scientific propositions, for the cultural critic so many examples of how differently things can be arranged. This is the language of authenticity – 'anthropological' accounts are either authentic or inauthentic; cultures are either 'real', and hence worthy of our interest, or they are synthetic, creolised, invented – and hence unworthy of our attentions.

This 'anthropological' language of culture and difference is, I would argue, an exclusivist one, a language that can be and frequently has been harnessed to the view that the world, or the nation, is made up of irreconcilably different groups of people. This exclusivist anthropological language, I would suggest, whether embedded in hegemonic projects, or in movements that counter existing cultural hegemonies, is inevitably linked with a project of power and domination. It is, one suspects, an inevitably statist ideology, whether employed by the state or by those seeking to challenge a particular mode of exercising state power. Under such conditions, I would argue, culturalism can become indistinguishable from racism. Apart from its uses in the writings of many contemporary anthropologists, such 'anthropological' language of radical cultural alterity is, for example, clearly manifest in the 'ethnic' conflicts in the former Yugoslavia. It is no longer a case of a 'civilising' imperial ideology to be sure, but it is a poor replacement for it.

However, as we have seen, the *anthropological* is not the only form taken by the modern language of culture and difference. While Béla Bartók retained an anthropological language in his (musical) representation of the Hungarian peasantry, from the 1920s his musical expressions changed rather dramatically. No longer did he write music purporting to be an authentic representation of the (musical) culture of the Hungarian peasantry – he now composed fusions or syntheses. These later works did not – and did not claim to – reflect an already existing, authentic peasant music. Nor were they mere continuations of earlier, Germanic, musical traditions. They were something new. Bartók's music provides a counterweight to the anthropological language of cultural difference. To see his musical representations of otherness as something new, in the same way as Gershwin saw his own music as arising out of an encounter with, but not claiming to reproduce/speak for African American jazz and spirituals, is to see them as *hermeneutic* rather than anthropological. One is here reminded of those radical Indonesian journalists of the 1920s who sought, not to simply resurrect 'tradition' or 'custom', but out of the fusion between custom and European notions of freedom and emancipation to create something new – an emancipation without the bland or even hegemonising cosmopolitanism of the French *philosophes*, the English utilitarians.

The language here is, perforce, not a language of authenticity, of discrete and mutually unintelligible cultures. A hermeneutic account of cultures and difference cannot assume that there are no connections between 'alien' worlds; it must locate the particular act of cultural interpretation within the context of the history of the act of cultural interpretation in general, and of encounters between the 'us' and the 'them' of ethnographic discourse in particular. B. Traven does not write as though Chiapas were first discovered by him – the bloodletting by the Spanish, the exploitation by gringos, the cultural brokers like himself are all there. Zora Neale Hurston does not write as though America were not actually occupying Haiti when she arrived to study Haitian culture.[6]

Hermeneutic languages of culture and difference, in contrast to anthropological ones, are inclusive rather than exclusive. By this I refer to the ways in which appeals to cultural differentiation represent a challenge to universalism, or better to the universalisation of what are in fact particularistic discourses. Such challenges, of course, are not restricted to discourses of cultural liberation. Feminism, for example, has long challenged the attempt to universalise what it takes to be androcentric discourses to all of humanity. In much the same way a hermeneutic language of cultural difference represents a challenge to attempts by hegemonic groups to impose their particular vision of the universal human condition on others. The implication here is not that universalism is itself of necessity a bad thing, only that existing universalisms are in fact particularistic. The conclusion to be drawn from such a project is an inclusive one, to the extent that it represents a plea for new, non-hegemonic forms of interaction and communication among diverse peoples. In this sense a hermeneutic language of cultural difference may play an important emancipatory role.

Doubtless the discourse of culture and difference is fractured along other lines as well. The point is that no simple and generalised 'explanation' proves adequate to the task of analysing and evaluating the role played by notions of cultural difference in the culture of modernity and in the discourse of the participants in modern mass social movements, politicians and populist leaders, political elites, colonial rulers, theologians, advertising executives, artists, musicians, novelists and academics, western and eastern. Given the overwhelming focus in the preceding chapters, by way of conclusion I want merely to offer some remarks on why it should be that in a particular period, it should have come to appear at least to some intellectuals and artists (rather than either the 'masses' or political elites), that the world was made up of a large number of distinctive cultures, rather than, as was previously thought, a diversity of peoples who could be ranked within existing racial or civilisational hierarchies, and why such images of cultural diversity should have been consumed so widely. Any attempt to answer this question requires two somewhat separate kinds of discussion: first, about the kind of globe that confronted these intellectuals and, second, about their own changing role within it.

A New Global Order in the Interwar Years

Classical social philosophy, as it developed in the nineteenth century particularly in Britain and France, while in many ways differentiated internally, and with certain notable exceptions, nonetheless was more or less united in the assumption that the modern social world would come to take on a homogeneous form – a form anticipated in the philosophy and political economy of the Enlightenment. What is commonly called social Darwinism in particular, while maintaining that eighteenth century social philosophy was naive in its commitment to a rational view of history and society, nonetheless accepted that the 'laws' of history and society would result ultimately in the achievement of the utopia of eighteenth century liberalism – a (future) society which, through technological and scientific advancement, industrialisation and political emancipation, would be characterised by an advanced division of labour and the liberation of autonomous human subjects from the ties of tradition and tyranny. No society as yet, it is true, had achieved this liberal utopia, but certain nations – particularly Britain and France – were assumed to be much closer to it than any other. The Marxist tradition certainly took issue with this typical nineteenth century social evolutionism in certain key respects. But Marxists were also generally wedded to the vision of a liberal utopia which needed to be achieved before it would in turn be superseded by the yet more rational system of socialism. Social Darwinism also had other sorts of critics, particularly in Germany as we have seen. But even here the language of progress through what Spencer called the differentiation of function within modern society was largely retained. Nineteenth century populists and conservatives alike merely placed a different value judgement on progress – bemoaning the loss of tradition rather than rejoicing in it.

By the end of the nineteenth century, however, severe doubts began to arise, at least in Europe, about the validity of this nineteenth century intellectual heritage. The prominence of *fin de siècle* thinkers – such as Freud, who drew our attention to the significance of the unconscious and the repressive facet of civilisation; or Weber, who raged against the 'iron cage' of a modern society governed by the principles of instrumental rationality; or the English Fabians who saw in the liberal project of emancipation an opportunity for the strong to prey unimpeded on the weak; or even Emile Durkheim who came to despair in his search for an integrating morality in modern society – testifies to an increasing disillusion with the classical narratives of modernity. By the 1920s, the most influential intellectual systems in Europe, and to some extent in the United States, were characterised by at least a sceptical attitude towards nineteenth century narratives of modernisation and capitalist development, and equally importantly, of the prevailing positivist epistemologies. Equally worthy of mention are the different but equally relativising linguistic theories of Saussure, Wittgenstein and Benjamin Whorf; the ontological philosophies of Rozenschweig and Heidegger; quantum physics (wave theory of matter) pioneered by Erwin Schrödinger, Max Born, Werner Heisenberg, Wolfgang Pauli and others in the mid-1920s; the relativism of early cultural anthropology; institutionalism in economic theory. Together these contribute to the picture of a substantial relativisation and questioning of the epistemological foundations of knowledge taking place in the early decades of the twentieth century.

Part of the reason for the emergence of what Robertson has called a global relativism by the time of the interwar years, a renewed despair of civilisation and of reason, was clearly that the world was not going according to plan. In general, Europeans may not have been particularly concerned about the ravages being wrought by colonialism from the end of the nineteenth century, but they could not help but be struck by the contrast between the aspirations of modernism and the brutal realities of the First World War.

But in other ways too the world was stubbornly refusing to follow the plan. For example, in the economic realm it was an article of faith that the application of science and of industrial organisation would bring untold material benefits to the modern world. Traditional farming systems and traditional systems of manufacture were to be swept away, to be replaced by more efficient, technologically advanced, large-scale production units. Taylor and Henry Ford promised that scientific management and the latest technology would transform American manufacturing, sweeping away the sweatshops and replacing them by large-scale, clean factories full of happy company *men*. In the colonial world modern plantations and mines, new systems of transportation and communication (shipping, railways, the telegraph) would generate heretofore untold levels of prosperity, bringing the benefits of western science and industry to all the peoples of the world. Even the social democratic critics of these forms of capitalist modernity accepted the benefits of the new capitalist regime. By creating a strong proletariat in both industry and agriculture, by sweeping away 'reactionary' classes like 'feudal' landlords and 'backward' peasantries, capitalist modernisation could only pave the way for a socialist system within which the benefits of scale and technology would be even greater.

But things did not seem to work out quite this way. Consider, for example, the nature of rural transformation in the period from the end of the nineteenth century.

Agrarian Change and Rural Dispossession

The scope and pace of the changes to the global landscape brought about by the world-wide agrarian transformation that began towards the end of the last century was nothing short of staggering. In spite of the major role assigned to the so-called 'industrial revolution' in much of the literature on the economic dimensions of modernisation, it can be argued that the direct impact of industrialism was relatively limited compared with the changes in agriculture and mining that followed 1870. This overwhelming pre-eminence given to industrialisation, even in studies which take the global rather than western economies as their focus, is as clear a case of Eurocentrism as one can find.[7] In fact in terms of the sheer number of people whose lives were transformed within a relatively short space of time, this 'non-industrial revolution' far outweighs in significance the industrialisation of a handful of western economies.

> In the course of the nineteenth century, agriculture on plantations underwent a major change – away from estates capitalized with the financial resources of planter families and of merchants, who advanced needed commodities against the crop, and toward highly capitalized corporate 'factories in the field', in which all the factors of production, including labor, were determined by the play of the ever-enlarging capitalist market. The 'fall of the planter class' was not confined to the Caribbean; it was worldwide. (Wolf, 1982: 317)

This transformation has been documented by others, although its significance has not always been fully appreciated. In terms of the impact of this change on the lives especially of the majority of the world's population who lived in rural areas in the late nineteenth century, several dimensions of the development of a corporatised and globalised mining and agricultural sector need to be briefly summarised.

First, the extent to which ownership of the earth's surface was transferred into the hands of global agricultural and mining conglomerates in this period cannot be underestimated. Data on the amount of land that fell into the hands of such giant 'producing and distributing organizations such as the United Africa Company, United Fruit, Harrisons and Crossfields, Brooke Bond, the Compagnie Française de l'Afrique Occidentale, and the Société Commerciale l'Ouest Africain', to name only the largest (Wolf, 1982: 317) would in any case inevitably underestimate the significance of this process – first, because there were many other global organisations not listed here; second, because it was not just the amount of land they owned, but its quality that was significant (local studies show that it was always the best land taken over by these enterprises); third, because figures on land ownership do not reflect the extent to which these companies effectively controlled land even when they did not actually own it; fourth, because related to this process of private land alienation were accompanying processes of land alienation by public institutions for state enterprises and infrastructural developments (such as the building of railways, or the creation of vast forest reservations) that were directly related to the rise of corporate agriculture; and, finally, because this does not include the huge mining/petroleum conglomerates that were given not just mining/drilling rights to large areas of arable land, but for whom 'exploration rights' to far larger areas were set aside for extended periods. Figures[8] therefore tell only a small part of the story, figures such as those showing that between 1855 and 1881 in the Irrawaddy Delta in southern Burma the amount of land given over to rice cultivation for export rose from 1 million to 9 million acres; or showing that the United Fruit Company acquired vast tracts of land in Costa Rica, Panama, Honduras, Columbia and Ecuador from the last few decades of the nineteenth century, in fact 'a great deal more land than it could use at any one time, to hold as a reserve against the future'; or that in Malaya between 1900 and 1913 the amount of land allocated to plantations for rubber cultivation rose from 5,000 acres to 1,250,000 acres; or that show that after 1856 in Mexico (and 1877 in Guatemala) with the abolition of communal jurisdiction over land, Tzeltal- and Tzotzil-speaking peoples around San Cristobal de las Casas had already lost almost their entire territorial base to private landowners (see Wasserstrom, 1983); or that on Sumatra's west coast, a province of the Netherlands East Indies (and a region where estate agriculture was not supposed to have been highly developed in contrast with the plantation belt of the northern coast) in 1926 17 per cent of all cultivated land was held on long lease (*erfpacht*) granted to foreign plantation companies, that at any one time more than half again as much land was reserved for mining exploration and rights and that 35 per cent of the total land area of the province was given over to state forest reserve (see Kahn, 1993: 187ff.).

It is more difficult yet to estimate the effects of this process of land alienation on groups of people living in the areas where land was being alienated in this way. But contrary to the official impressions given by colonial governments and the companies that they were merely taking possession of vacant land[9], local studies have shown that this land performed important functions – both material and symbolic – in the lives of indigenous peoples. Citing Yalman's research on Ceylon, for example, Eric Wolf argues that the rapid spread of tea plantations after 1870 took place on land alienated from Kandyan Sinhalese peasants, turned into royal land and sold to planters:

> By 1903 more than 400,000 acres had been planted with tea shrubs . . . the effect was to restrict the Sinhalese peasantry to the precincts of their irrigated rice villages, and to curtail their ability to open slash-and-burn fields in their land reserves. (1982: 340)

In the Netherlands East Indies, similarly, the alienation of uncultivated land by the colonial state deprived local villagers of not just access to land for the cultivation of cash crops, but also for opportunities to earn a cash income through cattle raising, the collection of timber and a whole range of lucrative forest products. Here, as in Ceylon, villagers were forced back into their villages where what was previously a part-time occupation – the cultivation of rice on irrigated and rain-fed fields – became their only source of subsistence.

Elsewhere indigenous inhabitants were simply driven out of areas where the large enterprises seized land into areas less accessible and/or less desirable to multinational capital. There are numerous cases in the anthropological literature where it has been found that a supposedly isolated tribe had been driven quite recently into its isolated terrain by necessity, a consequence of the alienation of their former lands to outsiders.

But did these changes bring prosperity to the colonial regions? Mines and capitalist farms required not just land but labour. As a consequence it is often assumed that the two processes – of land alienation and labour recruitment – dovetailed neatly, turning the majority of the world's people into an agricultural proletariat. This was often the case. In the 1870s the Tzeltal- and Tzotzil-speaking peoples of Chiapas, having been deprived of their communal lands, were then encouraged to re-settle in those areas where foreigners had set up coffee estates on formerly Indian land, thus solving an acute labour shortage in coffee cultivation (Wasserstrom, 1983). Similarly, of the some 94,000 unskilled workers required by South Africa's diamond mines in 1906, most were migrant Africans from as far away as Nyasaland and Mozambique. In the southern states of the United States after the Civil War, African Americans, now ostensibly free, endured a new kind of slavery as there was very little land not owned by plantations that they could farm as free peasants, and because northern factory owners refused to hire them. As a consequence the majority of former slaves became tenant farmers, providing most of the labour required by plantation owners for the production and processing of cotton, sugar, rice, and so on (Mandle, 1992).

But as often as not local people were not re-incorporated into the new economic system as full-time wage labourers. In areas affected by the agrarian transformation of the latter half of the nineteenth century, owners of plantations and mines were almost universal in their complaint of inadequate labour supplies. A closer look often turns up plenty of local people – what was clear is that coerced locals were unwilling to work for the pitiful wages plantation and mine owners were willing to pay. While in cases such as those mentioned, various forms of coercion – economic or extra-economic – were brought to bear to ensure adequate supplies of cheap labour, in many cases other means were found. Thus began a movement of peoples around the world that was perhaps as significant as the one that took place through the African slave trade. In the Caribbean, for example, the end of the slave trade together, sometimes, with local abolition meant that sugar planters and others lost their guarantee of cheap labour. In some places, as in the southern states of the United States, former slaves were in different ways coerced back into agricultural labour. Elsewhere – for example in Trinidad, Jamaica and Guyana – ex-slaves were able to gain access to their own land beyond the plantation regions, and thus resisted further plantation work. Here a new supply of labour – from the Indian subcontinent – was to save the day for the planters. As early as 1836 Guyana, Jamaica and Trinidad asked the British to supply them with Indian indentured labour. Even earlier, in 1833, the first indentured labourers had travelled from India to work on plantations in Mauritius, where by 1861 they constituted two thirds of the population. In 1860 Indian indentured labourers were sent to the tea plantations of Assam and Bhutan, where by 1900 more than 700,000 had been recruited. Then followed large-scale movement of Indian indentured labourers to Fiji in 1879, to Ceylon throughout the 1870s, to Burma in the 1880s, to Natal in South Africa in 1870 and to Malaya to work on rubber plantations after 1900. Tinker has estimated that by 1870 already 1 million Indians had gone overseas to work on indenture contracts (see Tinker, 1974 ; Mandle, 1973, on Guyana; Wolf, 1982: 369ff.).

While Indians comprised probably the largest of the late nineteenth century labour diasporas, they were not alone. Elsewhere people were moved internally to supply labour when indigenous peoples refused. The expansion of plantations and mines on Indonesia's Outer Islands, for example, took place almost entirely through the use of 'koelis' from the poorer and more densely populated island of Java (see for example Stoler, 1985; Breman, 1987).

And while Indians were most often employed in agricultural labour, a Chinese labour diaspora also emerged at around the same time, often in the mining industry. Hence Singapore and Penang became the metropolitan cores of the tin mining industry of peninsular Malaya, supplying capital and Chinese labourers to work in the mines (Wolf, 1982: 375ff.; Loh, 1988). Between 1849 and 1874, 90,000 indentured Chinese labourers replaced Hawaiians who had died working Peru's guano beds (Wolf, 1982:

377); between 1854 and 1859 the number of Chinese working in Australia's goldfields rose from 2000 to 42,000 (ibid.: 378); and large numbers of Chinese labourers were also involved in the American gold rush and the building of the American railroads.

Not only did indigenous people find their land alienated and then found themselves often excluded from the momentous commercial developments taking place around them, even where they did manage to find employment, they found their labour less and less in demand as what were initially quite labour-intensive operations became, in the manner of capitalist enterprise, increasingly 'productive', that is labour displacing. This held, of course, for immigrant labourers just as it did for indigenes. Mandle has shown, for example, how in Guyana's sugar industry initially high demands for labour – which had led among other things to the immigration of large numbers of indentured workers from the Indian subcontinent – gradually subsided in the first few decades of the twentieth century, a consequence of increased technological sophistication in the sugar industry (Mandle, 1992). Anne Stoler has shown how Sumatran tobacco and rubber plantations, which had initially caused large numbers of Javanese labourers to be brought in to join a permanent workforce in the latter decades of the nineteenth century, increasingly in the twentieth attempted to shed their permanent workforce, employing people as much as possible for relatively short periods when labour demands remained high (Stoler, 1985).

Finally, as we have seen in the case of Central America, the late nineteenth century scramble for land by corporate plantation and mining interests was not always matched by production. On the contrary, in this period a highly speculative land market developed, vast tracts of land in Asia, Africa and the Americas were alienated and placed under private or state control, local peoples were denied access to land that had previously been a major source of both subsistence and commodity production, and yet as often as not the land was simply left idle. There are various reasons for this. As Wolf shows for Central America, United Fruit acquired vast tracts of land as a hedge against future uncertainty. The extensiveness and wide distribution of their holdings meant that should anything untoward happen in one place – such as political unrest, environmental catastrophe, infrastructural problems – then they could always shift production elsewhere. After all, acquiring the land cost the company very little.

On the other side of the world, in the Netherlands East Indies, much the same thing happened. Plantation companies operating, for example, on Sumatra's east coast also acquired large amounts of land on the west coast as a reserve against problems in the east. Only a very small proportion of these reserve lands were ever cultivated. Much the same was the case for mining exploration rights. Huge tracts of land were set aside for 'exploration', and declared off limits to indigenous alluvial miners. But very few of these areas were developed for mining purposes – they acted either as reserves against current operations elsewhere, or as a means merely of staking a future claim against other European mining companies to ensure a monopoly over mining on the island.

In short, it would be a mistake to assume that the indigenous peoples of the world were suddenly transformed into a rural proletariat from the late nineteenth century. More often than not what the new global economy required of them was their land and their resources, not their labour. In taking their land, such forms of community as had existed were eroded or completely burst apart as the material resources on which such communities were based were drawn into a speculative global land market. As for the people themselves – when they were not being shipped off to work off indentures, or working in mines and on plantations, often for only part of the year for extremely low wages – they were expected largely to disappear into the hills, the jungles, the deserts.

Many of these peoples formed what the anthropologist Sidney Mintz has called a 'reconstituted peasantry', although this begs the question of whether we can speak of 'real' peasants in the previous period. They inhabited, fled to, or were forced into areas where for any number of reasons even foreign mining and plantation companies were loathe to go – to remote mountain areas, to deserts and drylands, to tropical jungles. In these mysterious other worlds they subsisted as best they could, seeking, as James Scott reminds us, as far as possible to reduce the risks involved in agriculture under harsh conditions, to reduce their needs for cash (but given the division of labour and the external demands for taxes this could never be a pure subsistence existence), and doing all this by attempting to find economic niches that had been left to them by outsiders.

Increasingly in this period, of course, the peasants fought back – intruding from their hidden worlds to fight against the forces that sought to coerce them into labour in the mines and on the plantations that continued to intrude on their land, that saw in them a source of taxes. The first few decades of the twentieth century was clearly a time of tremendous unrest in the rural areas of the emerging 'Third World'. Revolutions in Mexico, Russia and China, whether or not they were really peasant wars in the sense of being fought in the interests of peasants, were nonetheless often fought by them and in their name.

In short, unprecedented processes of economic transformation on a global scale in the early decades of this century nonetheless did not generate the kinds of changes that would have been predicted by classical theories of economic modernisation. Not only did the supposed economic benefits to the world's rural population not eventuate, but the large majority of them seemed to have been left out altogether. If these people still apparently eluded modernisation, then perhaps traditional economies and cultures would not disappear after all. Viewed through the grid of the classical metanarratives of modern economic evolution, most of the colonial world appeared still to be traditional. Balinese, Mexican, African American inhabitants of the American South had apparently not been assimilated to our world in spite of the promise/threat of modernisation.

Post-Fordism before Fordism: New York's Cultural Division of Labour

But much the same impression was given by economic changes in the industrial heartlands, even in the United States. In spite of the prevailing view that this period marks the beginnings of a Taylorist regime of large-scale, technologically-advanced manufacture and a Fordist regime of mass production and mass consumption by an increasingly homogeneous working class, large parts of the American economy failed to conform to the plan. Take the example of New York City. New York's manufacturing sector grew from the Civil War, producing first for the local market, then for an expanding national market, spurred on by the building of the Erie Canal and the railroads. But transport was always a significant constraint on the development of a manufacturing base. The high cost of transporting products to markets, and of bringing in raw materials prevented many industries from getting a foothold. As a result the sectors that did best were those with a high ratio of sales value to shipping cost. One industry that met this condition was the manufacture of apparel, and to a lesser extent the millinery business.[10]

New York's manufacturing industries have always been heavily dependent on immigrant labourers. Between 1825 and 1875 and subsequently between 1825 and 1925 the number of immigrants trebled. Until 1880 they came mostly from England, Ireland, Scandinavia, and Germany. In the later period the immigrants were mainly eastern and southern Europeans, as well as internal migrants from the South. The combination of a low wage labour market and a highly motivated immigrant labour force also contributed to the emergence of highly labour intensive industry in New York. Indeed the pattern of immigration coincided with the rise to dominance of the manufacture of apparel, especially women's apparel, a rise also made possible by new technological developments facilitating the shift in the production of garments from homes to factories. In 1869 Manhattan produced 32 per cent of women's apparel in the United States; by 1921 Manhattan's share had risen to 71 per cent. The industry was established mainly by German Jews, many of whom came with tailoring skills. By the twentieth century Eastern European Jews were in control. By then the production process was decomposed/deskilled into specialised, simpler-to-perform tasks making entry to the industry easier. The apparel business had become so dominated by Jewish owners and workers that in most shops the common language was Yiddish not English.

Apart from being characterised by a cultural division of labour, rather than the cultural homogeneity anticipated by a Henry Ford, the New York manufacturing sector was also characterised by the dominance of relatively small-scale firms. Garments were produced mainly in lofts – post Civil War and newly built, multi-storey industrial structures:

> Manhattan's resulting high-density environment offered a distinct competitive advantage to the typical apparel business, which was thinly capitalized, produced

small runs for a highly variable fashion-fickle market, and needed to be within walking distance of a large pool of low-wage labor. (Tobier, 1988: 84)[11]

The cultural distinctiveness of garment workers was also constituted through residential proximity. As the above suggests, the high cost of transportation made it necessary for garment workers to live within walking distance of their places of employment. In 1906 67 per cent of Manhattan's factory workers were employed below 14th Street, most in the 6th Assembly District on Lower East Side where there was a ratio of 304 factory workers per acre (Tobier, 1988: 87). By the First World War it had also expanded into nearby parts of the West Side – Chelsea, the West Village and Hell's Kitchen (now called Clinton). In these neighbourhoods garment workers lived very close together in tenements – five to seven storey walkups with tiny two- to three-room apartments – built by independent small businessmen (ibid.: 90).

Only with the beginning of the subway system could the workers live farther away. Thus from the Lower East Side, Chelsea, the West Village and Hell's Kitchen the garment industry after the First World War began to move to Brooklyn and the other boroughs where land was cheaper and where the subway system made it easier for workers to commute longer distances to work. Thus between 1899 and 1919 manufacturing employment in Manhattan grew by 36 per cent, but in the other boroughs it grew by 142 per cent. Only then did the population of the Lower East Side begin to fall (by 54 per cent between 1900 and 1930), a consequence of lower immigration rates, improved public transport, shifts in industrial location, and higher working class incomes.

The combination of small-scale industrial organisation, strong links between ethnic affiliation and class position, and ethnic links between workers and owners makes the New York garment industry apparently an exception in an age of corporate capital and Taylorist/Fordist production regimes. While the transformation of the garment industry beginning in the years after the First World War broke this nexus, it is clear that Lower Manhattan and particularly the Lower East Side continues to exercise a strong hold on the American Jewish imaginary, making New York America's first, and probably still most culturally-significant, Jewish homeland (see Sheskin, 1993). The history of the New York garment industry does not testify to the emergence of a culturally-homogeneous, industrially advanced modern world, but instead to the strong presence of cultural difference within the heart of the modernist project.

As the example of the garment industry shows, New York's economic modernisation has therefore been associated with the emergence of a significant 'cultural division of labour'.[12] The history of Harlem as a distinctly African American residential neighbourhood, and certainly as *the* black homeland not just for the United States, but for the whole of the African diaspora in the 1920s, is somewhat different.[13] The migration of African Americans from the South to the North was prompted at least in part by the demands of northern industry for workers during the First

World War. Previously excluded because of northern racism (see Mandle, 1992), the labour shortage created by conscription prompted northern manufacturers increasingly to hire African Americans, even sending trains directly to the South to recruit workers.[14] But through the operations of the real estate industry in New York, and the fact that a number of black real estate agents like Phil A. Payton Jnr were able to persuade the owners of empty buildings in what is now Harlem to rent to these new migrants, Harlem became a largely black neighbourhood, attracting not just American migrants, but also blacks from the West Indies who made up almost 20 per cent of the population of Harlem.

The constitution of a 'culturally' differentiated citizenry – rather than of that mass of autonomous and individual (cosmopolitan) subjects anticipated by nineteenth century narratives of modernisation – in New York City, the very heart of the new global order after the First World War, suggests that the daily experience of people in the West was not of the kind of cosmopolitan world that modernism had predicted. The 'discovery' of alterity and cultural difference would have made as much if not more sense of this experience than would any of the narratives of high modernism.

Intellectuals and Power

But as I have suggested the emergence of new languages of culturalism, multiculturalism, even postculturalism cannot be assumed to be mere reflections of developments in the world, as it were. Because the images of culture and difference with which we have been dealing are produced and consumed overwhelmingly by a particular group, namely the intellectuals, it is important that we ask about the conditions that led intellectuals in particular to produce and consume a new image of a multicultural world in this period.

To begin with, it is important to note that the period under consideration marks a time of tremendous absolute and relative growth in the size of the social group from which intellectuals are drawn, namely the educated middle classes, a growth which, while uneven, is notable throughout the world. In colonial regions like Indonesia, this growth was a result of a combination of factors, most notably a change in the form and function of the colonial state. Beginning in the latter part of the nineteenth century, the state in the Netherlands East Indies moved to establish a complete monopoly of violence within its territorial boundaries, to expand its influence over more and more areas of life by means of a larger and more differentiated bureaucracy, to increase the number of state functionaries with professional expertise both in administrative matters and also in areas (such as agriculture, industry, accountancy, science, and so on) that it was seeking to manage, and, consequently, also to expand the educational system both in the colony and in the Netherlands to train larger numbers of government servants (both Dutch and Indonesian).[15]

The expansion in the educational system in the colony involved both a greater number of Dutch medium schools where future employees of the colonial administration would be trained, and of vernacular primary schools for villagers. In addition Indonesians themselves opened schools to keep up with the immense local demand for education. Notable in this regard were the new-style Islamic schools run by Muslim modernists in which Islamic teaching was combined within a largely European-style curriculum (see Alfian, 1969). This pattern was repeated elsewhere in the colonial worlds of Asia and Africa.[16]

The West also witnessed a rapid growth of the middle classes in the early decades of this century. In this instance the reasons normally offered are somewhat different – namely the emergence of new forms of capitalist production requiring a stricter separation between 'skilled' and 'unskilled' workers, and hence between blue and white collar occupations, a development usually linked to Taylorist techniques of scientific management (see, for example, Abercrombie and Urry, 1983). In the United States the growth of an educated middle class in this period was particularly dramatic:

> One pertinent indicator of these developments in the USA was the extraordinary expansion in higher education between 1880 and 1930. . . . By 1930 the USA possessed more institutions of higher education than France possessed academic personnel and its university and college population was ten times higher than the secondary population in France. (ibid.: 103)

All this is to say that the early twentieth century saw the growth not just of an increasingly numerically significant educated middle class, but a growing 'professional' class, especially in the sciences and the social sciences, in business and government as a result of new productive technologies, and new forms of bureaucratic rule. Engineers, but also experts in scientific management and in the management of people by a growing welfare state were all part of this new class.

In fact, to speak of 'new middle classes' in this way is somewhat misleading. The tendency in much recent literature on this theme has been to attempt to conceptualise situations such as these by means of revisionist concepts, particularly here of concepts of a 'new middle class'. Following on from the work of writers like Bourdieu, Giddens, Abercrombie and Urry and others, many have suggested that these new middle classes are to be defined as groups differentiated, in class terms, from the bourgeoisie because they do not own/control the means of production and the proletariat because of their 'ownership'/'control' of credentials, information and/or cultural capital.

This is not the place for a detailed critique of such approaches.[17] Suffice it here to point out four related flaws in such analyses. First, there is a very real problem in assuming some kind of formal isomorphism between the Marxist ownership: non-ownership of the means of production distinction, and revisionist dichotomies such as 'ownership': 'non-ownership' of credentials, skills or cultural capital. The former generates a logical bipolarity, the latter does not. To attempt formally to define a class on the basis of the latter is certain to generate a misleading conflation of class understood in the Marxist sense, and class in its revisionist sense. Second, and following on from this, revisionist attempts to distinguish classes on the basis of degrees of control of cultural capital or credentials will never succeed in generating discrete classes, only a plethora or matrix of socio-cultural 'strata'. There can, in short, be no new middle class, only new middle classes. Third, once cultural differentiation becomes a part of class analysis, its application must extend beyond the confines of groups that could even be remotely linked to the new middle classes. I have in mind here in particular so-called 'underclasses', whose distinction from the proletariat is itself very often also 'cultural', since the groups we tend to label underclasses are very often defined by their culturally undervalorised and/or marginal status. Finally, there is that other dimension of cultural differentiation, namely power. Unequal power relations can never be considered the formal equivalent of class relations, since power is always best understood as a matrix or set of matrices of unequal relationships. Moreover it is always a mistake, particularly in conditions of late or neo-modernity, to reduce the matrix of power relations to the structure of class relationships as I have already suggested.

In sum, the processes of political, social and cultural differentiation that characterise modernity must be analysed as separate from the dominant process of class formation, and not, as a number of revisionists have done, be subsumed under an increasingly elaborate, but ultimately sterile conceptual apparatus of 'new' classes. Only in this way can we hope to provide an understanding of modernity that is sensitive to its specific multidimensional character.

In any case, the growth in the size of the educated middle class, or the often-discussed process of professionalisation, do not on their own explain the fact that some of their number will play the role of 'intellectuals'. To some extent this can be explained by reference to the very emergence of a group labelled intellectual within modern society.

There are, of course, many discussions of the role of intellectuals. But almost inevitably, precisely because they are themselves produced by intellectuals, not many go beyond normative assertions about what that role *should* be, and somewhat romantic complaints about the *decline* of intellectual life. One writer who has examined the relationship between the activities of intellectuals and the conditions from which they emerged is Zygmunt Bauman. He has argued that the category 'intellectuals', used to refer to a group offering a general (as opposed to specialised) view of the world and of society, a group that takes its vocation to be the insistence on culture and meaning as opposed to mere management and technical mastery, is in fact a classic example of self-definition, one moreover that articulated precisely a sense of loss. The rise of intellectuals is, in this formulation, seen as a consequence of a systematic change in modern society. The change, for Bauman, is best understood as the shift from a mode of governance based on the project of 'civilising' the masses (a project that involved, following Elias, a central role for 'trainers' whose job it was to educate the masses in the 'higher' culture of ruling elites), to increasingly panoptic systems (like the rule of law) for guaranteeing the obedience of the masses. This is, of course, linked to the rise of the professional, the 'white collar' worker, the scientific manager and the rational bureaucrat mentioned above. The declining importance of ideas for the reproduction of state power was, argues Bauman, accompanied by a professionalisation of the 'trainers' whose job was no longer to transmit a culture or civilisation to the masses, but now became a procedure to manage some part of the social machine.

Previously indistinguishable from the elite, the generalists now found their status considerably reduced – the very concept of a class of intellectuals being a part of their attempt to carve out a niche for themselves under the changed circumstances of later modernity.

> The self assertion (or was it, rather, self-formation?) of the intellectuals was therefore an act of rebellion, and a rebellion against at least two enemies, that demanded engagement on at least three different battlefronts. First of all, one had to oppose the political regime that hermetically sealed itself against any discussion of ethical principles or cultural values and downgraded – as politically irrelevant – those who insisted on the social importance of such discussions; one had to re-assert the political relevance of culture. Secondly, one had to brace oneself against the indifference or resentment, if not active opposition, from the majority of the educated elite well settled in their respective niches of functionally divided society and unlikely to risk the privileges attuned to professional membership and expert status; one had to re-assert the right to *vocation* (what one *does*) against the institutionalized rights of *professions* (what one *is*). Thirdly, one had to make a new bid for leadership over 'the people' – over those many whose assumed need to be guided justified the intellectuals in their desire to guide. (Bauman, 1992: 88)

One must not assume, however, that intellectuals everywhere spoke with one voice, indeed it has been almost a defining feature of the modern intelligentsia that they are deeply divided. This is partly a consequence of the fact that intellectuals appear to have a highly ambivalent attitude towards the state:

> The relation between the educated classes and modern state [sic] is not . . . one of perpetual contention. The relationship is, rather, of a *Haßliebe* type. Suspicion and dissent constantly alternate with a powerful attraction – nay, fascination – with the power of the state. Sometimes, they succeed each other with breath-taking speed. Most of the time, they cohabit uneasily within the same intellectual community; often inside the same 'split personality' of a single intellectual. (ibid.: 91)

One might add that there appears to be a similarly ambivalent attitude towards capitalism. Perhaps these attitudes are further shaped by the different employment situations of potential intellectuals. Here there are differences between places like the United States where academics, scientists, and artists tended to have a more direct relation to private capital than in Europe where they are more often directly employed by, or more directly rely upon, the welfare state for their means of subsistence. This may explain, for example, why American intellectuals have tended to be more critical of the state, while European intellectuals have at least in the past focused their critical eye more directly on capitalism.

What this suggests is that intellectual life is not everywhere and always the same. On the contrary the existence of intellectuals demands public intellectual activity around causes. A formative condition, therefore, for the intellectuals is a propensity to become involved in public debate not merely in their professional capacity – as experts – but in their generalist or vocational capacity, a propensity that, suggests Bauman, is related less to the sheer numbers of potential intellectuals and more to the extent to which the state is prepared to give some public role to the educated classes from which they are drawn. Paradoxically perhaps, it is precisely when self-defined intellectuals see themselves being excluded from public life that their presence is most strongly felt:

> Neither the intensity nor invisibility of intellectuals' public presence correlated with the numbers, or even with the socio-cultural weight of the learned professions from which 'the intellectuals' are normally recruited. They showed instead an intimate connection with the degree to which the educated professions in their totality were accommodated within the current socio-political order. (ibid.: 90)

This also explains for Bauman the temporal changes in intellectual activity. For example:

> As Nicole Racine-Furlaud has . . . found out, in the aftermath of the Great War discussions of the role and duties of intellectuals almost totally disappeared; yet from 1925 on, the term 'intellectuals' again 'figures prominently in the manifestoes . . . This lexical change seems to mark the end of hopes entertained immediately after the War – hopes that a new international order will arrive soon, or that the world will return to the traditional values of the Christian West'. The postwar armistice between the educated classes and the political powers and the dominant culture lasted as long as the hopes remained credible. (ibid.: 90)

In the light of Bauman's remarks, the eagerness with which at least a segment of the world's intelligentsia embraced a discourse of culture and difference in the interwar years is not perhaps very surprising. At a time when the intellectuals as a class were reconstituting themselves, when the size of the social group to which they belong was expanding rapidly, when populations in both the American and the colonial worlds were experiencing unparalleled processes of social and cultural differentation, when the hopes that followed the end of the Great War were evaporating, during a period of an unprecedented 'rationalisation' of political and economic life, in a time that also saw the spread of culturally homogenising ideologies such as Americanisation and unprecedented revivals of racism and Christian fundamentalism at least in the United States, that a self-defining class of intellectuals should articulate an expressivist critique of that political and economic order is also unsurprising. Many did this almost entirely as academics, by which I mean that in spite of the kinds of relatively short encounters anthropologists term 'fieldwork', they manipulated images of other cultures elsewhere, addressing audiences who would not have been concerned with the particular cultural others being re-presented to them. Significantly it is mostly in such internal contexts that the exclusivist discourses of difference were and continue to be most readily apparent. Here the other becomes an 'example', a 'case', a field for 'scientific' investigation, a terrain from which to launch a critique of techno-modernism.

But the turn to cultural otherness on the part of at least some of these intellectuals also makes sense in the context of Bauman's remarks about the political position of twentieth century intellectuals, many of whom in any case found themselves involved in their professional capacity as 'patrons', not of the working class which by this time already had its forms of institutional patronage (trade unions, labour parties, and so on), but of those almost entirely excluded from public life. Intellectuals, in seeking to re-present cultural others – in both the political and metaphorical sense of that term – can be seen to have been looking for political allies among groups that had previously been denied representation in the existing political arrangements – in colonial worlds and indeed in the heartlands of the West. As a consequence of their own expressivist intellectual projects, and hence critics of the kinds of civilisational discourses by which bearers of cultural otherness were denied patronage, representation or, to use a currently fashionable term, voice, some intellectuals – like B. Traven, Walter Spies, George Gershwin, Béla Bartók, Diego Rivera, Zora Neale Hurston, Franz Boas to name a few – found themselves in alliances with those they sought to re-present. Here the intellectuals' project, an expressivist critique of modernism, resonated more widely with the demands of colonised Indonesians, indigenous Mexicans, disenfranchised African Americans. Why particular 'anthropologists' and not others should have become politically involved with the 'objects' of their own investigations is not something we can easily explain. In some cases it may have been a result of their own marginality or exclusion from public life – the examples of American Jews like Boas or Gershwin unhappy with 'Americanisation', highly educated African Americans like Zora Neale Hurston, Minangkabau and Balinese on the bottom rungs of the colonial hierarchy, political exiles like B. Traven, homosexuals like Walter Spies spurned by a puritanical colonial bureaucracy come to mind. The point is that here the intellectual critique of techno-modernism was merged with a political project, and as a consequence expressivism once again escaped the boundaries of the private and erupted into the public sphere. And more often than not as a consequence the discourse of otherness was here inclusive rather than exclusive, anti-statist rather than statist.

What then of the present, when once again the language of culture, multiculture, postculture seems to be all around us? Here, perhaps because he seems caught up in the kinds of nostalgia he earlier seems to warn against, Bauman's analyses prove less useful. In the same article in which he attempts to account for the rise of intellectuals in the twentieth century, Bauman has also argued that there has been a demise in the 1990s. Bauman suggests that the time of the intellectuals has gone or is fast disappearing, a consequence of a number of factors including: a shift from *panoptic* to *seductive* techniques of social control and integration (the rise of consumerism), the nature of new forms of communication technology, and the increasing specialisation and professionalisation of the middle classes whose public role increasingly is that of *experts* rather than generalists. In the 1980s, these changes have undoubtedly affected in significant ways the project of constructing the world as being culturally differentiated. A language perhaps first developed by intellectuals in the 1920s has increasingly been integrated into the system of signs associated with late capitalist consumption – to sell commodities through the manipulation of images of culture, multiculturalism, ethnicity and difference; to highlight particular locations in the global competition for transnational capital, and so on. Similarly, the process of professionalisation has meant that particularly the language of multiculturalism is now more often spoken by states and employees of the state then it is by intellectuals resisting the imposition of state power. The (market-based) democratisation of the discourse of cultural difference, on the one hand, and the professionalisation of the knowledge of cultural otherness, on the other, has led not so much to a decline in prevalence of languages of culture and difference – in fact, such a language seems to be at present, if anything, more pervasive than ever – as to a radically changed context within which it is spoken.

But what then of intellectuals? Certainly the academy is if anything even more than ever a site for debates over cultural difference, a fact evidenced in the rapid rise of new interdisciplines like cultural studies and, at least in places like the United States, of African American, Asian American, Native American studies centres and programmes. But what is perhaps most striking about all this debate on culture and difference is how little it appears to relate to the world outside the academy, and how much it appears to focus on issues like curriculum, student selection, hiring practices, promotion, tenure and so on, that are of general concern largely to academics. It is symptomatic that of the books in recent years that have made the greatest impact in this area, most have been explicitly written about education and academic institutions.

In spite of this overwhelming academic concern with culture, multiculture and postculture, there is very little evidence that the defence of difference has permeated through to the general population (in fact the results of the 1994 American elections suggest just the opposite), that there is any credible political movement explicitly concerned to tackle the rising tide of American racism, that academics have been systematically involved in the debates taking place within those communities the representation of which their academic debates are so centrally concerned with. The kinds of long term interest in, involvement with and influence on the communities of difference of a B. Traven, a Walter Spies, a Franz Boas is strangely lacking today.

It remains to be seen, however, whether or not this signals a permanent demise of the culturalist projects of that earlier generation of intellectuals discussed here. Perhaps the less public role played by academics in general, and professional anthropologists in particular, signals instead a shift towards a different kind of intellectual. But for the moment, at least, the accomplishments of people like Spies, Hurston, Gershwin, Bartók, Heyward and Boas can only be admired, rather than merely dismissed as old-fashioned and orientalist.

Notes

1 It has recently been announced, for example, that Indonesia will shortly have two new pay TV music channels – one broadcasting 'western', the other 'Asian' rock music. Superficially we have here a classic case of a globalised technology generating cultural diversity. However, as it turns out *both* channels will be owned and operated by MTV.

2 It did not take the recent 'communications revolution' to produce knowledge of other cultures, an argument supported by the fact that it is precisely such an explanation that is now commonly offered to account for the discovery of the significance of human difference in the early nineteenth century. For example, Burrow (1966) has argued that it was precisely increased knowledge of the rest of the world that prompted nineteenth century evolutionists to criticise the simplistic accounts of human difference offered by the French *philosophes* and the British utilitarians.

3 A well-known case concerns the strong push among Jesuit theologians to argue for the inclusion rather than the exclusion of native Americans in the category 'humanity' (see Hanke, 1974). Similarly, eighteenth century European images of China were strongly influenced by the earlier Jesuit position in the so-called controversy over rites in which they committed themselves to a universalising rather than a particularising discourse (see Mackerras, 1989; Bitterli, [1986] 1989: Ch.6). Bitterli, among others, has demonstrated how encounters between Europeans and non-Europeans have produced different European images depending upon context (see Bitterli, [1986] 1989; see also Adas, 1989).

4 Some of these issues are raised by Spivak in her now famous critique of the subalternist school of Indian historians (of which she was herself a member) (see for example Spivak, 1988).

5 This is not the place for a book on the importance of non-European elements in the making of European culture. Suffice it to note that the American historian Donald Lach set out to document fairly exhaustively what he called the place of Asia in the making of Europe, and having written four volumes on visual arts, literature and scholarship found that he was still not past the sixteenth century (see Lach, 1965–77, 1992).

6 See Gordon (1990). Gordon's contrast between the rhetorical styles of Margaret Mead and of Hurston capture nicely this distinction between 'anthropological' and 'hermeneutic' languages.

7 See, for example, Eric Wolf's study of the effects of European expansion on the non-European world. Although Wolf provides a good deal of important information on the non-industrial revolution, he nonetheless follows established convention by seeing these effects as a follow-on from Europe's industrial revolution (Wolf, 1982: 265ff.).

8 Unless otherwise noted, these figures are all from Wolf (1982).

9 The government of the Netherlands East Indies, for example, simply declared all land not under current cultivation to be 'waste ground', hence to be allocated by the state to foreign capital. Australia's white settlement was premised on the judicial fiction of 'terra

nullius', that is the pronouncement that the land into which white colonists were moving was quite simply empty.

10 This account, unless otherwise noted, is based on Tobier (1988).

11 See also Selekman et al. (1925); Waldinger (1986).

12 B. Kahn uses this term to describe the division of labour among New York's African American, Jewish and Italian population in the early decades of this century (see Kahn, 1987).

13 For a useful account of the history of Harlem see Kahn (1987: 250ff.).

14 This foreshadowed a similar change in the lives of many American women during the Second World War, who were suddenly and conveniently reclassified as capable of manual labour when the conscription of men made for tremendous labour shortages.

15 A survey of changes in the patterns of colonial state formation in Southeast Asia is found in Elson (1992). By 1928 90 per cent of state functionaries in the Nertherlands East Indies were Indonesians (Anderson, 1983: 106n).

16 Between 1900 and 1904 an average of 2987 Indonesians received a 'primary Western-style education', in 1928 the number was 74,697 (Anderson, 1983: 106n). For an overview of similar developments in Africa and other parts of Asia see Anderson (ibid.: 108ff.).

17 For a very good critique of the analysis of the development of a, new, middle class, see Barbalet (1980). Barbalet also argues convincingly that we cannot, as some analysts have assumed, merely resurrect Weber's notion of 'status' in contexts such as these, since for Weber social differentiation on the basis of status has its origins in distinctly pre-modern cultural categories, while if nothing else the cultural distinctions at work in contemporary Malaysia are definitely not traditional.

References

Aas, S. (1980) The Relevance of Chayanov's Macro Theory to the Case of Java. In E. Hobsbawm, W. Kula, A. Mitra, K.N. Raj and I. Sachs (eds), *Peasants in History*. Calcutta: Oxford University Press.

Abercrombie, Nicholas and Urry, John (1983) *Capital, Labour and the Middle Classes*. London: Allen and Unwin.

Adas, Michael (1989) *Machines as the Measure of Men: Science, Technology and Western Dominance*. Ithaca and London: Cornell University Press.

Alfian (1969) *Islamic Modernism in Indonesian Politics: The Muhammadijah Movement during the Dutch Colonial Period*. PhD thesis, University of Wisconsin.

Alpert, Hollis (1990) *The Life and Times of Porgy and Bess: the Story of an American Classic*. New York: Alfred A. Knopf.

Anderson, Benedict (1983) *Imagined Communities: Reflections on the Origin and Spread of Nationalism*. London: Verso.

Anderson, Elijah (1994) The Code of the Streets. *The Atlantic Monthly*, May: 81–94.

Anon (1920) The Failure of the Melting Pot by an Unassimilated Foreigner. *The Nation*, 110 (2847): 100–2.

Antokoletz, Elliot (1988) *Béla Bartók: A Guide to Research*. New York and London: Garland.

Appadurai, Arjun (1990) Disjuncture and Difference in the Global Cultural Economy. *Public Culture*, 2(2): 1–24.

Appadurai, Arjun (1993) Patriotism and its Futures. *Public Culture*, 5(3): 411–29.

Asad, Talal (ed.) (1973) *Anthropology and the Colonial Encounter*. London: Ithaca Press.

Bach, H.I. (1984) *The German Jews: A Synthesis of Judaism and Western Civilization, 1730–1930*. Oxford: Oxford University Press.

Bailey, Anne and Llobera, J.R. (eds) (1981) *The Asiatic Mode of Production: Science and Politics*. London: Routledge and Kegan Paul.

Baker, Lee D. (1994) The Location of Franz Boas within the African-American Struggle. *Critique of Anthropology*, 14(2): 199–217.

Banks, David (1987) *From Class to Culture: Social Conscience in Malay Novels since Independence*. Yale University Monograph Series, 29, New Haven: Yale University Southeast Asia Studies.

Barbalet, J.M. (1980) Limitations of Class Theory and the Disappearance of Status: the Problem of the New Middle Class. *Sociology*, 20(4): 557–75.

Barkin, K.D. (1970) *The Controversy over German Industrialization: 1890–1902*. Chicago: University of Chicago Press.

Barth, Frederick (1989) The Analysis of Culture in Complex Societies. *Ethnos*, 54(3–4): 120–42.

Bateson, Gregory and Mead, Margaret (1942) *Balinese Character: A Photographic Analysis*. New York: The New York Academy of Sciences.

Bauman, Zygmunt (1992) Love in Adversity: On the State and the Intellectuals, and the State of the Intellectuals. *Thesis Eleven*, 31: 81–104.

Beaufort, H.L.T. de (1954) *Cornelius van Vollenhoven, 1874–1933*. Haarlem: H.D. Tjeenk Willink.

Berkovici, Konrad (1924) *Around the World in New York*. New York: Century.

Berman, Marshall (1983) *All That is Solid Melts Into Air*. London: Verso.

Billeter, Erika (1987) *Images of Mexico: The Contribution of Mexico to 20th Century Art*. Dallas: Dallas Museum of Art.

Bitterli, Urs ([1986] 1989) *Cultures in Conflict: Encounters Between European and Non-European Cultures, 1492–1800*. Cambridge: Polity.

Boas, Franz (1925a) What Is a Race? *The Nation*, February: 89–91.

Boas, Franz (1925b) This Nordic Nonsense. *Forum*, October, 74: 502–11.

Boas, Franz (1927) Fallacies of Racial Inferiority. *Current History*, 25 February: 676–82.

Boeke, Julius Herman (1910) *Tropisch – Koloniale Staathuiskunde: Het Problem*. Amsterdam: J.H. de Bussy.

Boeke, Julius Herman, et al. (1966) *Indonesian Economics: The Concept of Dualism in Theory and Policy*. The Hague: W. van Hoeve.

Breman, Jan (1987) *Koelis, planters en koloniale politiek*. Dordrecht: Providence.

Bronsen, D. (ed.) (1979) *Jews and Germany from 1860–1933: The Problematic Symbiosis*. Heidelberg: Carl Winter.

Bücher, Karl (1901) *Industrial Evolution*. London: G. Bell and Sons.

Burrow, J. (1966) *Evolution and Society: a Study of Victorian Social Theory*. Cambridge: Cambridge University Press.

Cahnman, W.J. (1987) *German Jewry: Its History and Sociology*. New York and Oxford: Transaction Publishers.

Chametzky, Jules (1986) *Our Decentralized Literature: Cultural Mediations in Selected Jewish and Southern Writers*. Amherst: The University of Massachussets Press.

Chatterjee, Partha (1986) *Nationalist Thought and the Colonial World*. London: Zed.

Chayanov, A.V. [Tschajanov] (1924) *Die Lehre von der bäuerlichen Wirtschaft. Versuch einer Theorie der Familienwirtschaft*. Berlin: Parey.

Chayanov, A.V. (1966) *The Theory of Peasant Economy*. Ed. D. Thorner, B. Kerblay and R.E.F. Smith. Homewood, IL.: Irwin.

Conrad, J. (1891) Bauerngut und Bauernstand. In J. Conrad, *Handwörterbuch des Staatswissenschaften*: 259–83. Stuttgart: G. Fischer.

Copeland, Aaron (1968) *The New Music: 1900–1960*. London: Macdonald.

Darcy, Anthony (1987) Franz Boas and the Concept of Culture: A Genealogy. In Diane J. Austin-Broos (ed.), *Creating Culture. Profiles in the study of culture*. Sydney: Allen and Unwin.

Dobow, S. (1989) *Racial Segregation and the Origins of Apartheid in South Africa, 1919–1936*. London: Macmillan.

Dutch East Indies, Commissie voor het adatrecht (1911–1945) *Adatrechtbundels*. The Hague: Koninlijk Instituut voor taal-, land- en volkenkunde van Nederlandsch-Indië.

Elson, Robert (1992) International Commerce, the State and Society in Southeast Asia: Economic and Social Change from the Early Nineteenth Century to the Depression. In Nicolas Tarling (ed.), *The Cambridge History of Southeast Asia*. Cambridge and Melbourne: Cambridge University Press.

Essback, Wolfgang (1987) A Language without Master: Marx Stirner's Influence on B. Traven. In E. Schuerer and P. Jenkins (eds), *B. Traven: Life and Work*. University Park and London: Pennsylvania State University Press.

Evans-Pritchard, E.E. ([1937] 1965) *Witchcraft, Oracles and Magic among the Azande*. Oxford: Clarendon Press.

Featherstone, M. (1993) Global and Local Cultures. In J. Bird (ed.), *Mapping the Futures: Local Cultures, Global Change*. London and New York: Routledge.

Fischer, Michael M.J. (1992) Orientalizing America. Beginning and Middle Passages. *Middle East Report*, Sept–Oct: 32–5.

Fleming, Ray (1992) Race and the Difference It Makes in Kleist's 'Die Verlobung in St. Domingo'. *German Quarterly*, 65(3–4): 306–17.

Fouchet, Max-Pol (1976) *Wifredo Lam*. New York: Rizzoli.

Frazier, E. Franklin (1962) *Black Bourgeoisie*. New York: Collier.

Furnivall, John Sydenham (1956 [1948]) *Colonial Policy and Practice*. New York: New York University Press.

Geertz, Clifford (1963) *Agricultural Involution*. Berkeley and Los Angeles: University of Calfornia Press.

Geertz, Clifford (1984) Culture and Social Change: The Indonesian Case. *Man*, 19: 511–32.

Gershwin, George (1935) *Porgy and Bess*. Music by George Gershwin. Libretto by DuBose Heyward. Lyrics by DuBose Heyward and Ira Gershwin. New York: Gershwin Publishing Corporation/Chappell and Co.

Giroux, Henry (1993) Living Dangerously: Identity Politics and the New Cultural Racism: Towards a Critical Pedagogy of Representation. *Cultural Studies*, 7(1): 1–27.

Gomez, Ermilio Abreu ([1940] 1979). *Canek: History and Legend of a Maya Hero*. Berkeley and Los Angeles: University of California Press.

Gordon, Deborah (1990) The Politics of Ethnographic Authority: Race and Writing in the Ethnography of Margaret Mead and Zora Neale Hurston. In Marc Manganaro (ed.), *Modernist Anthropology*. Princeton: Princeton University Press.

Gould, Stephen Jay (1981) *The Mismeasure of Man*. New York and London: W.W. Norton.

Greenblatt, Stephen (1991) *Marvelous Possessions: The Wonder of the New World*. Oxford: Clarendon Press.

Guillaumin, Colette (1991) Race and Discourse. In Maxim Silverman (ed.), *Race, Discourse and Power in France*. Aldershot: Avebury.

Gurewitsch, C. (n.d.) Die Entwicklung der menschlichen Bedürfnisse und die sociale Gliederung der Gesellschaft. *Staats- und Socialwissenschaftliche Forschungen*, 20(4).

Halbfass, Wilhelm (1988) *India and Europe: an Essay in Understanding*. Albany: State University of New York Press.

Handelman, Susan (1991) *Fragments of Redemption: Jewish Thought and Literary Theory in Benjamin, Scholem, and Levinas*. Bloomington and Indianapolis: Indiana University Press.

Hanke, Lewis (1974) *All Mankind is One: a Study of the Disputation Between. . .Las Casas and. . .de Sepulveda in 1550 on the Intellectual and Religious Capacity of the American Indians*. DeKalb: Northern Illinois University Press.

Harris, Nigel (1986) *The End of the Third World*. London: Tauris.

Hartt, Rollin Lynde (1921) More Irish than Ireland. *The Independent*, 106 (May): 68–70.

Harvey, David (1992) Social Justice, Postmodernism and the City. *International Journal of Urban and Regional Research*, 16(4): 588–601.

Havens, Thomas R.H. (1974) *Farm and Nation in Modern Japan: Agrarian Nationalism: 1870–1940*. Princeton: Princeton University Press.

Hawthorn, Geoffrey (1976) *Enlightenment and Despair: A History of Sociology*. Cambridge: Cambridge University Press.

Hegeman, Susan (1991) Shopping for Identities: 'A Nation of Nations' and the Weak Ethnicity of Objects. *Public Culture*, 3(2): 71–92.

Helms, Cynthia Newman (ed.) (1985) *Diego Rivera: A Retrospective*. New York and London: W.W. Norton.

Heyward, DuBose (1953 [1925]) *Porgy*. Garden City, NY: Doubleday (with foreword by Dorothy Heyward).

Hiassen, Carl and Montalbano, William D. (1981) *Powder Burn*. London: Pan Books.

Hoernlé, R.F. Alfred (1939) *South African Native Policy and the Liberal Spirit*. Cape Town: University of Cape Town Press.

Holleman, J.F. (ed.) (1981) *Van Vollenhoven on Indonesian Adat Law*. KITLV Translation Series, 20. The Hague: M. Nijhoff.

Holub, Robert C. (1992) Henrich Heine on the Slave Trade: Cultural Repression and the Persistance of History. *German Quarterly* 65(3–4): 328–39.

Hooker, M.B. (1978) *Adat Law in Modern Indonesia*. Kuala Lumpur: Oxford University Press.

Hoster, Germaine A. (1986) *Marxism and the Crisis of Development in Prewar Japan*. Princeton: Princeton University Press.

Huggins, Nathan Irvin (1971) *Harlem Renaissance*. New York: Oxford University Press.

JanMohammed, Abdul R. (1985) The Economy of Manichean Allegory: The Function of Racial Difference in Colonialist Literature. *Critical Inquiry*, 12(1): 59–87.

Jasper, Chris (1994) Clash of Civilisations. *Window* (7 January), 3(1): 32–7.

Jencks, Charles (1993) *Heteropolis: Los Angeles, The Riots and the Strange Beauty of Hetro-Architecture.* London: Academy Group and Ernst John & Son.

Jospe, A. (ed.) (1981) *Studies in Jewish Thought.* Detroit: Wayne State University Press.

Kahn, Bonnie Menes (1987) *Cosmopolitan Culture: The Gilt-Edged Dream of a Tolerant City.* New York: Atheneum.

Kahn, Joel S. (1993) *Constituting the Minangkabau: Peasants, Culture and Modernity in Colonial Indonesia.* Providence and Oxford: Berg.

Kalaidjian, Walter (1993) *American Culture Between the Wars: Revisionary Modernism and Postmodern Critique.* New York: Columbia University Press.

Kellner, Douglas (1992) Popular Culture and the Construction of Postmodern Identities. In Scott Lash and Jonathan Friedman (eds), *Modernity & Identity.* Oxford and Cambridge, MA: Blackwell.

Kerblay, B. (1966) A.V. Chayanov: Life, Career, Works. In A.V. Chayanov, *The Theory of Peasant Economy.* Ed. D. Thorner, B. Kerblay and R.E.F. Smith. Homewood, IL.: Irwin.

King, Anthony (1992) Rethinking Colonialism: An Epilogue. In Nezar AlSayyad (ed.) *Forms of Dominance: On the Architecture and Urbanism of the Colonial Experience.* Aldershot: Avebury.

Koens, A. (1925) Bedrijfsboekhouding voor den Inlandschen Landbouw. *Mededelingen van de Afdeeling Landbouw,* 9.

Koens, A. (1926–7) Tschajanow's leer van het boerenbedrijft. *Landbouw,* 2: 128–9.

Kolff, G.H. van der (1926) European Influence on Native Agriculture. In B. Schrieke (ed.), *The Effect of Western Influence on Native Civilisations in the Malay Archipelago.* Batavia: G. Kolff and Co.

Kornbluh, Andrea Tuttle (1987) From Culture to Cuisine: Twentieth Cerntury Views of Race and Ethnicity in the City. In Howard Gillette Jr and Zabe L. Miller (eds), *American Urbanism: A Historiographical Review.* New York: Greenwood Press.

Króo, G. (1974) *A Guide to Bartók.* Budapest: Corvina Press.

Kuper, A. (1988) Anthropology and Apartheid. In J. Lonsdale (ed.), *South Africa in Question.* London: James Curry for Cambridge University African Studies Centre.

Lach, Donald E. (1965–77) *Asia in the Making of Europe* (2 vols). Chicago and London: University of Chicago Press.

Lach, Donald E. (1992) *Asia in the Making of Europe, Vol. III: A Century of Advance.* Chicago: University of Chicago Press.

Leonard, Robert and McCormack, John (1993) Beyond the Pale: Dick Frizzell's Indigenuity. *Art and Asia Pacific* (June): 36–41 (in *Art and Australia,* 30(4), Winter 1993).

Linke, Uli (1990) Folklore, Anthropology, and the Government of Social Life. *Comparative Studies in Society and History,* 32(1): 117–48.

Littlejohn, G. (1977) Peasant Economy and Society. In B. Hindess (ed.), *Sociological Theories of the Economy.* London: Macmillan.

Loh, Francis Kok-Wah (1988) *Beyond the Tin Mines: Coolies, Squatters, and New Villagers in the Kinta Valley, Malaysia, c. 1880–1980.* Singapore and New York: Oxford University Press.

Lyotard, Jean-François (1985) Histoire Universelle et Différences Culturelles. *Critique,* 41 (456): 559–68.

McGrane, Bernard (1989) *Beyond Anthropology: Society and the Other.* New York: Columbia University Press.

Mackerras, Colin (1989) *Western Images of China.* Hongkong, Oxford, London: Oxford University Press.

McLellan, David (1974) *Karl Marx: His Life and Thought.* New York: Harper and Row.

McVey, Ruth (1965) *The Rise of Indonesian Communism.* Ithaca, NY: Cornell University Press.

Mandle, Jay (1973) *The Plantation Economy: Population and Economic Change in Guyana, 1883–1960.* Philadelphia: Temple University Press.

Mandle, Jay (1992) *Not Slave, Not Free: The African American Experience since the Civil War*. Durham and London: Duke University Press.

Marcus, George E. and Cushman, D. (1982) Ethnographies as Texts. *Annual Review of Anthropology*, 11: 25–69.

Marcus, George E. and Fischer, Michael M.J. (1986) *Anthropology as Cultural Critique: An Experimental Moment in the Human Sciences*. Chicago and London: University of Chicago Press.

Marx, Karl (1971) *Early Texts*, edited and translated by David McLellan. Oxford: Blackwell.

Miller, Zane L. (1992) Pluralism, Chicago School Style: Louis Wirth, the Ghetto, the City and 'Integration'. *Journal of Urban History*, 18(3): 251–79.

Morris-Suzuki, Tessa (1989) *A History of Japanese Economic Thought*. London and New York: Routledge.

Mosse, W.R., Paucker, A. and Rürup, R. (eds) (1981) *Revolution and Evolution: 1848 in German-Jewish History*. Tübingen: J.C.B. Mohr.

Murphy, Patrick (1987) B. Traven: Anarchist From the Jungle; Anarcho-primitivism in the Jungle Novels. In E. Schuerer and P. Jenkins (eds) *B. Traven: Life and Work*. University Park and London: Pennsylvania State University Press.

Murphy, Peter (1993) Romantic Modernism and the Greek Polis. *Thesis Eleven*, 34: 42–66.

Nevemore, J. (ed.) (1979) *The Treasure of the Sierra Madre*. Wisconsin/Warner Brothers Screenplay Services. Madison: University of Wisconsin Press.

Ossenbruggen, F.D.E. van (1976) Prof. Mr Cornelius van Vollenhoven. In *Hondert Jaar Studie van Indonesië: 1850–1950*. The Hague: Smits.

Peel, J.D.Y. (1971) *Herbert Spencer: The Evolution of a Sociologist*. London: Heinemann.

Phillips, P. and Howell, L. (1920) Racial and Other Differences in Dietary Customs. *Journal of Home Economics*, 12: 396–411.

Picard, M. (1990) Cultural Tourism in Bali. *Indonesia*, 49: 37–74.

Pierson, N.G. (1877) *Koloniale Politiek*. Amsterdam: P.N. van Kampen.

Pollman, T. (1990) Margaret Mead's Balinese: The Fitting Symbols of the American Dream. *Indonesia*, 49: 1–35.

Pulzer, Peter (1992) *Jews and the German State*. Oxford and Cambridge, MA: Blackwell.

Putre, John Walter (1991) *Death Among the Angels*. New York: Charles Scribner's Sons.

Rabinow, Paul (1992) Colonialism, Modernity. The French in Morocco. In Nezar AlSayyad (ed.), *Forms of Dominance: On the Architecture and Urbanism of the Colonial Experience*. Aldershot: Avebury.

Rathbun, C. (1972) *The Village in the Turkish Novel*. The Hague: Mouton.

Redfield, Robert (1956) *Peasant Society and Culture*. Chicago: University of Chicago Press.

Reinharz, J. and Schatzberg, W. (eds) (1984) *The Jewish Response to German Culture: from the Enlightenment to the Second World War*. Hanover and London: University Press of New England.

Rhodius, Hans and Darling, John (1980) *Walter Spies and Balinese Art*. Zutphen (Netherlands): Terra under auspices of Tropical Museum, Amsterdam.

Richarz, M. (ed.) (1991) *Jewish Life in Germany: Memoirs from Three Centuries*. Bloomington and Indianapolis: Indiana University Press.

Rieff, David (1993) Multiculturalism's Silent Partner. It's the Newly Globalized Consumer Economy, Stupid. *Harper's Magazine*, August 1993: 62–72.

Robertson, Roland (1992) *Globalization: Social Theory and Global Culture*. London, Newbury Park, New Delhi: Sage.

Romero, Mary (1992) *Maid in the U.S.A.* New York and London: Routledge.

S. Takdir Alisjahbana (1966) *Indonesia: Social and Cultural Revolution*. Kuala Lumpur/London/Melbourne: Oxford University Press.

Said, Edward (1978) *Orientalism*. New York: Pantheon.

Said, Edward (1989) Representing the Colonised: Anthropology's Interlocutors. *Critical Inquiry*, 15 (Winter): 205–25.

Said, Edward (1993) *Culture and Imperialism*. London: Chatto and Windus.

Sangren, P. Steven (1988) Rhetoric and the Authority of Ethnography. *Current Anthropology*, 29(3): 405–24.

Scheiffele, Eberhard (1991) Questioning One's 'Own' from the Perspective of the Foreign. In Graham Parkes (ed.), *Nietzsche and Asian Thought*. Chicago and London: University of Chicago Press.

Scheltema, A.M.P.A. (1923) De ontleding van het Inlandsch landbouwbedrijf. *Mededelingen van de Afdeling Landbouw*, 6.

Schöffer, I. (1978) Dutch 'Expansion' and Indonesian Reactions: Some Dilemmas of Modern Colonial Rule (1900–1942). In H.L. Wesseling (ed.), *Expansion and Reaction*. Comparative Studies in Overseas History, Leiden: Leiden University Press.

Schrieke, B. (1955) *Indonesian Sociological Studies*. The Hague: W. van Hoeve.

Schuerer, E. and Jenkins, P. (eds) (1987) *B. Traven: Life and Work*, University Park and London: Pennsylvania State University Press.

Scott, James (1976) *The Moral Economy of the Peasant: Rebellion and Subsistence in Southeast Asia*. New Haven: Yale University Press.

Scott, James (1985) *Weapons of the Weak: Everyday Forms of Peasant Resistance*. New Haven and London: Yale University Press.

Selekman, Benjamin M. (1925) *The Clothing and Textile Industries in New York*. New York: McGraw Hill.

Shahnon Ahmad (1987) *Kemulut [Crisis]*. Kuala Lumpur: Utusan Publications and Distributors Sdn Berhad.

Shanin, Teodor (1983) Late Marx: Gods and Craftsmen. In T. Shanin (ed.), *Late Marx and the Russian Road: Marx and the 'peripheries of capitalism'*. New York: Monthly Review Press.

Sharp, J. (1981) The Roots and Development of *Volkenkunde* in South Africa. *Journal of Southern African Studies*, 8(1): 16–36.

Sheskin, Ira M. (1993) Jewish Metropolitan Homelands. *Journal of Cultural Geography*, 13(2): 119–32.

Siegel, James (1969) *The Rope of God*. Berkeley and Los Angeles: University of California Press.

Silverman, Maxim (1991) Introduction. In M. Silverman (ed.), *Race, Discourse and Power in France*. Aldershot: Avebury.

Slavick, William H. (1981) *DuBose Heyward*. Boston: Twayne.

Smith, Anthony (1983) *The Ethnic Revival*. Cambridge and New York: Cambridge University Press.

Smith, Dennis (1988) *The Chicago School: A Liberal Critique of Capitalism*. London: Macmillan Education.

Smith, M.G. (1982) Ethnicity and Ethnic Groups in America: The View from Harvard. *Ethnic and Racial Studies*, 5(1): 1–22.

Sorkin, David (1987) *The Transformation of German Jewry 1780–1840*. New York and Oxford: Oxford University Press.

Spivak, G. (1987) *In Other Worlds: Essays in Culture and Politics*. London: Methuen.

Spivak, G. (1988) Can the Subaltern Speak? In Cary Nelson and Lawrence Grossberg (eds), *Marxism and the Interpretation of Culture*. Urbana and Chicago: University of Illinois Press.

Sprung, Mervyn (1991) Nietzsche's Trans-European Eye. In Graham Parkes (ed.), *Nietzsche and Asian Thought*. Chicago and London: University of Chicago Press.

Stein, Siegfreid and Loewe, Raphael (1978) *Studies in Jewish Religious and Intellectual History*. Birmingham: University of Alabama Press, London: Institute of Jewish Studies.

Stocking, George (1982) *Race, Culture and Evolution*. Chicago: University of Chicago Press.

Stoler, Anne Laura (1985) *Capitalism and Confrontation in Sumatra's Plantation Belt*. New Haven: Yale University Press.

Taguieff, Pierre-André (ed.) (1992) *Face au racisme*, vol II, analyses, hypothèses, perspectives. Paris: La Découverte.

Tal, U. (1975) *Christians and Jews in Germany: Religion, Politics, and Ideology in the Second Reich, 1870–1914*. Ithaca, NY and London: Cornell University Press.

Taufik, Abdullah (1971) *Schools and Politics: The Kaum Muda Movement in West Sumatra*. Ithaca, NY: Cornell University Modern Indonesia Project, Monograph Series.

Taussig, Michael (1980) *The Devil and Commodity Fetishism in South America*. Chapel Hill: University of North Carolina Press.

Taussig, Michael (1993) *Mimesis and Alterity: A Particular History of the Senses*. New York and London: Routledge.

Taylor, Charles (1975) *Hegel*. Cambridge: Cambridge University Press.

Taylor, William R. (1988) The Creation of a Commercial Culture: New York City, 1860–1930. In John Hull Mollenkopf (ed.), *Power, Culture, and Place: Essays on New York City*. New York: Russell Sage Foundation.

Thaxton, Ralph (1983) *China Turned Rightside Up: Revolutionary Legitmacy in the Peasant World*. New Haven: Yale University Press.

The Studio Museum in Harlem (1987) *Harlem Renaissance. Art of Black America*. New York: Harry N. Abrams, Inc.

Thernstrom, Stephan (1980) *Harvard Encyclopedia of American Ethnic Groups*. Cambridge, MA and London: Harvard University Press.

Thomas, Nicholas (1994) *Colonialism's Culture: Anthropology, Travel and Government*. Carlton, Victoria: Melbourne University Press.

Thompson, Leonard (1985) *The Political Mythology of Apartheid*. New Haven and London: Yale University Press.

Tinker, Hugh (1974) *A New System of Slavery: the Export of Indian Labour Overseas 1830–1920*. London: Oxford University Press.

Tobier, Emmanuel (1988) Manhattan's Business District in the Industrial Age. In John Hull Mollenkopf (ed.), *Power, Culture, and Place: Essays on New York City*. New York: Russell Sage Foundation.

Torgovnick, Marianna (1990) *Gone Primitive: Savage Intellects, Modern Lives*. Chicago: University of Chicago Press.

Traven, B. (1980) *The Treasures of B. Traven*. London: Jonathan Cape. Contains English versions of *The Treasure of the Sierra Madre* (1934 English original); *The Death Ship* (1940 English original) and *The Bridge in the Jungle* (1940 English original).

Trouillot, Michel-Rolph (1990) *Haiti: State Against Nation*. New York: Monthly Review Press.

Tuchman, Gaye and Levine, Harry Gene (1993) New York Jews and Chinese Food: The Social Construction of an Ethnic Pattern. *Journal of Contemporary Ethnography*, 22(3): 382–407.

Van Doorn, C.L. (1924) De productie-elementen in het boerenfamiliebedrijft. *Koloniale Studiën*, 8(2): 276–9.

Van Vechten, Carl (1926) *Nigger Heaven*. London: Alfred A. Knopf.

Van Vollenhoven, Cornelius (1909) *Miskenningen van het Adatrecht*. Leiden: Brill.

Van Vollenhoven, Cornelius (1919) *De Indonesiër en zijn Grond*. Leiden: Brill.

Vickers, Adrian (1989) *Bali: A Paradise Created*. Harmondsworth: Penguin.

Waldinger, Roger (1986) *Through the Eye of the Needle: Immigrants and Enterprise in New York's Garment Trades*. New York: New York University Press.

Walicki, A. (1969) *The Controversy over Capitalism: Studies in the Social Philosophy of the Russian Populists*. Oxford: Clarendon Press.

Wasserstrom, Robert (1983) *Class and Society in Central Chiapas*. Berkeley: University of California Press.

Wertheimer, J. (1987) *Unwelcome Strangers: East European Jews in Imperial Germany*. New York and Oxford: Oxford University Press.

Weyant, R.G. (1973) Helvetius and Jefferson. Studies on Human Nature and Government in the 18th century. *Journal of the History of Behavioral Sciences*, 9: 29–41.

Whitton, Brian (1988) Herder's Critique of the Enlightenment: Cultural Community versus Cosmopolitan Rationalism. *History and Theory*, 27(2): 146–68.

Williams, John (1991) *Into the Badlands: Travels Through Urban America*. London: Flamingo.

Williams, Michael C. (1982) *Sickle and Crescent: The Communist Revolt of 1926 in Banten*. Ithaca, NY: Cornell University Modern Indonesia Project, Monograph Series.

Williams, Raymond (1976) *Keywords: a Vocabulary of Culture and Society*. London: Fontana Croom Helm.

Wilson, A. Leslie (1964) *A Mythical Image: The Ideal of India in German Romanticism*. Durham, NC: Duke University Press.

Wolf, Eric (1982) *Europe and the People Without History*. Berkeley and Los Angeles: University of California Press.

Woolen, Peter (1993) *Raiding the Icebox: Reflections on Twentieth Century Culture*. Bloomington and Indianapolis: University of Indiana Press.

Wyatt, Will (1980) *The Man Who Was B. Traven*. London: J. Cape (US title: *The Secret of the Sierra Madre*. New York: Doubleday).

Young, Iris Marion (1990) *Justice and the Politics of Difference*. Princeton: Princeton University Press.

Index

ADV4451